Wisconsin
History Highlights

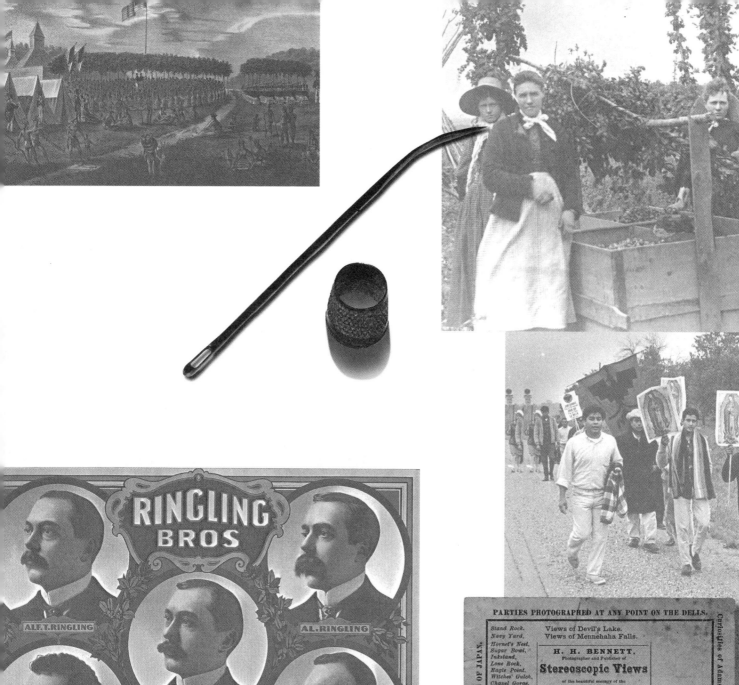

BADGER ORDNANCE WORKS

★ ★ ★

YOU'RE WORKING

to BRING THE BOYS

HOME SOONER!

PASS WITH CARE

Wisconsin
History Highlights
DELVING INTO THE PAST

Jon Kasparek   Bobbie Malone   Erica Schock

Ask for WISCONSIN STATE BRAND

Cheese

DATED
MILD · MELLOW · NIPPY · SHARP

DEPT. O
AGRICULT
& MARK
MADISON

Published by the
Wisconsin Historical Society Press

Photographs identified with PH, WHi, or WHS are from the Society's collections; address inquiries about such photos to the Visual Materials Archivist at the above address.

Publications of the Wisconsin Historical Society Press are available at quantity discounts for promotions, fund raising, and educational use. Write to the above address for more information.

Printed in the United States of America
Designed by Garry Harman, The ArtWorks

The publication of this book was made possible through a collaborative project with the D.C. Everest School District and the Fund for the Improvement of Education Earmark Grant Award entitled Teaching the Art of Historical Inquiry: Expanding the National History Day Model. PR Award # R215K020021

07 06 05 04 03   5 4 3 2 1

Library of Congress Cataloging-in-Publication Data

Kasparek, Jon.
  Wisconsin history highlights : delving into the past / Jon Kasparek, Bobbie Malone, Erica Schock.
    p. cm.
  Includes index.
  ISBN 0-87020-358-4 (alk. paper)
  1. Wisconsin—History. 2. Wisconsin—History—Research. I. Malone, Bobbie, 1944– II. Schock, Erica. III. Title.
F581.5.K37 2004
977.5'0072'0775–dc22
                      2004011246

∞ The paper used in this publication meets the minimum requirements of the American National Standard for Information Sciences—Permanence of Paper for Printed Library Materials, ANSI Z39.48-1992.

Contents

Chapter 8: Arts, Entertainment, and Sports ——— 206

Chapter 9: Government ——— 228

Preface for Teachers

In an era where test-driven accountability dominates the K–12 educational environment, critical and creative thinking sometimes are given short shrift. How can students be involved not only in the short term by achieving good scores on standardized tests, but in the longer term by identifying and strengthening skills and habits of mind that carry over from one content area to another? Historical inquiry offers a productive process that can yield positive outcomes in responding to both of these concerns. Asking students to embark upon a research project of their own choosing, engages their interest and becomes a key in helping them take responsibility for their own learning. When a student selects a historical topic, plans and carries out research, reflects upon that subject's relation to the historical context in which it occurs, analyzes the sources and the data gathered, then writes a paper, creates a presentation, or designs a project, that student is demonstrating far more than content mastery. Such a process reflects not only the student's analytical grasp of the subject, but a synthetic interpretation of its historical importance and impact. Student learning becomes synonymous with self-improvement and self-empowerment—skills that are absolutely critical to any independent thinker in a democratic society. This publication has been designed to facilitate students' achieving this worthwhile goal.

Wisconsin History Highlights is a student handbook for research in Wisconsin history. It introduces 100 topics in the state's history to middle-and high-school students who are interested in creating historical research projects. Students will find subjects in a wide variety of categories and will have the opportunity to use relevant primary and secondary sources to

WHS Archives

Learn more about the UW-Extension in Chapter 6: "Agriculture."

document their research. The events and personalities highlighted range from the well-known to the lesser known, but all are significant samplings in their own right that span the broad spectrum of our state's history. Each one appeals to students' interests and is linked to other similar topics. The entire publication is designed to familiarize readers with important historical eras and stories, giving students a variety of compelling choices for further study.

If students are working within a National History Day framework, *Wisconsin History Highlights* makes an excellent starting point from which to begin a project. The introductory pages outline the basics of historical research, and the rest of the book has two-page stories (or vignettes) that function as topical overviews. Within each vignette, students will find a Getting Started on Research feature that provides information on relevant sources to help them initiate their research. Complete citations for each of these resources are included in the bibliography at the end of each chapter. This section also classifies the resources as primary or secondary. Relevant Model Academic Standards are noted in the appendix at the end of the book.

Acknowledgments

The genesis of *Wisconsin History Highlights* began as a collaborative project with a team from the D.C. Everest Area Schools—Paul Aleckson, Grant Project Director; Nancy Gajewski, Project Consultant; Lori Bychinski, Project Consultant; and James Kegel, Project Consultant; who conceived of, sought funding for, and reviewed the publication. Through the efforts of Congressman David Obey, they received a Federal Earmark Grant Award (PR Award # R215K020021) from the Fund for the Improvement of Education for the project "Teaching the Art of Historical Inquiry: Expanding the National History Day Model." The D.C. Everest team wanted students to have more information on Wisconsin topics appropriate for National History Day research. The Wisconsin Historical Society would also like to thank the Hugh Highsmith Family Foundation whose generous gift helped support this publication.

From the Society, Michael Stevens and Kent Calder worked to establish the parameters of such a publication. The authors could not have done their work without supporting project staff: Sarah Clement, whose detective skills uncovered outstanding secondary and primary resources; Sarah's research assistant, Janet Piehl; Emma Starzewski, Coordinator for National History Day in Wisconsin, who helped shape the introduction; and Diane Drexler, who kept everyone on track.

Beyond the editorial assemblage, state archaeologists Bob Birmingham, John Broihahn, and Russ Green made sure our pre-contact Wisconsin materials were archaeologically sound; architectural historian Jim Draeger helped supply information for anything relating to historic structures; Andy Kraushaar, Harry Miller, and others in the archives and library helped unearth materials; Fay Stone, UW-Platteville, J.P. Leary from the Department of Public Instruction, and Patty Loew from UW-Madison added insights into selections dealing with Wisconsin Indian Nations. For specific topics, we called on many more people for images and guidance: The River Alliance of Wisconsin (dam removal); Alice Ridge (Yellowstone Trail); Sauk County Historical (hops); Chippewa Falls Main Street Program (saving downtowns); Douglas County Historical Society (Fairlawn and the Dionne quintuplets); Wisconsin Maritime Museum (Manitowoc submarine); Steve Sundell at the Mills Music Library (German polka); UW-Milwaukee Archives (Golda Meir); and Kenosha Public Museum (woolly mammoths). Tracy Will helped us conceptualize the book, and Abby Markwyn contributed additional written materials. Bill Malone generously offered his usual support in editing the manuscript.

Introduction for Students

Wisconsin History Highlights is not a textbook. There are no facts here to be memorized and used to answer any multiple-choice exam. Instead, it is handbook for research in Wisconsin history in which you will find 100 topics from the state's distant and recent past. The topics are not necessarily the most significant events or people to have affected Wisconsin history, nor are they the only events or people of interest to you, but they may lead you to a topic that you *would* want to explore more fully. Also, they will lead you to resources that will help you refine your search and get you started on your own historical investigation.

If you're interested in housing segregation in Milwaukee, see Chapter 7: "Social Issues."

How to Use *Wisconsin History Highlights*

A quick glance through the table of contents will show you 100 historical vignettes (brief stories) that are two pages in length and have been classified into thematic chapters. Select a chapter you find appealing and choose a few vignettes to look through. Every story has a brief overview of the subject, questions to think about, and a Getting Started on Research feature to introduce you to sources that will help you take the first steps toward creating your project. At the end of each chapter, you'll find additional information to help you track down these sources. With this information, you will be able to move more easily from this book to the research itself. But, before you begin, here are some important things to know about historical research so you can get off to a good start.

Thinking Like a Historian

If this is the first time you've done historical research, you might be surprised to find that it's very different from reading a textbook or other history book. Historians don't simply read about the past, they *investigate* the past. They enter into a dialogue with the past and ask probing questions, much the way a scientist conducts research or a detective tries to solve a case. Historical research is about problem-solving—not just fact-gathering—and researchers begin the process by posing questions.

Historians ask questions to tease out new interpretations or to draw tentative conclusions from the clues presented by the past. After all, no one can ever truly come to terms with the past. We cannot replay an event on a video screen, and even if we could, we could only focus on one image at a time. If we were trying to revisit the Black Hawk War, for example, our "camera" could only see one event from one perspective at a time, and we know each battle

Learn more about Black Hawk in Chapter 1: "Discovering the Past."

WHS Archives

Life of Black Hawk

During our encampment at the Four Lakes, we were hard put to obtain enough to eat to support nature. Situate in a swampy, marshy country, (which had been selected in consequence of the great difficulty required to gain access thereto,) there was but little game of any sort to be found — and fish were equally scarce. The great distance to any settlement, and the impossibility of bringing supplies therefrom, if any could have been obtained, deterred our young men from making further attempts. We were forced to *dig roots* and *bark trees*, to obtain something to satisfy hunger and keep us alive! Several of our old people became so much reduced, as actually to *die with hunger!* And, finding that the army had commenced moving, and fearing that they might come upon and surround our encampment, I concluded to remove my women and children across the Mississippi, that they might return to the Sac nation again. Accordingly, on the next day, we commenced moving, with [131] five Winnebagoes acting as our guides, intending to descend the Ouisconsin.

Ne-a-pope, with a party of twenty, remained in our rear, to watch for the enemy, whilst we were proceeding to the Ouisconsin, with our women and children. We arrived, and had commenced crossing them to an island, when we discovered a large body of the enemy coming towards us. We were now compelled to fight, or sacrifice our wives and children to

153

Learn more about Black Hawk in Chapter 1: "Discovering the Past."

involved winners (with their point of view) and losers (with theirs). Not every U.S. militiaman viewed a given situation as an imminent threat to the Union. Similarly, individuals from various Wisconsin Indian Nations supported, sympathized with, were indifferent to, or disagreed with Black Hawk. And the same is true for every other historical event. Since we cannot revisit the past or completely understand the way different people thought about the times in which they lived, historians look for new ways to tell the story of any given event, person's life, or idea from the past. Historians search for clues to help them fill in missing parts of the story, and when they find enough of them to build a compelling argument, they put them together to form a new interpretation.

What questions do historians ask? Basically, they ask what a historical person, event or idea *has meant* to history. They might ask about the impact of one event, such as the Great Depression of the 1930s, on the lives of those who experienced it. They might examine how an idea, such as abolition of slavery, changed the experiences of blacks and whites both in the North and South in the mid-1850s. Historians definitely don't answer these questions in the same way. You can see proof of this every time you go to your local

library. The history section might contain dozens of books on Abraham Lincoln, perhaps all written by different authors. How can this be? The facts of President Lincoln's life haven't changed. He hasn't made any new decisions, written any new letters, or made any new speeches. After reading one Lincoln biography, you might assume that there would be nothing new to tell. But, of course, that's not the case at all. Hundreds of historians have written books about Lincoln. Why? The reason is simple: Each historian brings his or her own ideas, experiences, and interpretations to the topic, and each one finds different *meaning* in the subject. This is the process of historical interpretation.

As a quick exercise, ask yourself what question comes to mind when you think of Abraham Lincoln. You might think of a large, general question such as: "What meaning did he have to the Civil War, slavery, or the Northern attitude toward the South?" or you might be curious about something more specific: "What was the impact of Mary Todd Lincoln's influence on the president's decision to free southern slaves through the Emancipation Proclamation of 1863?" and "Did her influence have a minor impact or a major one?" The evidence that both leads to more questions and supports the conclusions you ultimately draw will come from both primary sources and secondary materials.

Explore Joshua Glover's story in Chapter 7: "Social Issues."

TWO SIMPLE STEPS TO THINKING LIKE A HISTORIAN

1. Change your mind.

Forget about history as an unchanging, static story. Start looking at the past as a jigsaw puzzle of facts that can be put together in many different ways, depending upon your knowledge of the subject and your convictions. Remember that you are a historian as you do your research, and, as a historian, you are entitled to your own opinion. Put the puzzle together in your own way and answer your historical question however you see fit, based upon the information you deem important and interesting. Your conclusions might agree with other historians' views or you might come up with a unique interpretation. The choice is yours.

2. Change our minds!

Whenever you present your ideas in a research paper or in a creative format such as an exhibit, a documentary, or a dramatic performance, you are not simply presenting your audience with information, but you are drawing conclusions about your historical question that express your own interpretations. Your goal is to change your audience's mind and have them agree with your interpretation. Keep this in mind as you're going about your research. Don't forget: Look for more than just information. Look for proof.

Now that you're prepared to think like a historian, you'll need to initiate the research process.

WHS Archives

The Badger Ordnance Works is covered in Chapter 5: "Industry."

The Research Process

First, decide what general topic interests you (**Big picture**). Next, try to figure out why that subject is intriguing (**What's the hook?**). Then, choose a specific part of the broader topic that you want to explore and

determine the direction you want to take. That direction (**Narrowing the search**) is where you begin to ask the questions (**What do I want to know?**) that will help you define and guide your investigation. For historians, that's where the fun begins. From this point, focus on what you need to read in order to get answers to your questions, or to lead you to new questions.

Step 1: The Big Picture

Let's pick a topic from one of the chapters to see how this process works. If you are interested in the Civil War, this topic becomes your big picture. Check the *Wisconsin History Highlights* index to see if the book covers anything about the Civil War. You will find, among many related topics, that Hans Christian Heg led Wisconsin's famous 15th Regiment (the "Norwegian" regiment) in the Civil War and that Cordelia Harvey worked hard to build hospitals in the North for wounded Union soldiers. Either one of these would be a great topic to research.

Getting Started on Research in each vignette and the Resources section at the

Learn more about Cordelia Harvey in Chapter 7: "Social Issues."

end of each chapter are important starting points because they list relevant secondary materials and primary sources. **Secondary** materials such as books, Internet articles, reports in periodicals, maps, documentaries, and more will help you focus your

The vignette on Colonel Hans Christian Heg is featured in Chapter 2: "Immigration in Wisconsin History."

ABOUT RESEARCH MATERIALS

You'll find references to secondary and primary materials in every Getting Started on Research feature tucked into each historical story and in the Resources section at the end of each chapter. Why are these sources so necessary to the research process? What's the difference between them?

Secondary materials include all kinds of articles (in print and on the Internet), books, and other materials written about a historical person or event by historians, journalists, or other interpreters of the past. These materials are interpretations of those people or events by those who did not witness them or live during that time period. Secondary sources provide valuable overviews and insights, but are not principal accounts.

Primary sources are documents from the actual time period, event, or person under investigation. These sources provide the critical evidence upon which future historians base their interpretations. Because you'll be doing real historical research, you must use primary sources to help you tell your version of the story. Artwork, government documents, photographs, maps, city directories, census data, journals, correspondence, interviews, and newspaper accounts from the period are common primary sources. A critical part of the historian's work is to figure out how such sources can help support the arguments the historian is trying to make. Without primary sources, you have no argument!

Calvin Coolidge's trip to Wisconsin is related in Chapter 4: "Tourism."

Robert La Follette is discussed in several chapters, including Chapter 9: "Government."

research. These sources provide the historical context that will help you understand how the topic you ultimately select fits into the big picture. Secondary sources help you get to the What's the hook? step in the process.

At this point, your exploration will begin with secondary literature, materials that were written about your subject by someone else. You might find biographies of Hans Christian Heg or Cordelia Harvey at the library or locate quality resources online. You might even visit an archive to

Great Lakes Fishery Commission

The vignette about lampreys is found in Chapter 3: "Environmental History."

see available primary sources. All this legwork has two purposes: First, it will help you determine the general topic you want to learn more about. Don't rush to a final decision without looking at a few different options! Sometimes the best topics are ones you discover while investigating something else. Second, it will help you answer the very important "What's the hook?" question.

Step 2: What's the Hook?
By now, you've conducted preliminary research and learned several important things by asking "What's the hook?" Using

the Heg and Harvey examples, you've discovered how they fit into the overall themes and chronologies of the Civil War. Second, you now know which of these topics you find more intriguing and worth pursuing. If you've discovered that neither of these topics are strong enough to hook you in, hopefully your reading so far may have introduced you to some promising alternatives. The point of selecting your own topic of historical research is to uncover an event or personality that you find interesting enough to explore more fully. You may find it helpful to ask "What parts of the story need to be told in more depth?" or "How can my research bring more compelling evidence to light?"

Step 3: Narrowing the Search
To conduct true historical research, it's not enough to read and report on just what other people have written or said about your topic. As part of narrowing the search, you need to make sure that you can find historical evidence to support your investigation. That's where **primary** resources become essential. Primary sources are important especially after you decide "What do I want to know?" Footnotes and bibliographies in the secondary materials you use will often lead to many primary resources. Look for illustrations or other artwork, government documents, photographs, maps, city directories, census data, journals, and personal or official correspondence.

Step 4: What do I want to know?
This is the step that will help you define your project. This is where you pose the questions that will help you establish the

Wisconsin's milk strikes are discussed in Chapter 6: "Agriculture."

WHS Archives, Milwaukee Journal photo

WHS Museum 1991.161.2

Learn more about treaty rights in Chapter 9: "Government."

WHS Museum 1988.203

kind of evidence that will lead you to *answer* your questions and *shape* your argument. You may find that a primary resource doesn't make sense and that you need to consult the secondary literature or talk to an expert to re-establish your big picture. Staying flexible in these early stages may mean that you move back and forth through the steps while putting your project together. This is a natural part of the process.

If you're doing research for a National History Day project, you must decide how the topic you choose addresses the overall theme for the year. By framing your topic so that it deals with the annual theme, you will naturally focus your investigation on the "What do I want to know?" question and how it relates to the NHD theme.

Making a Case for Your Topic

By now you will have recognized that the research process involves a series of steps and decisions that bring you to the point of starting to develop your project. The crucial question now becomes "What is my main point?" For your project to be effectively presented, you have to convince your audience that your research led you to a new conclusion. And your task is to demonstrate that the historical evidence you found supports the claim, argument, central point, or thesis that you are making. Your main point needs to be (1) supported by both primary and secondary evidence, (2) significant and straightforward enough for you to explain in one sentence, (3) directly and specifically related to the overall topic or theme you're investigating. Use these criteria to help you keep your topic within reasonable limits and to help you weigh the historical evidence you find "How useful is this to me?"

DON'T PLAGIARIZE!

As you move through the process of researching, creating, and presenting your project, you will collect ideas, words, images, and other material from the sources you use. Together, this material forms the evidence you need to support your argument. You *HAVE* to state clearly that these materials are not yours! You *MUST* cite them carefully, and completely in your bibliography and in footnotes for a paper. When you fail to do these things, you are claiming that the information is yours, and this is illegal. In other words, you're stealing. This kind of theft is called **plagiarism**, and it can mean serious consequences for you, including disqualification from any competition (National History Day, for example) or a lower, even a failing, grade. Nowadays, it's very easy to slip something from the Internet into a paper without citing the source, but teachers and competition judges are very aware of how to spot and track down this kind of plagiarism.

For these and other reasons, it's important to make source citation a habit right from the start. Always include complete bibliographic information in all notes you take. Label every individual photocopy. Collect the Web addresses of the sites you access. Just copy the address from the browser window, then paste it into a storage document. Storing addresses in categories is a quick, easy, and very useful approach. A big mistake researchers can make is to think that they'll remember where they found the information without writing it down. Don't fall into that trap! Any historian will tell you that this attitude almost never works. If you think recording bibliographic information isn't much fun, just remember that it's a lot less painful than being disqualified from a competition or getting an F. It's also easier than retracing your steps later on in search of information that you could have easily written down right away!

Where to Find Research Materials

For recent historical events, such as World War II or the Civil Rights movement, look for ways to interview people who actually participated or were directly affected. Depending upon the topic you choose, your local or county historical society, library, museums, churches, social and political organizations, government agencies, or businesses may help put you in touch with living individuals (such as WWII veterans) to interview. In addition to the sources listed in the Resources section, local and state historical societies and museums, as well as national archives such as at the Smithsonian Institution can lead to a different kind of primary source. Artifacts, as they are called, are objects from the past such as medals, furniture, and clothing. It's good to acquire a diversity of primary resources so

that you can see a historical era, event, or person from several perspectives. Good sources help you find the puzzle pieces of "real evidence" that ultimately will help you make a convincing presentation of your case.

Evaluating Resources

All historians know that *not all research materials are equal!* Especially in the

You can learn more about hops production in Chapter 6: "Agriculture."

Sauk County Historical Society

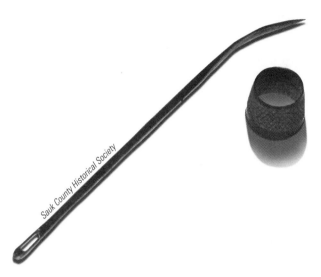

Sauk County Historical Society

Needle and thimble used to sew bales of hops for shipping.

twenty-first century when we have access to so much information on the Internet, we have to remind ourselves to "consider the source." Remember that every item from the past and every interpretation from the past tells someone's story; that is, a story from a very particular point of view. Articles from reference books contain only the briefest topic summaries and are only useful in the early stages of your research. They should not count as sources.

When using primary and secondary materials, you need to be able to ask "Whose past is this?" to make sure you get more than one perspective on any event or historical question. Ask "Where did this information come from?" Did it come from a museum, local historical society, university, or governmental agency (such as the Wisconsin Department of Natural Resources, the National Archives, the Library of Congress, or the Wisconsin Historical Society), an official Indian Nation Web site, or other institution of higher education? When you find information from a Web site or other source that may be questionable, verify what you have found by asking an expert (librarian, computer teacher, etc.) about the reliability and validity of the

information and its source. You are building your case on reliable *evidence*. The more reliable it is, the more persuasive your research and presentation will be. Annotate your bibliography to reflect this understanding.

A word of warning: Historical research can be habit-forming—habits you will find extremely useful in a lot of ways! Throughout your school and work careers, you'll be required at times to express your ideas by finding, evaluating, and presenting information. Whenever you do a research project, you're practicing these same skills. So, even if you don't plan on becoming a professional historian or full-time researcher, your research skills will help you prepare for life and the very real requirements it sometimes brings.

Jack Pfefer Collection, University Libraries of Notre Dame

Find more about Ed "Strangler" Lewis in Chapter 8: "Arts, Entertainment, and Sports."

Chapter One

Discovering
the Past

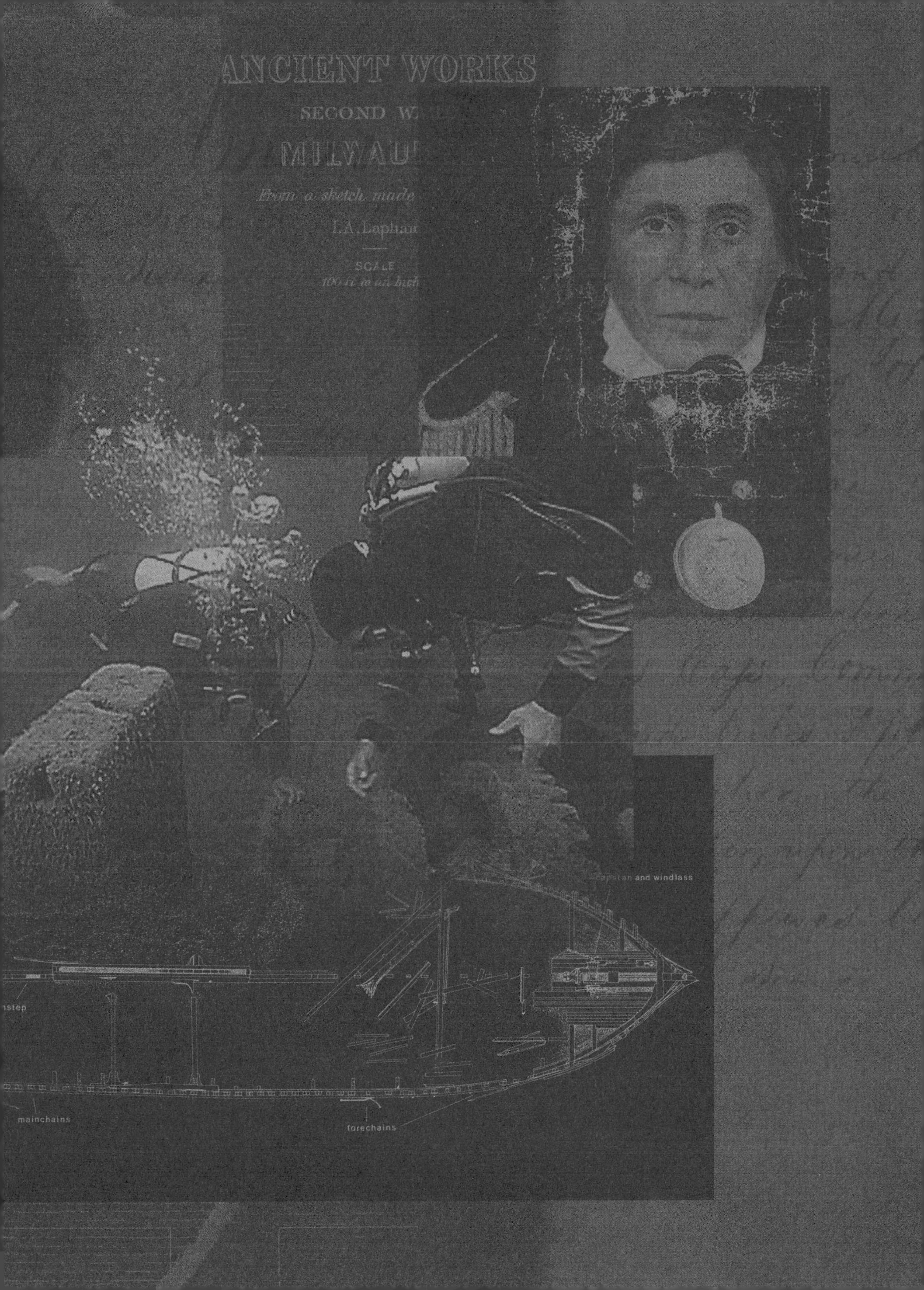

capstan and windlass

step

mainchains

forechains

Finding the Mammoth Hunters
Kenosha Public Museum

In 1964, Kenosha County farmer Frank Schaefer was tilling his field when he struck something so hard it broke his tilling machine. The buried object he discovered that day was a bone from a woolly mammoth. Woolly mammoths were large, elephant-like creatures with large tusks and shaggy long hair that roamed North America during the Ice Age (about 8000 B.C.). The first Native people, called Paleo-Indians by archaeologists, hunted these mammoths for food.

An amateur archaeologist named Phil Sander drew a map of the find, then Schaefer donated the bone to the Kenosha Public Museum. The bone sat in the museum for more than 25 years before museum volunteer Dave Wasion reexamined the museum's collections. In 1990, he noticed cut marks on some bones from another part of Kenosha County. The old bones in the museum and the new discovery raised new questions about how woolly mammoths lived and died.

Wasion shared his findings with the museum's curator Dan Joyce, who agreed that the marks may have been made by a stone tool from a human being, rather than

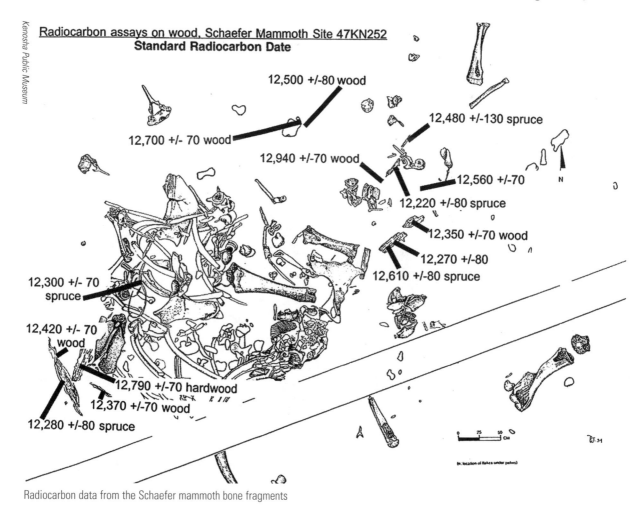

Kenosha Public Museum

Radiocarbon data from the Schaefer mammoth bone fragments

the teeth or claws of a natural predator. The two men began studying the bone found by Schaefer. They noticed similar marks. These cut marks indicated that the mammoth was probably killed, or at least butchered, by Stone Age people!

Mammoth bones excavated at Schaefer site

Kenosha Public Museum

Intrigued by the discovery of the cut marks, Joyce and Wasion set out to excavate the rest of Schaefer's mammoth. They used Sander's map to guide their project.

At first, they found nothing. The Sander map gave precise measurements oriented to a nearby fencepost, but the archaeologists found no evidence there. Then, Schaefer told them that he had moved the fence post after Sander drew the map. They suddenly realized that they had been reading the map correctly but were digging in the wrong place. After finding Sander's original beginning point, Joyce and Waison soon found other mammoth bones, including some of the stone tools used by the hunters who had killed it.

During the excavations, Schaefer's neighbor, John Hebior, showed the archaeologists a similar bone he had found several years earlier. This led to a second excavation and the discovery of a second mammoth nearby. After the bones were excavated and cleaned, the archaeologists analyzed bone fragments to determine the approximate time period that the mammoth lived. Amazingly, the results indicated that mammoths had inhabited the area about 12,500 years ago. Then the men learned that the mammoth unearthed on the Hebior farm was the largest and most complete mammoth ever found in North America. Today, you can visit the Schaefer mammoth on display at the Kenosha Public Museum.

The discovery of these mammoths did more than just create a curiosity for tourists. It was a unique opportunity to study early American Indian hunting techniques. Because the mammoth bones were so old and because the animals had been butchered, the two sites proved that people lived in North America even earlier than archaeologists had previously realized. Prior to the Kenosha excavations, the oldest known evidence of human existence on the continent dated to about 11,000 years ago. Archaeologists had speculated that American Indians had crossed the Bering Strait from Asia to North America about 13,000 years ago. But, the Kenosha discoveries showed that humans had arrived many, many years earlier.

Archaeologists began to dramatically revise their theories about the spread of human beings across the globe. Everything changed because of the accidental discovery of a bone by a Kenosha County farmer! And fortunately, he gave that bone to a museum for all of us to see, study, and admire!

Getting Started on Research

Find interesting facts and photographs of the Schaefer and Hebior sites online at http://www.woollymammoth.org/. Learn more about the Kenosha Public Museum at http://www.kenosha.org/museum/. View a "virtual excavation" by clicking on the "Mammoth Mystery" link at http://www.wisconsinhistory.org/kids/.

For a fascinating history of mammoth hunters, read chapter 1 of *Indian Nations of Wisconsin* or *Native People of Wisconsin* by Patty Loew. Learn even more about hunting and early Wisconsin Indians in *Digging and Discovery: Wisconsin Archaeology* by Diane Holliday and Bobbie Malone.

Discovering Aztalan
Samuel Barrett and the Milwaukee Public Museum

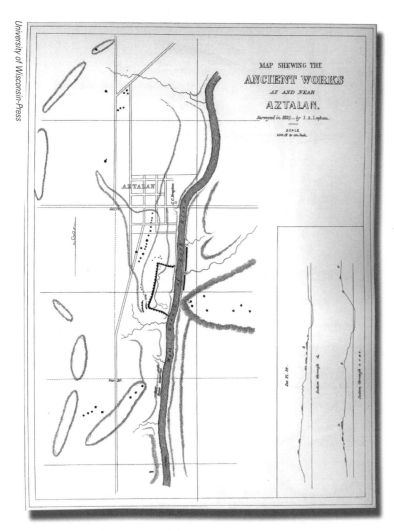

MAP SHEWING THE
ANCIENT WORKS
AT AND NEAR
AZTALAN.

Surveyed in 1850 by I. A. Lapham.

SCALE
1000 ft. to an Inch.

Increase Lapham's map of Aztalan, 1850

When American settlers began moving into southern Wisconsin in the 1820s, they were often astonished at what they found. Scattered throughout the area were hundreds of mounds formed in the ground. Many were effigy mounds, or great piles of earth that were in the shapes of birds and other creatures. Some of these mounds were quite large. The largest mounds, discovered in 1836, were not effigies built in any image, but actually were the remains of a town built along the Crawfish River near what is now Lake Mills in Jefferson County. This site

contains three large platform mounds and the remnants of fortifications.

Most early European and Euro-American settlers thought the Wisconsin Indian inhabitants they encountered or heard about were "uncivilized." Because the settlers did not respect or understand Indian cultures they encountered, few believed that these Native people or their ancestors could have made such monuments. Instead, these early settlers compared the mounds to Aztec pyramids in Mexico and speculated that the site, which they dubbed "Aztalan," may have been a distant outpost of the Aztec Empire.

Then came Wisconsin's distinguished natural scientist Increase Lapham. He studied the site in 1850 and prepared detailed drawings of the area (before much of it was cleared and turned into farmland). For nearly seventy years, the site remained unexcavated and became something of a mystery. As farming continued, it eroded many of the surface features. No one made a systematic survey of the site, although occasional treasure-hunters tried their luck in search of treasures. Finally in 1919, Samuel Barrett, the director of the Milwaukee Public Museum, undertook a careful study.

The more Barrett learned about Aztalan, the more excited he became. His party traced out the wall that once surrounded the site. They also found several mounds and places where houses had once stood. Most thrilling was the discovery that the Crawfish River had cut a ravine through the site. This revealed a four-and-a-half-foot layer of garbage. To an archaeologist, this was a dream come true! From the broken pottery, stone tools, bones, and other trash, Barrett learned more about Aztalan than anyone had ever known before.

In his writings, Barrett mentioned the remains of a rectangular enclosure. It was about 700 by 1,500 feet and covered about 21 acres. Remnants of logs showed that a stockade about 10 feet high and plastered inside and outside the enclosure had once encircled the site. At each of the enclosure's corners stood towers from which inhabitants could watch the surrounding countryside and guard the main entrance gates. Inside the fortress, or palisade, three flat-topped pyramids still remained. One had steps leading to a platform 15 feet high, and it covered an area about 53 square feet.

Later archeological excavations by the Wisconsin Archaeological Survey, Wisconsin Historical Society, University of Wisconsin–Milwaukee, and University of Michigan revealed a lot about the people who once lived at Aztalan. For example, the studies showed that the Aztalan dwellers possessed sophisticated knowledge of agriculture and used it to create intricate and artistic pottery and ornaments. Also, archaeologists found items that were not made in the region. This indicated that these Native people

Archaeological excavation at Aztalan

had engaged in trade relations with other populations. The fortifications indicate that the Aztalan dwellers lived in hostile territory and went to great lengths to protect themselves.

Early clues helped Barrett and others figure out just what kind of people were responsible for building Aztalan. Aztalan very likely was a village outpost for a cultural group centered around Cahokia, near present-day East St. Louis in Illinois. This is almost certain because Aztalan dwellers displayed aspects of that culture. Barrett's work confirmed that North American Indian populations, like those at Aztalan, had developed a highly organized and refined way of life long before Europeans arrived on the shores of the Americas.

The only mystery that remains is why people abandoned Aztalan. Whatever happened to the people who once lived there? Perhaps a hostile population forced them out and destroyed their settlement. Perhaps the Aztalan dwellers simply decided to move on. What do you think about why the Wisconsin outpost no longer remains? What reasons can you think of that would explain how and why the culture stopped being a vital part of the region?

Getting Started on Research

Barrett described his work in the book *Ancient Aztalan*. During his excavations, Barrett relied heavily on Increase Lapham's *Antiquities of Wisconsin*, which was first published in 1855. The reprinted text describes how the region changed between 1855 and 1919. Also, Leslie E. Eisenberg and Robert A. Birmingham write extensively about mound builders in *Indian Mounds of Wisconsin*. Visit the Wisconsin Department of Natural Resources Web site to find information and photos of the state park at Aztalan at http://www.dnr .state.wi.us/org/land/parks/specific/aztalan/.

WHS Archives

Increase Lapham
Wisconsin's First Scientist

In 1836—the same year Wisconsin became a territory—a 25-year-old engineer arrived in Milwaukee. He had come to work on a canal that its developers hoped would connect that city to the Rock River some 80 miles to the west. The canal was never built, but the young man stayed anyway. His name was Increase Lapham. Within a few years of his arrival, he had become the leading expert on Wisconsin's geography and geology.

One of 13 children, Increase Allen Lapham was born in 1811 in Palmyra, New York. His father was an engineer who worked on the Erie Canal. Young Increase was working on the canal as a common laborer when he made a startling discovery. He split open a rock that revealed a collection of fossils. This event captured his vivid imagination and inspired him to pursue scientific research for the rest of his life, which he did whenever and wherever he could. Every place he went, he noted details of his surroundings, collected specimens, and documented what he gathered. Within his first year in Wisconsin, Lapham wrote a *Catalogue of Plants and Shells, Found in the Vicinity of Milwaukee, on the West Side of Lake Michigan*. It was one of the first publications of its kind in the new territory.

Wisconsin proved to be fertile ground for Lapham's curiosity. As he traveled the countryside, he collected samples of grasses and flowers. He also studied the legends and traditional stories of the Ho-Chunk and other Native peoples. Most importantly, Lapham investigated and documented the many mounds built in the southern part of the state by peoples of the late Woodland culture. These people had populated the region 600 to 1,200 years earlier. Because construction and farming have since destroyed many of the mounds, Lapham's surveys provide an invaluable resource. He also mapped Wisconsin's first farming village, the early Indian site of Aztalan in Jefferson County. His drawings were so accurate that they were used a century later when the site was partially restored and turned into a state park.

In 1844, Lapham published the first history of Wisconsin, perhaps the first major publication in the territory. The book was titled *A Geographical and*

Lapham's map of effigy mounds in Milwaukee's Second Ward, 1836

Getting Started on Research

Chapter 21 of *Badger Saints and Sinners* by Fred L. Holmes describes Increase Lapham's life. His papers can be found in the archives at the Wisconsin Historical Society in Madison. Among them are his original survey notes, the diaries he wrote as a young man, and the numerous scrapbooks he kept. Lapham's most influential book *Antiquities of Wisconsin* has been republished recently, and it remains the earliest and best documented source of ancient mounds in Wisconsin.

More current information about the mounds and the people who built them can be found in *Indian Mounds of Wisconsin* by Robert Birmingham and Leslie Eisenberg, which is available at many public libraries and bookstores.

Topographical Description of Wisconsin; with Brief Sketches of Its History, Geology, Mineralogy, Natural History, Population, Soil, Productions, Government, Antiquities, etc. Within a few years, Lapham worked with Lyman Copeland Draper to found the Wisconsin Historical Society and served for 22 years as its president. Because of his familiarity with the state's geography, he became Wisconsin's first state geologist as well.

Lapham also wanted to put scientific inquiry to practical use. Early on, he began to keep detailed records of the weather. He reasoned that if records were kept long enough, a pattern would become apparent. This, he argued, would mean that the weather could actually be predicted. Lapham's primary interest was in predicting storms on the Great Lakes in order to warn ships of dangerous conditions. In 1869, after 15 years of research and numerous accurate predictions of Great Lakes storms, Lapham finally convinced the

federal government to establish a National Weather Bureau. On November 8, 1870, Lapham issued the first official weather forecast from the Bureau's Chicago office.

For 34 years after his arrival in Milwaukee—from documenting archaelogical remains in the countryside to his work in establishing the National Weather Bureau—Increase Lapham devoted himself to scientific inquiry. He had a unique energy and unflagging curiosity about the natural world, and in particular, about Wisconsin and its past. The $128.03 monthly salary he earned from the weather bureau was the first money he ever received for his scientific work.

In 1875, while fishing near Oconomowoc, Lapham died after suffering a heart attack. From start to finish, he spent his life exploring his adopted state, and he donated his vast collection of books, shells, fossils, minerals, and plant specimens to the University of Wisconsin for the benefit of future scholars.

WHI Image ID 2219

Portrait of Increase Lapham, undated

Think of all the curiosity sparked by a small rock that a young boy found while digging a hole!

Are you naturally curious like Increase Lapham? Have you ever been surprised by something you found while playing in your backyard or on your way to school? If you were to find a fossil, a strange rock, or an odd formation in the ground, how could you find out more about it? Where might you go? Your school library, the local public library, and the Internet are three excellent places to start. How many other sources can you think of?

Otter Spring
Protecting Wisconsin's Sacred Sites

For most people, the phrase "sacred sites" brings to mind images of churches or cathedrals. Perhaps you might think of St. Peter's Basilica in Rome, the Wailing Wall in Jerusalem, or a local place of worship in your community. American Indians consider all that is part of the earth worthy of being treated with reverence and respect. Indians who lived in Wisconsin before Europeans arrived established certain locations important not only for everyday use but for sacred rituals as well.

One such site for the Forest County Potawatomi is Otter Spring. During the 1600s, the Potawatomi moved into eastern Wisconsin to escape conflicts generated by the fur trade. They established several large settlements along Green Bay and the Milwaukee River. But when the United States took control of the area in the 1800s, many Potawatomi were forced to move west.

In 1833, the Treaty of Chicago required the Potawatomi to abandon Wisconsin for reservations west of the Mississippi River. Many did leave, but others remained in the state, moving farther north, ahead of non-Indian settlement.

By the late 1890s, many Potawatomi were settled in Forest County. Their population numbered about 450 by 1910. In 1913, the federal government finally abandoned its attempts to convince the tribe to move to a reservation in Kansas, where other Potawatomi bands had already settled. Instead, the Forest County band members used tribal trust money to purchase parcels of land throughout the county. Members of

WHS Historic Preservation

Interior, Otter Spring, undated

the tribe now owned land and were able to make a living in the logging and tourism industries. Many worked as guides for sportsmen or sold baskets and beadwork to growing numbers of tourists flocking to what was becoming prime vacation land.

Otter Spring was an important place for these members of the Forest County Potawatomi. Because their houses had neither indoor plumbing nor outdoor wells, the spring provided a prime source of fresh water, especially during cold winters and other natural hardships. For decades, Potawatomi families hauled water from Otter Spring in barrels and used it for drinking, cooking, and washing. In the difficult early years of the twentieth century, Otter Spring sustained the people and began to acquire spiritual significance. To the Potawatomi, the water brought life, and they saw the spring as an important connection between their tribe and the earth itself.

In 1933, the Civilian Conservation Corps (CCC), a federal program during the Great Depression, moved unemployed men to the area to improve roads, construct fire lanes, restock fish habitats, and stabilize lake and river banks. One of their projects was the construction of a log structure over Otter Spring. After the CCC left in 1935, local residents continued to use Otter Spring to obtain water, and the "spring house" greatly facilitated this and other uses.

WHS Historic Preservation

Exterior, Otter Spring, undated

As more and more Potawatomi members drilled wells, Otter Spring became less critical for their daily needs. But, the spring continued to be used for sacred purposes. Traditionally, the Potawatomi grew to consider the spring sacred because the water bubbled up from below the ground, a "natural" gift of life from the earth itself. Potawatomi spiritual leaders referred to the spring water as "living water" or "holy water." When drawing water from the spring, the Potawatomi people customarily include a prayer of thanks to the earth. They also use the water in a variety of ceremonies, such as when a boy is honored for catching his first fish or for capturing his first game. Traditional feasts begin with a ritual sharing of the spring's water as a symbol of the tribe's common link to the earth. Because of its historical significance and continued spiritual importance to the Potawatomi people, the Otter Spring House was listed on the State and National Register of Historic Places in 1999.

Getting Started on Research

Do you know any natural sites in your area of the state that are considered sacred to some Native community? What sites were sacred to Indians who no longer live here?

To learn more about Native people in Wisconsin and their spiritual connection to the natural world, read *Indian Nations of Wisconsin* by Patty Loew or *The Woodland Indians of the Western Great Lakes* by Robert E. and Pat Ritzenthaler. Also, the Forest Country Potawatomi Web site can be found at http://www.fcpotawatmi .com/ Several links take you to information about the tribe. To contact the Forest County Potawatomi reservation, follow the links to phone numbers and addresses.

Henry R. Schoolcraft

The 1820 Expedition to the Western Michigan Territory

Henry Schoolcraft, undated

Today, Wisconsin's many roads and highways crisscross the state, and you can easily find your way around it with a good map. But for many years after 1873, when the United States took possession of the land that would become Wisconsin, the area was completely unknown to most Americans. Those who chose to move to the Great Lakes region traveled into uncharted territory, found American Indian settlements, and discovered some remarkable natural landmarks. Beginning in the 1820s, the federal government sent expedition parties to this unexplored area to learn about its people and places. These expeditions encountered many wonders and surprises.

One of the earliest of these exploratory missions into Wisconsin occurred in 1820. The area was then part of the Michigan Territory, and its governor Lewis Cass decided to personally explore the portion of his territory that lay west of Lake Michigan. On May 24, he and 40 others departed Detroit in a flotilla of canoes and paddled up Lake Huron to the straits of Mackinac on the upper peninsula of Michigan. They traveled into Lake Superior and went across to the head of the lake and down the Mississippi River. After landing at Fort Crawford (modern day Prairie du Chien), they paddled up the Wisconsin and Fox Rivers to Green Bay. They then headed down Lake Michigan to Fort Dearborn (modern Chicago) before traveling back to Detroit. The trip lasted four months and covered 4,200 miles.

Accompanying Cass were his secretary James Duane Doty, who would later become governor of the Wisconsin Territory, and a geologist named Henry Rowe Schoolcraft. The New York-born Schoolcraft had taken part on a similar mission in Missouri in 1818. His task was to make topographical surveys of the areas through which they traveled. Schoolcraft's intense curiosity quickly became evident as he encountered American Indian communities and early non-Indian settlements. He recorded detailed descriptions of everything he experienced, from geographic formations to plants and animals. The expedition found Lake Itasca in northern Minnesota, which he believed to be the source of the Mississippi river. The lead mines in southwest Wisconsin also caught his attention. He knew the history of the territory, and by interspersing historical background freely throughout his narrative, he created a lively and thoroughly interesting account. His work is the earliest known documented descriptions of Wisconsin.

On August 20, he recorded his first glimpse of Fort Howard on Green Bay: Nothing, he wrote, "can exceed the beauty of the intermediate country—chequered as it is, with farm houses, fences, cultivated fields, the broad expanse of the river—the

Getting Started on Research

Ask your librarian to help you find a copy of Schoolcraft's *Narrative Journal.* From this primary source, what areas does Schoolcraft describe that are in or near your community? What did the expedition find interesting about this area? What areas did you find most interesting? Did your hometown exist in the early 1800s? If so, what was it like? An excellent secondary account of Schoolcraft's journey is in *James Duane Doty* by Alice Smith.

bannered masts of the vessels in the distant bay, and the warlike array of military barracks, camps, and parades."

After he returned to Detroit, he published his account of the voyage, which he titled *A Narrative Journal of Travels through the Northwestern Regions of the United States: Extending from Detroit through the Great Chain of American Lakes, to the Sources of the Mississippi River.* The 419-page

LXXXIX. Day.—(*August, 20th.*)—A heavy fog in the morning, prevented us from quitting our encampment until seven o'clock.—Six miles below, we passed the rapids of the little Kakalin, which, however, oppose no serious obstacle to the navigation of the river, on the descent. Here, we found a small party of United States soldiers, who were engaged in preparing the foundation for a saw mill, which is to be erected at that spot for the accommodation of the garrison, and settlement at Green Bay. There is another small rapid, seven miles below, called Rock rapid, from which it is five more to the garrison, where we arrived at one o'clock P. M. The settlement of Green Bay commences at the little Kakalin, twelve miles above the fort; and is very compact, from the Rock rapid. Here, we are first presented with a view of the fort; and nothing can exceed the beauty of the intermediate country—chequered as it is, with farm houses, fences, cultivated fields, the broad expanse of the river—the bannered masts of the vessels in the distant bay, and the warlike array of military barracks, camps, and parades. This scene burst suddenly into view, and no combination of objects in the physiognomy of a country, could be more happily arranged, af-

ter so long a sojournment in the wilderness, to recall at once to the imagination, the most pleasing recollections of civilized life; and indeed, the circumstances of our return, would have produced a high degree of exhilaration; without the additional excitements of military music, which now saluted our ears, and the peals of artillery which bid us welcome to the fort.

WHS Archives: Rare Books

Schoolcraft's description of approaching Green Bay, from his travel journal, 1821

book appeared in 1821. The first 1,500 copies sold out quickly. People all over the country were getting the opportunity to experience his journey for themselves. Schoolcraft then turned from geology to ethnology. In 1822, he became an Indian Agent posted at the straits of Mackinac. He married the daughter of a fur trader, an Ojibwe woman, and learned the language and traditions of the Ojibwe. Later, he wrote extensively on American Indians and published a six-volume history of the tribes in America.

Juliette M. Kinzie
Pioneer Encounters on the Wisconsin Frontier

Imagine traveling to a place where you have never been before; a place with few people like yourself and almost no roads at all. An adventure like that may seem pretty scary to most people today, but that's exactly what Euro-American men and women who came to Wisconsin in the early 1800s experienced.

One of the women who made the journey was Juliette Kinzie. In 1830, her husband John Kinzie was sent by President Andrew Jackson to be the Indian Agent at Fort Winnebago, near Portage. The Ho-Chunks and non-Indian Americans had recently fought over the settlers' encroachment on Indian land. After the Ho-Chunk leader Red Bird surrendered, John Kinzie came to maintain peaceful relations with the Ho-Chunks. Kinzie had lived his entire life on the frontier, and he spoke many

Portrait of Juliette Kinzie, 1855

Indian languages. This was one of the reasons why he was such a good choice to represent the U.S. government. His wife, Juliette, accompanied him, and the two lived at the Indian Agency House near Fort Winnebago for three years.

Juliette described their journey and life at the Indian Agency House in *Wau-Bun: The "Early Day" in the Northwest,* which was first published in 1855. The Kinzies traveled from Detroit on a steamboat, to Green Bay, then on a smaller boat, up the Fox River to their new home. During her travels, Juliette met a number of important people in Wisconsin, including the future governor of Wisconsin Territory, James Duane Doty. She described the landscape and the inhabitants of the territory in great detail, remarking about the beauty of the land and the culture of the Indians she encountered.

Life on the frontier was hard. Juliette was from New England, and she missed the comforts of town and the company of her friends. She struggled to build a respectable settlement at the fort and tried to create a comfortable, though smaller, version of New England town life. Although she missed her native Connecticut, she developed a strong interest in the local Ho-Chunk people. Juliette recorded many of their customs and traditional stories, such as the legend of how the Fox River was formed—by a great

Juliette Kinzie's drawing of Fort Winnebago from *Wau-Bun*

80 THE EARLY DAY IN THE NORTH-WEST.

sight of the white walls of Fort Winnebago, looking down from a rising ground upon the vast expanse of low land through which the river winds.

The Indians have a tradition that a vast serpent* once lived in the waters of the Mississippi, and that taking a freak to visit the Great Lakes, he left his trail through the prairies, which, collecting the waters from the meadows and the rains of heaven as they fell, at length became the Fox River.

The little lakes along its course were probably the spots where he flourished about in his uneasy slumbers at night. He must have played all the antics of a kitten in the neighborhood of the Portage. When the Fort was first pointed out to me, I exclaimed with delight, "Oh, we shall be there in half an hour!"

"Not quite so soon," said my husband, smiling. "Wait and see." We sat and watched. We seemed approaching the very spot where we were to disembark. We could distinguish the officers and a lady on the bank waiting to receive us. Now we are turning our backs on them, and shooting out into the prairie again. Anon we approach another bank, on which is a range of comfortable-looking log-houses. "That s the Agency,"—the largest house belongs to Paquette, the interpreter, and the others are the dwellings of our Frenchmen. The little building, just at the foot of the hill, is the blacksmith's shop, kept there by the

Juliette Kinzie's description of her arrival in Portage in her memoir *Wau-Bun*

serpent moving from the Mississippi River to the Great Lakes.

As Indian Agent, John was responsible for delivering the annual payment to the Ho-Chunks, and Juliette got to know several families who visited the Agency House regularly. Her narrative makes clear the affection she had for them. Among the many examples of her compassionate spirit was her description of a young man with the unlikely name of "Talk-English" and the elaborate funeral ceremony for a departed Ho-Chunk leader named Four Legs. At Christmastime, she played hostess to a group of Ho-Chunk women and served them doughnuts. The women had never

before seen white sugar. At first, they refused the treats, thinking that they had been sprinkled with salt!

Juliette also witnessed some tumultuous times on the Wisconsin frontier. In 1832, the Sauc leader Black Hawk led a group of Sauc and Fox Indians through southern Wisconsin. They were being pursued by Ho-Chunks and the United States army. The incident terrorized non-Indian settlers, and Juliette described the strained atmosphere of the time. Her family prepared to defend the Agency House in case Black Hawk's party drew near.

Many other women traveled to Wisconsin in the 1830s and 1840s, and although very few of them recorded their impressions of settling the frontier, Juliette Kinzie's account provides a vivid assessment of what life was like for many of them. From a twenty-first century perspective, some of her descriptions of the Ho-Chunks may seem patronizing, even racist. But, Juliette reflected the prejudices of her times. Her writings show that she admired many aspects of Ho-Chunk culture and the people she met. But, as was common in her day, it is clear that she and other non-Indian settlers believed that Native people were inferior. Despite this, Juliette was able to paint a sympathetic, even respectful, portrait of the Indians she grew to know, and her writings show how she often saw them as individuals.

Can you imagine traveling to frontier Wisconsin and trying to make it feel like the home you left? How would you have dealt with the challenges you would have encountered while living on this frontier?

Getting Started on Research

To learn more about Juliette Kinzie, her book *Wau-Bun* is an excellent place to start. It is still available in most libraries. Patty Loew's *Indian Nations of Wisconsin: Histories of Endurance and Renewal* is a good source of information about the Ho-Chunk people and other tribes.

A Potawatomi family at Skunk Hill in Wood County, 1920

WHi (X3) 35356

Skunk Hill, also known as Powers Bluff or Tah-qua-kik, in Wood County was home to a community of Native Americans from the late 19th into the early years of the 20th century. The area remains a significant spiritual center for Native American communities. Part of the importance of Skunk Hill derives from its association with the Dream Dance, a Native religious ceremony that began in the Great Plains and spread into Wisconsin. Communities like Skunk Hill were places where Native people could share traditional values, practices, languages, and ceremonies away from the intrusions of outsiders.

In the mid-1870s, a young Lakota woman in Minnesota named Wananikwe experienced a vision and began traveling throughout the northern plains. She shared her belief that Native people could liberate themselves from the United States and reclaim their lost land if they drummed with special songs and danced for four days. This ritual, she felt, would paralyze non-Indians

and would restore ancient tribal ways. Many American Indian communities began practicing the Dream Dance in the hopes that it would relieve the poor conditions they lived in and the ill treatment they received at the hands of non-Indians. Eventually, the message became one of spiritual renewal, and numerous tribes adopted the dance as an important part of their culture.

A variety of historical documents and oral histories—from the people who were children during that era—have provided information about the Skunk Hill community. The rocky, 250-foot hill itself is an easily recognizable landmark with strong spiritual meaning for Native people. The Prairie Band Potawatomi from Kansas—descendants of the Potawatomi people who lived in Wisconsin in the early nineteenth century—are believed to have settled much of this bluff in the 1870s. About 80 people briefly lived at Skunk Hill. They established it as a ceremonial center before moving further north. In the late 19th century, Skunk Hill had

WHS Archives

Dance ring at Skunk Hill, 1920

been the center of logging and iron-mining operations. After the logging and mining ended, another group of Prairie Band members settled at Powers Bluff. For important ceremonies, members of the Forest County Potawatomi Band, as well as other Wisconsin Indian people such as the Ho-Chunk, Menominee, and Ojibwe joined the residents.

In 1910, the census indicates that nearly a hundred Native Americans were living in the vicinity, and many likely lived on Skunk Hill itself. Deeds in Wood County show that Native people owned several parcels of land there, and photographic and archaeological evidence has uncovered much about the community, its life, and its ceremonies. Photographs show log cabins and shacks, including a traditional elm-bark structure used for ceremonial purposes, along the top of the bluff. Remnants of these structures are still visible, and a recent archaeological investigation revealed fragments of dishes and bones from butchered deer and other wildlife. Two separate dance rings remain evident. One is 80 feet in diameter, and the other is 100 feet in diameter. Evidence shows that earthen embankments once surrounded the rings, and photographs indicate that a tall fence encircled them. Potawatomi elders have reported that two rings were necessary to accommodate the large number of people who participated in ceremonies. The Skunk Hill inhabitants practiced traditional

Getting Started on Research

A good place to start reading about the Potawatomi and their beliefs and ceremonies is *The Prairie People: Continuity and Change in Potawatomi Culture, 1665–1965* by James Clifton. For more on the Wisconsin Potawatomi, see *Indian Nations of Wisconsin* by Patty Loew. This secondary source contains several photographs of Skunk Hill, and it documents some of the evidence mentioned in this section. To find primary documents, search the Wisconsin Historical Society's online Archives Catalog at http://arcat.library.wisc.edu/. Type in the keywords "Potawatomi" and "Skunk Hill."

subsistence of hunting and gathering food, but they also worked the area's farms, sold baskets, and created beadwork.

During the 1920s, the Skunk Hill community declined to only about 20 residents, and by 1930, the ceremonial dance rings were abandoned. But strong ties remained, as did the commitment of Native American tribes to come together for ceremonial and social purposes. Today, Wisconsin tribes host many powwows that serve these important functions. Their drumming, singing, and dancing preserve important American Indian traditions and honor the ancestors who lived in Wisconsin before and since Europeans arrived in North America.

WHS Archives: P88-185

see this change take place.

The Indian Dance.

On Saturday last the Indians at Skunk Hill commenced a sacred dance that lasted four days. Our curiosity had been aroused to attend one of these functions, and last Sunday it was our pleasure to have that ambition gratified. Through the courtesy of Mr. and Mrs. Geo. E. Martin, the editor and wife and Mrs. Sarah Gibbs were given an auto trip to the summit of Skunk Hill where the dance was in progress. The road leading to the top of the hill was rough and rocky, and we believe this was the first auto to make the summit of the hill.

The Indians hold several dances during the year to celebrate certain events, and the dance varies accordingly. This dance was of a religious nature in which the Indians make sacrifices and otherwise do homage to the Great Spirit. So in the whole this dance did not abound in the usual glitter of costume and was

Article from *The State Center,* October 10, 1912

Treaty Councils
From Prairie du Chien to Madeline Island

Did you know that of all the states east of the Mississippi River, Wisconsin has a greater diversity of Native American tribes? Wisconsin's geography—its navigable waterways between two Great Lakes and the Mississippi River—made it a popular crossroads for many different Native tribes long before Europeans arrived.

The 11 federally recognized Native American communities in Wisconsin are made up of three linguistic groups. These are the Siouan, Algonquian, and Iroquoian. Within these groups are many tribes, and the Creation stories in their oral traditions—the Ho-Chunk and Menominee nations, for example—explain that these tribes have been in Wisconsin for many, many years. The Ojibwe, too, have been present here for hundreds of years, and as Euro-American settlement displaced Native populations in lands to the east, even more tribes moved from the east into the area.

Other factors contributing to the state's diversity were changing U.S. government policies toward Native peoples. During the first half of the nineteenth century, the federal

Original color lithograph depicting the Treaty at Prairie du Chien in 1825

WHI Image ID 3142

government negotiated many treaties with Wisconsin tribes. The government forced some tribes to leave, assigned some others to reservations, and also encouraged eastern tribes to move west into Wisconsin. The many attempts by Wisconsin's Indian nations to maintain, return to, or reclaim their ancestral lands attests to their perseverance and great desire to maintain and nurture their "roots."

However, American Indians found the concept of "owning" land very strange. They never claimed ownership of any lands on which they lived. Treaty negotiations between Wisconsin tribes and the federal government began in 1804 when the

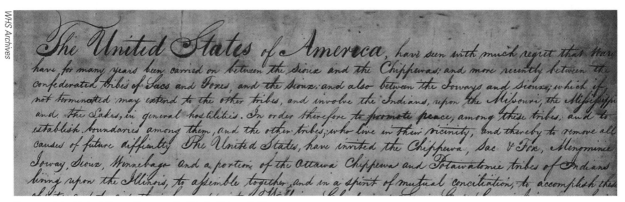

WHS Archives

Excerpt of the United States Treaty at Prairie du Chien, 1825 government purchased large tracts of land in southwestern Wisconsin from the Sauk and Mesquakie tribes. The members of the Potawatomi and Ho-Chunk nations had lived in the same area even longer, so in 1816 and 1832, the U.S. government negotiated additional treaties to purchase their lands.

To try to clarify the ownership situation, the federal government began holding "treaty councils" with all the Wisconsin tribes. The first of these councils was held in 1825, when 5,000 members of different tribes met at Prairie du Chien. On the pretext of promoting peace among the tribes, the government requested that all Indian nations establish clear boundaries. But, these boundary agreements only gave the government a clear map to use to negotiate for the land!

To further clarify the 1825 arrangements, two other treaty councils took place. In 1826, the government held a second treaty council with the Ojibwe. This event occurred at the head of Lake Superior. In 1827, a third council was held with the Menominee at Little Lake Butte des Morts.

The federal government then began a series of negotiations with Wisconsin tribes to persuade them to cede their land. Between 1829 and 1848, the federal government purchased land from every Wisconsin tribe. However, not everyone in the tribes had agreed to the outcomes. Often, treaties were signed by just a few Native individuals who had not received authority from tribal elders to negotiate with the federal govern-

ment or to sell any land. At other times, federal agents deliberately misled the tribes. For example, the tribes were sometimes told that they had years to leave when, in reality, they had only months. For these and other reasons, tribal members often resisted dealing with the federal government.

WHi Image ID (X3) 35395

Lithograph of Grand Council held at Little Lake Butte des Morts, 1827

Then in 1848, federal policy toward Native tribes changed. Instead of continuing their efforts to remove the tribes, the government wanted them to settle in one location. Some Wisconsin tribes were successful in petitioning the federal government for a different outcome. In 1854, Menominee leaders negotiated a treaty that reserved a tract of 276,000 acres on the Wolf and Oconto rivers. The Ojibwe tribe resisted removal and held the last treaty council in 1854 on Madeline Island. In these negotiations, the Ojibwe secured four reservations: Red Cliff, Lac du Flambeau, Bad River, and Lac Courte Oreilles (which totaled more than 270,000 acres). The St. Croix and Sokaogan (Mole Lake) Bands, however, did not receive reservation lands until the 1930s!

What tribe originally held the land where you currently live? When was the area ceded? What was the name of the treaty and what were the terms? How did the negotiations affect the tribes living in your area?

Getting Started on Research

Find your county on maps of tribal lands in *Wisconsin Indians* by Nancy O. Lurie. For more details on the tribes before, during, and after the treaties, see *Indian Nations of Wisconsin* by Patty Loew. To study the verbatim copies of actual treaties, consult Charles J. Kappler's *Indian Treaties 1778–1883.*

Chief Buffalo and His Mission to Washington

By the mid-1850s, the Ojibwe people had survived many of the challenges thrust upon them by the French, British, and American governments. U.S. officials had ordered the Ojibwe leader Chief Buffalo to move his people much farther west. In 1852, when he was more than 90 years old, Chief Buffalo went to Washington. He traveled by foot, canoe, and railroad in an effort to convince the American president and federal officials to allow the Ojibwe to remain on their land. He was especially committed to staying on Madeline Island, the spiritual home of the Ojibwe.

Through treaties signed in 1837 and 1842, the Ojibwe ceded their Wisconsin lands to the United States, but they clearly reserved the right to continue hunting, fishing, and gathering on the land that they had ceded. The treaties allowed the Ojibwe to remain there until the president ordered them to move west. The removal order came in 1850, when President Zachary Taylor directed the Ojibwe to leave Wisconsin. That same year, federal officials moved the annual federal payments required by the treaty from Madeline Island to Minnesota Territory. More than 400 Ojibwe men, women, and children endured cold and disease to travel to Sandy Lake in Minnesota. Along the way,

Portion of the Treaty of 1854

many died of cold and starvation.

"Our women and children do indeed cry … on account of their suffering from cold and hunger," wrote Chief Buffalo the following year, 1851. His letter went to the Commissioner of Indian Affairs. "We wish to … remain here where we were promised we might live, as long as we were not in the way of the Whites." Finally in 1852, he decided to take his case directly to the federal government. Guided by his adopted son Benjamin Armstrong, an Alabama native who settled in Wisconsin and married into the tribe, Chief Buffalo made his way to Washington. He met with President Millard Fillmore (who had taken office after Taylor died in 1850) in the White House. Chief Buffalo was so persuasive that the president rescinded the removal order and promised to restore annuity payments to Madeline Island. As Chief Buffalo made his way back to his home, he told the bands of Ojibwe he encountered the happy news that they would be able to stay.

As a result of Buffalo's direct appeal to the president, new treaty negotiations to establish reservations took place in 1854. Armstrong interpreted for 2,000 Ojibwe members who attended the treaty signing. The new treaty established four reservations for the Ojibwe: Lac Courte Orielles, Bad River, Red Cliff, and Lac du Flambeau. (Two additional reservations for the Mole Lake and St. Croix bands were not established until 1934.) The 1854 treaty also

WHI (X3) 41266

Portrait of Chief Buffalo, undated

reaffirmed the rights established in earlier treaties that the Ojibwe could hunt, fish, and gather into perpetuity in ceded areas. Chief Buffalo's success in securing land in Wisconsin for his people assured a continuing Ojibwe presence in the state.

Chief Buffalo made a second trip to Washington in 1855. The president (now Franklin Pierce) had requested a meeting with Ojibwe chiefs to finalize some minor remaining matters. While he was there, Chief Buffalo sat for artist Francis Vincenti, who sculpted a portrait bust of him in marble. Chief Buffalo returned to Madeline Island and died a few months later, just as many of his people were beginning to move onto reservations. The Vincenti bust of Chief Buffalo remains in the United States Capitol. It is a fitting tribute to the Ojibwe Nation's determination to retain their ancestral home.

Getting Started on Research

The tale of Chief Buffalo is told by his adopted son Benjamin Armstrong in *Reminiscences of Life Among the Chippewa,* which is printed in several consecutive issues of the *Wisconsin Magazine of History.* Patty Loew's *Indian Nations of Wisconsin* gives a good account of the Ojibwe and their efforts to secure their land in northern Wisconsin. The treaty-making process is described by Nancy Lurie in *Wisconsin Indians.* Another excellent source is Ronald Satz's *Chippewa Treaty Rights: The Reserved Rights of Wisconsin's Chippewa Indians in Historical Perspective.* Chapters 4 and 5 are especially relevant.

The Lucerne

Preserving Wisconsin's Great Lakes Shipwrecks

Underwater archaeologists explore the wreckage site of the *Lucerne*.

You might think life aboard a large lake schooner would be exciting and fun, especially with a crew that traveled and visited many places, but such a life could be very dangerous. There are many shipwrecks on the Great Lakes to prove it, and each one has its own story to tell.

One of these is the schooner *Lucerne*. On November 15, 1886, the *Lucerne* departed Ashland laden with more than 1,200 tons of iron ore bound for Cleveland. Many schooners just like the *Lucerne* regularly sailed the Great Lakes moving ore from Wisconsin, Michigan, and Minnesota to industrial cities in the East. But, November storms on Lake Superior are notorious for sweeping in without warning. Within a day of the ship's departure, the weather turned stormy, and the *Lucerne* pitched and rolled in the gale-force winds and heavy snow. Unable to find safe harbor in the Apostle Islands, the ship's captain, George Lloyd, dropped anchor and hoped to wait out the storm. Sometime that night, the ship and its crew sank in the cold waters of Lake Superior.

The wreck of the *Lucerne* was discovered on November 19, when the keeper of the La Pointe light-house spotted two masts poking up from the water just off the shore of Long Island. The ice-covered bodies of three men were found, bundled in clothing and lashed to the rigging in a futile attempt to protect themselves from the freezing Lake Superior water. The other four or five crew members were never found. For the people who made their living on the lake, the sinking of the *Lucerne* was a grim

Article about the sinking of the *Lucerne* from the *Ashland Weekly Press*, November 20, 1886

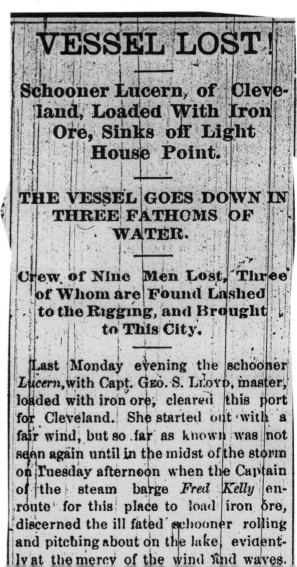

VESSEL LOST!

Schooner Lucern, of Cleveland, Loaded With Iron Ore, Sinks off Light House Point.

THE VESSEL GOES DOWN IN THREE FATHOMS OF WATER.

Crew of Nine Men Lost, Three of Whom are Found Lashed to the Rigging, and Brought to This City.

Last Monday evening the schooner *Lucern*, with Capt. Geo. S. Lloyd, master, loaded with iron ore, cleared this port for Cleveland. She started out with a fair wind, but so far as known was not seen again until in the midst of the storm on Tuesday afternoon when the Captain of the steam barge *Fred Kelly* enroute for this place to load iron ore, discerned the ill fated schooner rolling and pitching about on the lake, evidently at the mercy of the wind and waves.

Getting Started on Research

For more information on the *Lucerne* and its continued importance as an archaeological site, see *By Fire, Storm, and Ice* edited by David J. Cooper. Also, the University of Wisconsin Sea Grant Institute Web site can be accessed at http://www.wisconsinshipwrecks.org/. The Web site contains information on many shipwrecks on the Great Lakes. You can also visit the Lake Superior Marine Museum Association in Duluth's Canal Park or go online to view artifacts from the wreckage. Your local library, historical society, and many Internet Web sites provide access to reports from old newspapers, especially those published in nearby port communities. These newspapers commonly reported on the immediate reactions of people and early details about shipwrecks that happened in the nineteenth or twentieth centuries.

reminder of the dangers facing sailors. "Of the sufferings of that crew," wrote a reporter for the *Ashland Weekly Press*, "there will never be a written account, but in the unwritten annals … will undoubtedly be found tales of heroism and bravery in the meeting of deaths in the terrible manner which came to them."

Today, the fateful tale of the *Lucerne* and its crew is more than just a scary story to be told by the fireplace on a dark and stormy night. Like many such wrecks on the Great Lakes, the *Lucerne* offers us a chance to investigate our maritime heritage first-hand. The wreck is still in the same place where it sank and is accessible to archaeologists and others who want to learn more about it. Because the shallow waters make it easy to get to, the wreckage is a popular spot for divers who can explore its hull, take photographs, and make videos. The hull is largely intact, and the ship's windlass and capstan—the machinery used to raise the anchor—are still in place. Iron ore is scattered around the wreck.

The *Lucerne* was listed on the National Register of Historic Places in 1991 and is owned by the Wisconsin Historical Society, which maintains the site in cooperation with the National Park Service. The preservation of shipwrecks is very important. State and federal laws protect these sites from being looted and having any artifacts illegally removed. As historical places, the sites belong to everyone and are preserved and made available for research and educational purposes.

What do you think life was like for sailors on the Great Lakes during the 1800s? What other shipwrecks in the Great lakes or near your town do you know about? Librarians, teachers, and archivists at your local or county historical society can help you learn more about the *Lucerne* and other important shipwrecks.

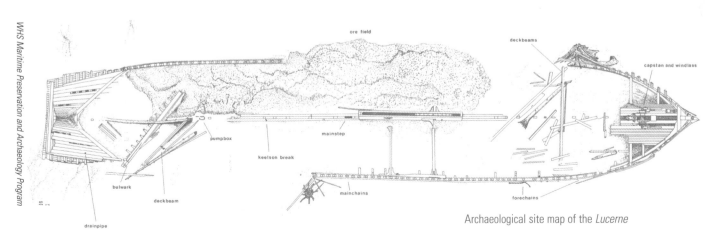

WHS Maritime Preservation and Archaeology Program

Archaeological site map of the *Lucerne*

Black Hawk's Return
"The Land Cannot Be Sold"

Portrait of Black Hawk, undated

In the summer of 1832, U.S. troops pursued a band of Sauk and Mesquakie Indians across southern Wisconsin in the last major confrontation between the U.S. Army and Native Americans east of the Mississippi River. The conflict's roots date back to 1804, when treaties required the Sauk and Mesquakie nations to cede their lands east of the Mississippi River to the United States. At that time, the two Indian nations lived near rivers in what is now southwestern Wisconsin and northwestern Illinois. Although the Indians retained the right to remain until ordered to leave by the federal government, pressure mounted as more and more non-Indians settled on Indian land. The eager search for lead in this area only increased the tensions.

When the land on the lower Rock River was offered for sale to settlers in 1829, the government ordered the Sauk and Mesquakie to go west. Some moved peacefully. Others, like Black Hawk, a warrior chief who had fought with the British during the War of 1812, disliked American settlers and firmly resisted. But after first refusing, he finally relented and moved his people west

Once west of the Mississippi River, Black Hawk's people began to suffer. They were forbidden to visit their ancestors' graves, even though the sites were now being disturbed. The U.S. government did not deliver the food promised to the removed tribes. Watching his people agonize, Black Hawk's anger grew. He made plans to reoccupy his old village. Joined by members of other tribes in April 1832, he led about a thousand people back across the Mississippi River.

The news of Black Hawk's movements alarmed local settlers, and they formed a militia to protect themselves. The U.S. army was ordered to ensure the return of Black Hawk back across the Mississippi River. Black Hawk hoped that other Indian tribes in the area and the British in Canada would help. For safety, Black Hawk moved his band

Site of Battle of Wisconsin Heights painted by Samuel M. Brooks and Thomas M. Stevenson, 1857

up the Rock River, but neither the British nor any of his Indian allies came to his aid.

The military and militia greatly outnumbered Black Hawk's hungry and tired people, so he sent a small delegation under a white flag of truce to a militia encampment. Some militia members panicked when they saw the Sauk men approaching and started a battle in which people on both sides were killed. The militiamen fled in terror.

Getting Started on Research

Black Hawk wrote his own account of the attempted return to Wisconsin in his autobiography *Life of Black Hawk.* **Another account is in the recent biography** *Black Hawk and the Warrior's Path* **by Roger L. Nichols. For more about the Sauk and Mesquakie, see** *Wisconsin Indians* **by Nancy O. Lurie.**

Life of Black Hawk

During our encampment at the Four Lakes, we were hard put to obtain enough to eat to support nature. Situate in a swampy, marshy country, (which had been selected in consequence of the great difficulty required to gain access thereto,) there was but little game of any sort to be found — and fish were equally scarce. The great distance to any settlement, and the impossibility of bringing supplies therefrom, if any could have been obtained, deterred our young men from making further attempts. We were forced to *dig roots* and *bark trees*, to obtain something to satisfy hunger and keep us alive! Several of our old people became so much reduced, as actually to *die with hunger!* And, finding that the army had commenced moving, and fearing that they might come upon and surround our encampment, I concluded to remove my women and children across the Mississippi, that they might return to the Sac nation again. Accordingly, on the next day, we commenced moving, with [131] five Winnebagoes acting as our guides, intending to descend the Ouisconsin.

Ne-a-pope, with a party of twenty, remained in our rear, to watch for the enemy, whilst we were proceeding to the Ouisconsin, with our women and children. We arrived, and had commenced crossing them to an island, when we discovered a large body of the enemy coming towards us. We were now compelled to fight, or sacrifice our wives and children to

153

WHS Archives

Description of the Battle of Wisconsin Heights from Black Hawk's autobiography

Black Hawk believed that the safest decision was to move his people north along the Rock River before heading west in order to get back across the Mississippi. Near the Wisconsin River, they successfully resisted the militia in the Battle of Wisconsin Heights. On August 1, Black Hawk and his band reached the Mississippi River and tried to cross. Despite another white flag of truce, the steamboat *Warrior* blocked their escape and fired on the band, while the military and militia attacked from the rear. Although Black Hawk and about 50 of his party escaped, many Indian people, mostly women and children, were massacred in the Battle of Bad Axe.

Black Hawk was captured a short time later and imprisoned. In his autobiography, Black Hawk wanted to communicate his people's frustration and explain his resistance. He clarified the cultural differences between the Indian and the Euro-American concepts of land use, when he stated, "My reason teaches me that the land cannot be sold ... Nothing can be sold, but such things as can be carried away."

How did Black Hawk's ideas about land motivate him to return to his village on the east bank of the Mississippi River? Why do you think the settlers were so alarmed at Black Hawk's return? Why did the militia, and later, those on the ship *Warrior,* not believe his flag of truce?

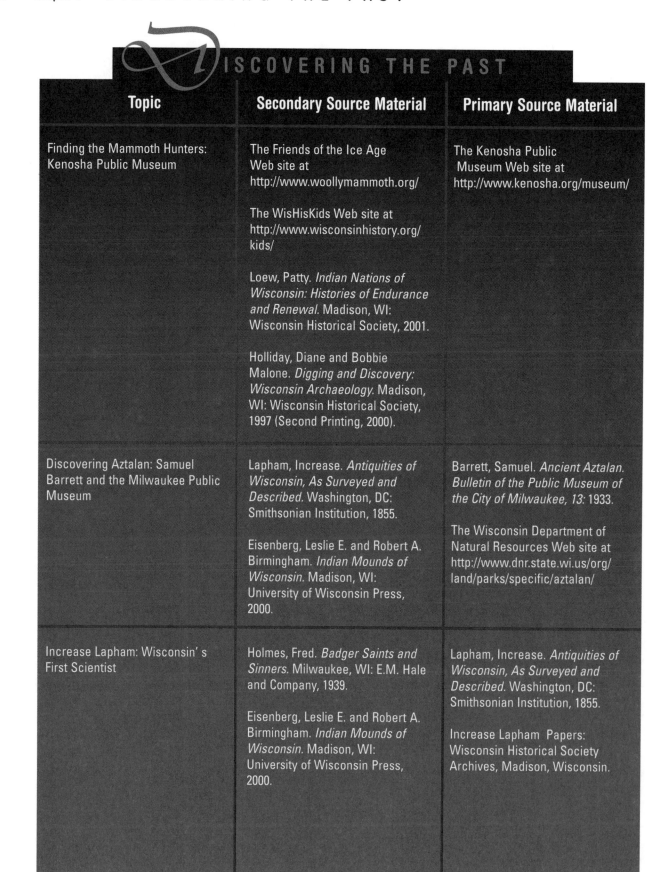

DISCOVERING THE PAST

Topic	Secondary Source Material	Primary Source Material
Finding the Mammoth Hunters: Kenosha Public Museum	The Friends of the Ice Age Web site at http://www.woollymammoth.org/ The WisHisKids Web site at http://www.wisconsinhistory.org/kids/ Loew, Patty. *Indian Nations of Wisconsin: Histories of Endurance and Renewal.* Madison, WI: Wisconsin Historical Society, 2001. Holliday, Diane and Bobbie Malone. *Digging and Discovery: Wisconsin Archaeology.* Madison, WI: Wisconsin Historical Society, 1997 (Second Printing, 2000).	The Kenosha Public Museum Web site at http://www.kenosha.org/museum/
Discovering Aztalan: Samuel Barrett and the Milwaukee Public Museum	Lapham, Increase. *Antiquities of Wisconsin, As Surveyed and Described.* Washington, DC: Smithsonian Institution, 1855. Eisenberg, Leslie E. and Robert A. Birmingham. *Indian Mounds of Wisconsin.* Madison, WI: University of Wisconsin Press, 2000.	Barrett, Samuel. *Ancient Aztalan. Bulletin of the Public Museum of the City of Milwaukee, 13:* 1933. The Wisconsin Department of Natural Resources Web site at http://www.dnr.state.wi.us/org/land/parks/specific/aztalan/
Increase Lapham: Wisconsin's First Scientist	Holmes, Fred. *Badger Saints and Sinners.* Milwaukee, WI: E.M. Hale and Company, 1939. Eisenberg, Leslie E. and Robert A. Birmingham. *Indian Mounds of Wisconsin.* Madison, WI: University of Wisconsin Press, 2000.	Lapham, Increase. *Antiquities of Wisconsin, As Surveyed and Described.* Washington, DC: Smithsonian Institution, 1855. Increase Lapham Papers: Wisconsin Historical Society Archives, Madison, Wisconsin.

Topic	Secondary Source Material	Primary Source Material
Otter Spring: Protecting Wisconsin's Sacred Sites	Loew, Patty. *Indian Nations of Wisconsin: Histories of Endurance and Renewal.* Madison, WI: Wisconsin Historical Society, 2001. Ritzenthaler, Robert E. and Pat Ritzenthaler. *The Woodland Indians of the Western Great Lakes.* Milwaukee, WI: Milwaukee Public Museum, 1983.	The Forest County Potawatomi Web site at http://www.fcpotawatomi.com/
Henry R. Schoolcraft: The 1820 Expedition to the Western Michigan Territory	Smith, Alice. *James Duane Doty: Frontier Promoter.* Madison, WI: State Historical Society of Wisconsin, 1954. Doty's journal was reprinted in the *Wisconsin Historical Collections,* volume 13, pages 163–219.	Schoolcraft, Henry R. *Narrative Journal of Travels through the Northwestern Regions of the United States: Extending from Detroit through the Great Chain of American Lakes, to the Sources of the Mississippi River.* Albany, NY: E. & E. Hosford, 1821. Doty, James Duane. Journal (papers): Madison, WI: State Historical Society of Wisconsin (Wisconsin Historical Collections 13), 1856: 163–219.
Juliette M. Kinzie: Pioneer Encounters on the Wisconsin Frontier	Loew, Patty. *Indian Nations of Wisconsin: Histories of Endurance and Renewal.* Madison, WI: Wisconsin Historical Society, 2001.	Kinzie, Juliette M. *Wau-Bun: The "Early Day" in the North-west.* Chicago, IL: University of Illinois Press, 1992.
Skunk Hill: Where the Dream Dance Came to Wisconsin	Clifton, James. *The Prairie People: Continuity and Change in Potawatomi Indian Culture, 1665–1965.* Lawrence, KS: Regents Press of Kansas, 1977. Loew, Patty. *Indian Nations of Wisconsin: Histories of Endurance and Renewal.* Madison, WI: Wisconsin Historical Society, 2001.	Wisconsin Historical Society Archives Catalog Web site at http://arcat.library.wisc.edu/ keywords: Potawatomi, Skunk Hill

Topic	Secondary Source Material	Primary Source Material
Treaty Councils: From Prairie du Chien to Madeline Island	Loew, Patty. *Indian Nations of Wisconsin: Histories of Endurance and Renewal.* Madison, WI: Wisconsin Historical Society, 2001. Lurie, Nancy. *Wisconsin Indians.* Revised and expanded edition. Madison, WI: Wisconsin Historical Society Press, 2002.	*Indian Treaties 1778–1883.* Compiled and edited by Charles J. Kappler. New York: Interland Publishing, 1972.
Chief Buffalo and His Mission to Washington	Loew, Patty. *Indian Nations of Wisconsin: Histories of Endurance and Renewal.* Madison, WI: Wisconsin Historical Society, 2001. Lurie, Nancy. *Wisconsin Indians.* Revised and expanded edition. Madison, WI: Wisconsin Historical Society Press, 2002. Satz, Ronald N. *Chippewa Treaty Rights: The Reserved Rights of Wisconsin's Chippewa Indians in Historical Perspective.* Madison, WI: (Transactions 79) Wisconsin Academy of Sciences, Arts, and Letters, 1991.	Armstrong, Benjamin. "Reminiscences of Life Among the Chippewa" (Parts 1–4). *Wisconsin Magazine of History* 55–56, nos. 3, 4, 1, and 2 (1972–73).

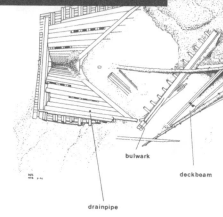

bulwark

deckbeam

drainpipe

Topic	Secondary Source Material	Primary Source Material
The Lucerne: Preserving Wisconsin's Great Lakes Shipwrecks	Cooper, David J. ed. *By Fire, Storm, and Ice: Underwater Archaeological Investigations in the Apostle Islands.* Madison, WI: Underwater Archeology Program, Division of Historic Preservation, State Historical Society of Wisconsin, 1991. The University of Wisconsin Sea Grant Institute (Wisconsin's Great Lakes Shipwrecks) Web site at http://www.wisconsinshipwrecks.org/	The Lake Superior Marine Museum Association Web site at http://www.lsmma.com/
Black Hawk's Return: "The Land Cannot Be Sold"	Nichols, Roger. *Black Hawk and the Warrior's Path.* Arlington Heights, IL: H. Davidson, 1992. Lurie, Nancy. *Wisconsin Indians.* Revised and expanded edition. Madison, WI: Wisconsin Historical Society Press, 2002.	Black Hawk. *Life of Black Hawk, or Ma-ka-tai-me-she-kia-kiak.* London, England: R.J. Kennett, 1836.

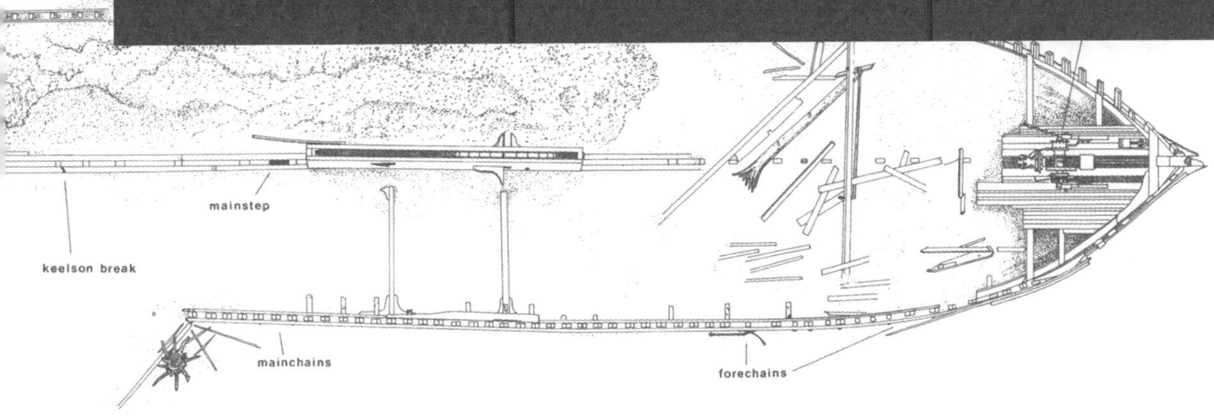

keelson break

mainstep

mainchains

forechains

Chapter Two

Immigration in Wisconsin History

- **From Factory to Farm and Back: The British Temperance Emigration Society and Savings Fund**

- **Finnish Co-ops: Fair Trade in the Northwoods**

- **Colonel Hans Christian Heg: A Norwegian Regiment in the Civil War**

- **The Niagara: Great Lakes Palace Steamer Fire Kills Hundreds**

- **Poles in Portage County**

- **Iron Mining and Italian Community Building in Hurley**

- **From Logging to Farming: Selling Northern Wisconsin to Immigrants**

- **Attracting Newcomers to a New State**

- **German Music in a German State**

- **Freedom Ride!: Grant County's African American Pioneers**

- **Escape from Laos: The Harrowing Journey of the Hmong to Wisconsin**

From Factory to Farm and Back

The British Temperance Emigration Society and Savings Fund

Have you ever wanted to move to another place and change your life? Millions of European, Asian, and Latin American immigrants did just that when they moved to the United States. They often risked a great deal to leave the homelands they knew, and they found life here very different from the life they had lived before.

Map of the British Temperance Emigration Society lands in Wisconsin

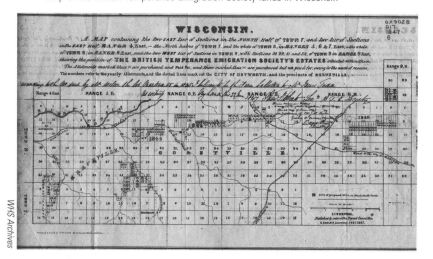

WHS Archives

During the Industrial Revolution of the 1700s and 1800s, factories in England were hazardous places. The primitive machinery was dangerous to operate, and many workers were killed or injured in industrial accidents. Also, the harmful chemicals being used often ruined workers' health if it didn't kill them immediately. Children, like adults, worked long hours, often six days a week for very low pay. Only decades later did the government begin to establish workplace safety rules and child labor laws. However, in the 1840s and 1850s, the British Temperance Emigration Society, a church-based group in England, wanted to change the situation. The group "indentured" (or contracted) factory workers in England to start farms in Wisconsin.

Society leaders believed that the long hours kept workers apart from their families. They also believed the difficult working conditions caused men to abuse alcohol and gamble away their meager paychecks, forcing their families into financial ruin. Because factories did not always pay a living wage, entire families were often forced to work just to make ends meet. In addition, the group's leaders believed that all these conditions made it difficult for workers and their families to worship regularly.

To address these problems, the Society did several things. It loaned money to poor families, helped them move out of communities where factory work had been their only option, and provided opportunities for them to experience an agricultural lifestyle. Because land was too expensive in the United Kingdom (UK), the Society relocated workers to Wisconsin. At that time, the best land in the state was both available

A member's share card from the British Temperance Emigration Society

WHS Archives

32

Getting Started on Research

On the topic of British immigration to Wisconsin, begin with the index in *Forward! A History of Dane: the Capital County* and *The History of Wisconsin, Volume 1: From Exploration to Statehood,* p. 490. The footnotes and bibliography provide archival sources. For primary and secondary sources of general information on British immigration to Wisconsin and the British immigrant experience, see the Resources section at the end of this chapter.

and inexpensive. The new immigrants signed a contract allowing them to borrow the funds needed for travel and land purchases. The contract also bound them to a promise to repay the loan.

The families who settled in Dane, Iowa, and LaFayette counties came from central England's main industrial cities. Between 1843 and 1850, the Society purchased tickets for them to travel by steamship from the port of Liverpool, England to New York, then overland to Wisconsin. Many settled in the Dane County towns of Berry, Cross Plains, Mazomanie, and Vermont. Others traveled southwest to the lead-mining region in Iowa, Grant, and Lafayette counties where they farmed and worked in lead and zinc mines.

When the British factory workers arrived on their new lands, they were shocked. Most had lived their entire lives in urban areas and had never experienced farm life. The unfamiliar tasks of building houses, clearing land, plowing, and raising crops loomed ahead. They discovered, however, that their neighbors, as well as other British immigrants who already lived in the region, helped them get started.

When the Milwaukee and Mississippi railroad was built through Dane County in the mid-1850s, many British immigrants started small factories to manufacture agricultural tools. They operated small workshops in villages that sprang up along the rail line, and they shipped tools to stores throughout Wisconsin, Iowa, and Minnesota. Within a few years, many of these settlers had sold their farms to other new immigrants and moved to town.

What social reforms have affected your community? Did church groups bring in orphans or immigrant groups from other countries? There are dozens of different ethnic groups in every Wisconsin community. Although many families have lived in the United States for a long time, others have been here for only a few generations. How did the particular groups in your community come to live there? How did the experiences of immigrants in your community differ from those of the British immigrants? What kinds of businesses have immigrants started in your community?

Official land certificate belonging to the British Temperance Emigration Society

WHS Archives

Finnish Co-ops
Fair Trade in the Northwoods

Have you ever heard of a co-op? Co-ops, or cooperatives, are groups of people working together and sharing profits from the services they provide. Because co-ops also buy products in bulk, they can offer low-priced goods to their members. There are food co-ops, electric co-ops, and dairy co-ops. Did you know that Finnish immigrants began a co-op movement that today serves millions of rural people in the upper midwest region of our state?

The story of Finnish co-ops begins more than 90 years ago in the community

After seizing Finland in 1810, the Russian Czars treated the country like a slave state, taking the Finns' resources and forcing them to pay high taxes. The Finns wanted to be independent. But the Russians made life so difficult that, in the late 1800s large numbers of Finns left for North America.

Many Finns immigrated to the Northwoods of the Upper Great Lakes where they established small communities. Although the climate suited the Finns well, they (like so many new immigrants) found the language to be a major barrier to a smooth integration into American society. Sometimes, merchants took advantage of newly arriving immigrants who did not understand English.

Coming from a heavily forested region, the Finns fit well into the logging economy. Many worked for logging companies that controlled important aspects of workers' lives, including access to food and supplies. Some logging companies ran "company stores" and paid their workers in "scrip,"

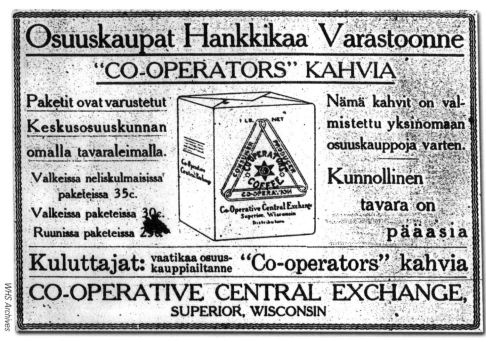

This advertisement for coffee appeared in the Finnish daily newspaper *Tyomies,* 1918

WHS Archives

of Oulu, in northern Wisconsin. The co-ops helped their communities in many ways, but they also promoted the cooperative movement that continues to aid farmers today. The Finns banded together, overcame challenges in their new home, and reformed their communities' economies.

instead of money. With their scrip, workers could buy merchandise only at the company store. The company stores charged high prices for goods and earned a profit at the expense of the workers. Because the Finns were a tightly knit community, they united to solve these problems.

In 1909, Finnish farmers started the Oulu Co-operative Creamery Association of Iron River in the town of Oulu in Bayfield County. The creamery provided the Finnish community with fresh milk, butter, cheese, and other goods. These products were sold to members at cost, rather than for a profit. The co-op approach also enabled members to earn cash for their goods, instead of the virtually worthless scrip.

The immigrants' strong support of Finnish independence also united them. As their cooperatives spread across northern Wisconsin, Minnesota, and the Upper Peninsula of Michigan, the Finns' hopes of creating an independent Finland also grew. This dream, combined with the rise of the Russian Bolsheviks (communists), forged a kindred socialist spirit that appealed to the Finnish immigrants. In small, close-knit communities, Finns would gather to build log cabins, barns, and pens for livestock and share their farm produce with one another. The success they achieved from sharing resources showed them how a socialist approach could improve their communities.

such as coffee, at reduced prices. In Wisconsin, cooperatives became a popular way to meet day-to-day needs and accomplish economic goals, especially in rural areas.

Where else in our state have Finnish communities established cooperatives? How did Finns interact with their non-Finnish neighbors? How did all the different kinds of cooperatives survive and even profit? What were common conflicts among the members? Many dairy and electric cooperatives still operate today. Pick one in any part of the state and tell its story. Try to include descriptions of larger trends in the movement and the economic and social contributions made by co-ops.

Finnish Co-op in Brantwood, Wisconsin, in the early 20th Century

WHS Archives

Getting Started on Research

To get an overview of the topic using secondary sources, the following two articles are good places to start: Frank G. Swoboda's "Agricultural Cooperation in Wisconsin" in the *Wisconsin Magazine of History* 10 (1926): 164–169 and Samuel Mermin's "Consumer Cooperatives in Northern Wisconsin," in *Monthly Labor Review* (1937): 1327–1344. You'll find more articles on cooperatives and several primary sources in the Resources section at the end of this chapter.

In 1915, the co-ops organized the People's Co-operative Society at Superior in Douglas County. As a major lake port, Superior and its neighbor Duluth offered direct access to European goods. The co-ops there provided members with prized goods,

Colonel Hans Christian Heg

A Norwegian Regiment in the Civil War

Have you ever wondered what it takes to be a real leader? What would it take to organize and direct people to support a cause you believe in? Hans Christian Heg's life story has all the attributes of effective leadership.

Hans Christian Heg was the son of Norwegian immigrant Even Heg, a pioneer settler in Muskego. From 1839 to the 1850s, Heg's family barn was an overnight stop for Norwegian immigrants traveling from Chicago or Milwaukee to the new Norwegian immigrant settlements at Koshkonong Prairie and Blue Mounds in Dane County, as well as other enclaves in Coon Valley, Viroqua, and Westby. Hans Heg arrived in the United States as a ten-year-old boy. As a young man, he spent two years (1849–1851) prospecting in California. After his father's death, he returned to Wisconsin to manage the family farm. In 1859, he moved to Waterford and operated a mill and general store. For the next two years, he served as the State Prison Commissioner at Waupun, the first Norwegian elected to a statewide office in Wisconsin. During his tenure as commissioner, Heg was an advocate for vocational training and for more humane treatment of prisoners.

When the Civil War broke out in 1861, Governor Alexander Randall asked Hans Heg to form a Norwegian regiment. This group later became the Wisconsin 15th Regiment. Heg agreed to take on the task because he believed that the Civil War was a just cause and that his skills as a leader could contribute to the preservation of the Union. The Norwegian-language newspaper *Emigraten*, which was read by many Norwegian immigrants in Wisconsin, assisted Heg's recruiting effort. He traveled to Norwegian communities across the state telling audiences that serving in the Civil War was an opportunity "to fight for a noble cause, to win an honored name, [to make] proud memories for the future, and [to have an] experience that could not be had elsewhere." Norwegian men answered Heg's call. By March 2, 1862,

Colonel Heg's letter describing Wisconsin's 15th Regiment at Chickamauga, 1863

Our brigade, (commanded by Col. Carlin of the 38th Ills.,) was marched up near the ground then occupied by McCook's corps, and where the fight was raging fearfully, and then filed to the right and ordered to support Sheridan's Division. We formed in the woods immediately behind an open field, with the 21st Ills. on our right, and the 101st Ohio on our left. I sent one company of my regiment in the advance as skirmishers, who soon engaged the enemy in the field. In the meantime we were ordered to advance in line of battle, and engage the enemy in force. No sooner did the 21st Ills. and 15th Wis. emerge from the woods, than the rebels retreated under the protection of their artillery, leaving several dead and wounded. Here commenced a chase. The enemy's artillery played on us lively, but the broken country afforded protection, and we advanced steadily at double quick, and in passing exposed positions at a run.

Getting Started on Research

An excellent place to find information about Wisconsin's role in the Civil War is Brett Barker's *Exploring Civil War Wisconsin: A Survival Guide for Researchers*. To learn more about Hans Christian Heg, you can begin with "Colonel Hans Christian Heg," in the *Wisconsin Magazine of History*. See the Resources section at the end of this chapter for help in finding these publications.

he had filled the ranks of the Wisconsin 15th Regiment and departed Camp Randall in Madison to fight.

In the "Western Campaign," the Norwegian 15th Regiment fought many close battles in Missouri, Kentucky, Tennessee, Mississippi, Alabama, and Georgia. As a reward for his leadership at the Battle of Stone River, Colonel Heg was placed in command of the 3rd Brigade of the 1st Division (Army of the Cumberland).

Colonel Hans Christian Heg

WHi (x3) 31683

Later, his commanding officer further demonstrated confidence in Heg by assigning him to conduct an assault across the Tennessee River.

In September 1863, Heg led his troops into the Battle of Chickamauga in Georgia. During the battle, Confederate and Union troops engaged in hand-to-hand fighting back and forth for two days. One of the bloodiest battles of the war, Chickamauga saw Heg's brigade suffer tremendous losses.

Ultimately, however, Union troops forced the Confederates to retreat back to their positions in Chattanooga, Tennessee. Heg was killed at Chickamauga and he is recognized as the highest-ranking Wisconsin soldier ever killed in Civil War combat. When the battle was over, the 15th Regiment of hundreds of men had been reduced to only seventy-five! Today, a statue outside the Wisconsin State Capitol at the King Street entrance commemorates Heg's service and sacrifice with the 15th Regiment.

Did any regiment from your area fight in the Civil War? If so, what was its impact on the families in your community? How did the war affect your community's identity? How would you find information about military regiments and stories of bravery and sacrifice in which individuals or groups risked their lives to make life better for your community?

Photo by Joel Heiman

Statue of Colonel Heg at the Wisconsin State Capitol

The Niagara

Great Lakes Palace Steamer Fire Kills Hundreds

WHS Archives

EVERGREEN CITY TIMES.

OM MADISON.

from the Select Committee
rant Bill reported the same on
ding, as a basis for legislative
Corporators in the North East.
Messrs Haertel of Milwaukee;
zaukee; Hiller of Sheboygan;
itowoc; Loy of Brown; Bal-
mie; Doty and Wright of
oore and Phillips of Fond du
of Madison; and J. Bradley
re to be appointed by the
his is the bill for the Road to
Fond du Lac.

nment Bill has not yet passed,
tless soon will do so.

essional Convention.

r is up (Friday evennig) we
oom to announce the result of
tional Convention at Fond du
e learn from Capt. SMITH, of
Tribune who was a delegate.
BILLINGHURST was re-nomi-
usly on the first informal bal-
LLIAMS, Esq., of this city, was
for this District. Both capi-
The Convention was full
s.

TERRIBLE DISASTER!

STEAMER NIAGARA BURNED.

ONE HUNDRED LIVES LOST!!

WRECK SUNI—CARGO A TOTAL LOSS!

Again are we alled upon to record one of
those fearful disaters, the thought of which
almost palsies th. heart with horror—the
burning of a thinly peopled steamer upon
the water, out of the reach of land.

Yesterday (Wednesday) the steamer Niagara, Capt. F. MILLER, from Collingwood,
landed at our pir, left a large number of
passengers, and started, about 2 P. M., for
Chicago. Early this morning the Huron
came in from Milwaukee, bringing the startling report that the Niagara was burned to
the water's edg about 5 o'clock last evening, some five niles off Port Washington,
and that but 25 or 30 persons were saved,
among whom was Capt. MILLER.

From Mr. GEORGE HART, Express Mes-
senger, who was on the Huron, we gather
the following particulars:

Capt Sweeney, of the
great credit for his despa
and his energy in savin
to the half naked and be
He furnished many with
a manly part every way.
Port Ulao, 10 miles o
South, and with steam
men got up steam as rapi
turned about to our help.

I think that a number
by the vessels went ab
Illinois. There were ab
and waiters, 80 cabin and
gers. We could only m
saved. The clerk is amc
lieve.

It did not seem more
utes from the time the fla
every soul had left the
clinging to the guard, a
whom I picked up and
and other passengers fel
were struggling around
let the child go. I saw
except Capt. Miller, an
got back to the boat. T
explosions before we lef
thought were of powder
and many reports of pi
man, Mr. H. Ainsworth
was saved, lost all of hi
several ladies and ch
amount of property.

His party consisted of
children, the eldest a gi

Evergreen City Times headlines announcing the burning of the *Niagara*

Whenever you and your family take a trip,
what safety precautions do you take? When
European emigrants left their homelands in
the mid-1800s, they often faced dangers on
their journeys. Crossing the Atlantic meant
dealing with the distinct possibility of a
shipwreck, catching a disease, or facing a
fire that could destroy the ship. Once immigrants arrived in New York, Baltimore, New
Orleans, or Canada, the dangers continued
as they traveled to their new homes.

For immigrants coming to Wisconsin,
traveling over land was slow. Roads were
primitive, and railroads weren't built until the
1850s. So, ports on the east-
ern Great Lakes provided
important shipping routes
to their new homes. Water
travel was inexpensive and
relatively quick. Also,
steamships and lake
schooners followed sched-
uled routes that allowed
for access to and from
Great Lakes ports.

In the early 1850s,
palace steamers were the
largest ships on the Great
Lakes, and 25 of them
brought settlers and immigrants west to the newly
opened lands of
Wisconsin. These ships
returned with furs, live-
stock, manufactured
goods, raw materials, and
agricultural produce. Built
in Erie, Pennsylvania, the
steamers were also the
fastest vessels, offering the
best way to travel from Buffalo, New York, to
the Great Lakes port at the end of the Erie
Canal.

For a time, the *Niagara* was the fastest
steamer around, having won several races
across Lake Erie to Detroit. Steamboats tra-
versed the
Great Lakes
during this
period at
about fif-
teen miles
per hour.
With stops
at ports

WHS Maritime Preservation
and Archaeology Program

Drawing of *Niagara*

38

along the way, a trip across the water could last four or five days. The *Niagara* made the round trip to Chicago every two weeks. When the vessel first arrived in Milwaukee, the *Milwaukee Sentinel* reported that it was "in truth, a noble boat; well-modeled, capacious, convenient, swift and most strongly built."

During this time, European immigrants who arrived in Montreal or Toronto traveled to Buffalo to board steamers for the trip west. In late 1855, a rail link from Toronto to Collingwood on Lake Huron offered immigrants a speedier trip to the Wisconsin frontier. Dozens of immigrants bound for Wisconsin and Chicago boarded the *Niagara* at Collingwood.

In 1855, the *Niagara* was a ten-year-old ship, and it was starting to look a bit run down inside and out. In its prime, it had broken speed records. But newer technologies were producing larger steamships that could speed right past it. On September 24, 1856, the ship made its way across northern Lake Huron into Lake Michigan and docked at Sheboygan, where several passengers had disembarked earlier in the day. The captain took a mid-afternoon nap as soon as the *Niagara* left Sheboygan. Bound

for Port Washington thirty miles south, the vessel never made it.

That afternoon, the captain awoke to cries of, "Fire, fire, fire!" In the panic that followed, frightened passengers jumped into lifeboats that bobbled and dumped them into the lake. Most people onboard were wearing wool clothing that, once wet, made staying afloat very difficult. Only a few of the passengers could swim, so the thin warm layer of surface water did little to keep the cold water beneath from quickly numbing the victims. Those who remained in the water for more than a few minutes met an untimely end. A few fortunate passengers floated to safety by holding onto planks, but nearly sixty passengers drowned.

Immigrants journeying to Wisconsin by land and across the water in the nineteenth century have many interesting stories to tell. Many of these stories, including the *Niagara,* and more recent ones involving Hmong, Latino, and other newcomers, make outstanding resources for historical research. Every immigrant journey has its own harrowing and fascinating episodes. What compelling stories do you know about immigrants in your family or community?

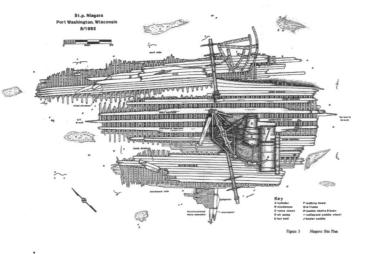

Wisconsin Historical Society Maritime Preservation and Archaeology Program

Niagara site map

Poles in Portage County

From what you know of the immigrant groups that came to Wisconsin in the 1800s and 1900s, in what areas of the state did they choose to settle? What types of jobs did they usually fill after arriving? For many Polish immigrants, central Wisconsin was their choice as a new homeland because other areas of the state had already been populated. Also, the land in the central region was very affordable.

In 1857, immigrants from Poland's German-controlled northern region of Kaszuby sailed for the United States. Several factors motivated them. The main ones were small agricultural holdings, rising death rates, high taxes, lack of adequate machinery, falling grain prices, required military service, and political tensions. Promotional efforts by railroad companies, lumber companies, and Wisconsin itself actively encouraged immigrant groups to occupy previously ignored areas of central Wisconsin. The Poles who came settled in a variety of different geographical areas. These separate communities have made it difficult for historians to prove exact numbers of ethnic Poles who traveled to Wisconsin. However, the *Polish Courier* newspaper, which began in

POLISH CATHOLIC CHURCH
Polonia, Wisconsin

WHi (x3)21088

Third Sacred Heart Church, Polonia, Wisconsin, 1920

Milwaukee in 1888, has estimated that there were 115,000 first-and second-generation Poles in Wisconsin by 1896 and 225,000 by 1915.

Poles in Wisconsin lived very much as they had in their homeland. Agriculture was still one of the primary work opportunities. In fact, 23% of Poles in Wisconsin in 1900 were working in agriculture. During the winter, these farmers often supplemented their incomes by working in lumber camps or on railroad gangs. Catholicism remained a central part of their social life. Poles built many Catholic churches in the months and years immediately after their arrival.

Immigrant Poles to the United States found limited land options. Much of the east was already settled by earlier arrivals of other groups, who were already spreading out and populating other sectors of the midwestern United States. Wisconsin, however, offered an alternative because the Menominee Indian Treaty and land cessions of 1848 provided inexpensive land in Portage County. Of course, this land was cheap because the more fertile, agriculturally rich lands were already claimed. And timber barons held onto the heavily forested areas in the north. The "sand counties" in

Getting Started on Research

For secondary resources, consult the chapter entitled "Shrines and Crosses in Rural Central Wisconsin" in James P. Leary's *Wisconsin Folklore* or Michael Goc's *Native Realm: The Polish-American Community of Portage County, 1857–1992*. Various other resources can be found in *Wisconsin History: An Annotated Bibliography*. You can find more details about the publications in the Resources section at the end of this chapter. Primary documents include a number of photographs and other materials you can find online at http://www.wisconsinhistory.org/archives/.

central Wisconsin, by contrast, were less appealing. Nevertheless, a hardy Polish community began to spring up there.

Portage County is recognized as the location of Wisconsin's oldest rural Polish community. The first families arrived in 1857. Despite the hardships associated with working sandy soil, Polish families wrote happily to their relatives about the inexpensive land. By 1864, more than forty families had settled in the area. By 1920, the Poles constituted 11% of Wisconsin's foreign-born population and ranked second only to the Germans in numbers.

In May of 1883, John and Malwina Konkol arrived in New York with their two children. They had lived in Klukowa hutta in the Kartuzy district west of Gdansk. The next year, they purchased a farm in Portage County. Malwina was a skilled midwife who delivered many of the local babies. John was a carpenter and beekeeper, as well as a farmer.

When he retired in 1912, John used his skills to build a red brick shrine near his home at the intersection of county highways B and K, a spot commonly called Konkol's Corners. Shrines

devoted to the Virgin Mary and the saints are popular along roadsides in Pole-settled regions, especially at crossroads. The tradition of shrine-making reaches back to pre-Christian times, and the shrines in Wisconsin today are considered daily reminders of their Catholic faith. Throughout central Wisconsin, fourteen roadside shrines and crosses currently dot the landscape, and accounts from older residents indicate that many more used to exist.

How does the Polish experience resemble that of other immigrant groups in Wisconsin? How does it differ? What were some of the advantages and disadvantages of moving to Wisconsin for the Poles?

Polish roadside shrine, 1942

WHi (v51)46

Iron Mining and Italian Community Building in Hurley

The Gogebic Iron Range stretches from Michigan's Upper Peninsula through parts of Iron and Ashland counties in northern Wisconsin and into southeastern Bayfield County, where it terminates. Many immigrants were encouraged to move to this district in the late 1800s and early 1900s to work in the mines. Italian immigrants formed a significant number of these arrivals. Unlike many who mined earlier, the Italians stayed. At first, they only mined, but later, they established businesses and cultural activities. Their largely untold story gives us a unique glimpse of life "up north."

Several Italians first entered the Gogebic Range as part of the French colonial service during the Fur Trade era. But like most of the traders, they did not stay. After mines opened in the range and railroads allowed commerce to spread to Ashland in the mid-1880s, European immigrants began to be attracted to the area. The earliest arrivals hailed from England, Ireland, and Sweden. But much of the second generation resisted mining and moved west. The Finns, Poles, and Italians followed in their wake. Hurley became the center of the state's Italian community, filled with those who had immigrated from communities in Tyrol, Piedmont, Venetia, Abruzzi-Molise, Calabria, and Sicily.

Italian boarding house in Hurley, Wisconsin

Early photograph of Hurley, Wisconsin

Few Italians spoke English when they arrived in the United States, and as a result, they tended to work in low-skilled jobs. While many Italians headed for the population centers of Racine and Milwaukee, those who settled in Hurley performed grueling work. The lowest-level job was "tramming," or shoveling, ore into rail cars that moved the ore to docks at Superior and Ashland. More capable workers rose to become miners or foremen.

By 1910, Italians made up nearly 20% of the immigrant regional labor force, second only to Finns. Most of the initial arrivals were single men who were intent upon making enough money in the mines to return to Italy and buy land. Once in Wisconsin, however, most brought their families and settled in Hurley. Few intended to remain miners, and their wives and children often worked small jobs to help save enough money to start independent businesses. Running a tavern required only a small investment, and Italian saloons quickly established themselves as social centers. Enterprising Italian businessmen also opened bakeries and grocery stores and stocked them with specialties such as olive oil, cod fish, and dried pasta. By 1920, the Italian community had members with enough capital to organize the Hurley National Bank, which initially prospered. Unfortunately, it later went bankrupt during the Great Depression of the 1930s.

Hurley was a transitional community where people worked in low-skilled, low-paying mining jobs for short periods of time before moving on. But the Italians who stayed strengthened their own ethnic ties even as they integrated into the larger community. These immigrants established a number of economic and social organizations, such as the Italian Mutual Benefit Society. This organization provided important economic benefits to those without insurance. It also offered compensation to workmen who got injured in difficult and often dangerous mining occupations. Other organizations, such as the Italian Library Club and the Sons of Italy, helped ease the social and cultural transition of newcomers.

Such businesses and institutions in Hurley demonstrate the way new immigrant groups could transform the local economy and cultural life of a community. Are there immigrant families selling vegetables in your local farmer's market or selling baked goods? Are there ethnic restaurants and grocery stores near your home? What might you be able to find out about the diverse cultural mix in your hometown?

Getting Started on Research

Other than a short pamphlet by Russell Magnagli titled *The Gogebic Range's Italian Immigrants*, little has been written about the Italian immigration to Hurley. Some excellent ways to conduct research on Italian immigration in our state include calling your local (city or county) historical society and investigating city directories in your local library. You can also visit local churches to find out about the ethnic groups associated with them. Interview longtime residents, especially those with ties to local historical societies, to discover great stories of the immigration experience. Visiting a local cemetery is another great way to explore your community's history. A search for keywords "Gogebic range" online at http://www.wisconsinhistory.org/archives/ will yield primary documents about this topic.

From Logging to Farming
Selling Northern Wisconsin to Immigrants

In the late nineteenth century, the Northwoods of Wisconsin contained large forests and was dominated by the highly prized great white pine. Consequently, it became one of the primary centers for the world's timber industry. However, within 20 years, the entire landscape changed. Better logging equipment and the railroad's ability to deliver lumber to town builders on the prairies devastated the area's timber population. This intersection of advanced technologies transformed the pineland region into what became known as the "cutover," a wasteland of stump-covered fields.

Into this now inhospitable land came new settlers. How could anyone be convinced to move to an area like that? At least part of the answer came in 1895, when William Henry, dean of the College of Agriculture at the University of Wisconsin, secured permission from the state legislature to create *Northern Wisconsin: A Handbook for the Homeseeker* with the intent "to draw to Wisconsin a desirable class of farmers."

Cheap land was readily available. Once the pinery had been cut down, lumber companies were eager to sell their property. Cornell University in Ithaca, New York, sold clear-cut lands in the Chippewa River Flowage for ten dollars an acre to avoid paying property taxes. Other landholders were just as eager to sell. All the area needed were farmers.

Professor Henry's heart was in the right place. He intended for the handbook to provide valuable scientific information, but his research was based on only a few years of study, and it painted a far too optimistic picture of the agricultural potential of the region. Henry argued, "We have shown the best of the marvelously fine crops found growing ... during the season of 1895." The accompanying photographs in this "picture book" provided additional evidence to convince homeseekers. The publication seemed to provide an astounding assurance of success!

He briefly mentioned the swamps, boulders, and stump-laden landscape, and even warned that no one looking to get rich quickly should think of farming the region. But his overall appraisal was glowing. It presented a picture of hard-working farmers able to make the cutover region flourish. The handbook offered detailed descriptions of topography, soil types, and climate variations, and it spelled out the kinds of crops and conditions that would suit these circumstances well. The photographs (with

Handbook for the Homeseeker, page 27

WHS Archives

Getting Started on Research

In the Resources section at the end of this chapter, you can find some excellent secondary sources that provide insight into dealing with the cutover. Lucille Kane's article, "Settling the Wisconsin Cutovers," in the *Wisconsin Magazine of History* and Arlan C. Helgenson's *Farms in the Cutover* make good places to start. You can find many others referenced in the index of *Wisconsin History: An Annotated Bibliography,* published by Greenwood Press. As a primary source, *Northern Wisconsin: A Handbook for the Homeseeker* provides a treasure trove of images and text.

vivid captions) only served to underscore Henry's enthusiasm.

The handbook convinced many to try their hand at farming in the cutover region. Henry's flawed theories, however, assured an economically tragic experience for most newcomers. Many of his crop production examples came from a single year's output. The forest soils with their thin topsoil lost fertility after a few years. Forest fires temporarily fertilized soil by releasing nutrient-rich wood ash, but poor drainage, clay soils, and different weather patterns created worsening soil conditions year after year. Although Henry warned that clearing for farmland would be difficult, the new pioneers were completely unprepared for the task. Limited equipment and primitive technology forced them to dig out stumps by hand and horse, which was labor intensive and backbreaking work.

The difficulties did not end once fields were successfully cultivated. In the years leading up to World War I, new commercial fertilizers came to the market, and wartime needs for agricultural products led to increased productivity. Efforts by the University of

Wisconsin's Agricultural Extension Service, which had helped farmers grow crops more efficiently, now worked against them. When European farmers returned to their fields after the war, demand for American agricultural products decreased and prices plummeted.

Despite Henry's honorable intentions, his well-packaged handbook never transformed the Northwoods into an agricultural paradise. In fact, it wasn't until the reintroduction of forestry and the development of tourism, which the railroads actively promoted, that the region began to recover economically.

What other ideas or opportunities were promoted around the state that turned out to be too good to be true? Did your community have to overcome difficult beginnings to create the strong, stable community that it is today? Has your community ever been hit hard by an industry that moved away and left many people out of work? How did the community respond to challenges? What efforts were initiated to help people adjust and overcome them?

Handbook for the Homeseeker, page 95

WHS Archives

Attracting Newcomers to a New State

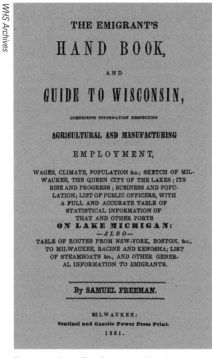

THE EMIGRANT'S

HAND BOOK,

AND

GUIDE TO WISCONSIN,

COMPRISING INFORMATION RESPECTING

AGRICULTURAL AND MANUFACTURING

EMPLOYMENT,

WAGES, CLIMATE, POPULATION &c.; SKETCH OF MIL-
WAUKEE, THE QUEEN CITY OF THE LAKES; ITS
RISE AND PROGRESS; BUSINESS AND POPU-
LATION; LIST OF PUBLIC OFFICERS, WITH
A FULL AND ACCURATE TABLE OF
STATISTICAL INFORMATION OF
THAT AND OTHER PORTS
ON LAKE MICHIGAN:
—A L S O—
TABLE OF ROUTES FROM NEW-YORK, BOSTON, &c.,
TO MILWAUKEE, RACINE AND KENOSHA; LIST
OF STEAMBOATS &c., AND OTHER GENER-
AL INFORMATION TO EMIGRANTS.

By SAMUEL FREEMAN.

MILWAUKEE:
Sentinel and Gazette Power Press Print.
1851.

Title page from *The Emigrant's Handbook and Guide to Wisconsin* (1851)

Today, advertisements for travel are just about everywhere. You can find them on billboards, in newspapers and magazines, on the radio and television, and even on the Internet. But 150 years ago, before some of these media had even been invented, the young state of Wisconsin was already in the business of promoting itself to newcomers.

Within three years after Wisconsin achieved statehood in 1848, the new state government established an agency to encourage immigration. Local publishers followed suit and produced vivid and persuasive handbooks and guidebooks to attract potential European immigrants to new land in Wisconsin.

In 1851, Samuel Freeman wrote *The Emigrant's Handbook and Guide to Wisconsin* containing valuable information and advice for newcomers. His purpose was "to present to the Emigrant the advantages he has in directing his course to Wisconsin" and to warn him about "the dangers he has to encounter before he reaches here." As the title page clearly points out, Freeman intended the ambitious handbook to be a useful collection of practical information for English-speaking immigrants. Its contents are not presented as well as one might expect, but Freeman manages to offer a convincing glimpse of the state's strengths and its potential for growth at a crucial juncture in its early history. This is what makes *The Emigrant's Handbook and Guide to Wisconsin* a fascinating source of early information about our state.

Although Freeman provides no table of contents for his book, his introduction does tell prospective settlers what he plans to offer them. He includes a short description of the way the democratic government of the United States functions, of how Wisconsin presents a "favorable field" for those seeking to work in agriculture or manufacturing, and of estimates of Wisconsin's "wages and their relative value." Also, he presents a "sketch" of Milwaukee as the "Queen City of the Lakes" and shows travel routes from Boston and New York to the southeastern

The Emigrant's Handbook and Guide to Wisconsin provided immigrants with useful information.

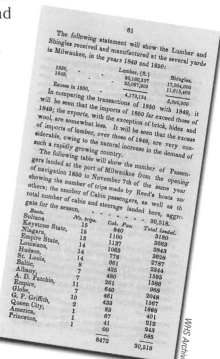

Wisconsin ports of Milwaukee, Racine, and Kenosha. Throughout the book, Freeman provides valuable tips to help immigrants find what they might need for daily living.

Based upon this introduction, the reader might expect a fairly straightforward presentation of information. But the charm of this resource is in the way Freeman's writing resists this expectation. He highlights employment opportunities in shoe factories, mines, mills, and logging camps. He points out public accommodations in the major cities and lists locations of churches for all faiths and fraternal societies that cater to travelers. Freeman also warns new immigrants of the dangers of large metropolitan cities, such as New York City. He directly urges newcomers to stay away from taverns and easy employment and to "lose no time, then, in working your way out of New York and directing your steps westward." To lure them across the Great Lakes, Freeman's closing section is an illustrated directory of Milwaukee businesses and services waiting to support every new immigrant who comes to Wisconsin.

In 1852, the Wisconsin Legislature created the Office of the Commissioner of Immigration and staffed an office in the port of New York to assist immigrants. The organization also provided pamphlets (written in German, Welsh, Norwegian, and French) to agents stationed abroad. These materials described Wisconsin's favorable attributes in

hopes of attracting potential settlers. The next year, the commission published an annual report to document its progress. It claimed success from the very beginning, explaining that nearly 60,000 immigrants arrived at Wisconsin ports in 1852—a number that increased to 80,000 the following year.

From what you've learned about newcomers to Wisconsin, what were the peak years of immigration to the state? In what ways has our state reached out to attract or support immigrant populations? Promoting Wisconsin remains a priority at both the state and local levels. How have governmental and non-governmental agencies worked to encourage immigration to the state? What positive features of the state and its economy do they publicize? How has your city or community promoted job opportunities and business activities to attract others? In what ways has your community reached out to potential companies, groups, or individuals?

The Emigrant's Handbook and Guide to Wisconsin contains many such ads.

WHS Archives

German Music in a German State

Did you know that Wisconsin is the most German state in the Union? In the 1990 census, nearly 54% of Wisconsin citizens identified themselves as German. Surprisingly, most of these people did not think of themselves as German until after they had settled in Wisconsin. Prior to 1871, there was no country named "Germany." Instead, people living in several small, independent, neighboring nations in north central Europe spoke a variety of German dialects. Their religious faiths

The Alte Kameraden Band

were different, too. Some immigrants to Wisconsin were Catholic, and others were Protestant; in particular, Lutheran. Still others were revolutionaries who came to the United States seeking political freedom.

From the 1850s through the 1890s, thousands of families from Bavaria, Saxony, Prussia, and the Rhineland came to the United States to find permanent homes, and many settled in Wisconsin. They created a culture based on a shared language and customs, including German food, literature, and music. People from nearby states who settled in Milwaukee and other parts of southern

and eastern Wisconsin proudly embraced this newly defined German identity.

Polka music became a major component of German identity in Wisconsin. A polka is a kind of fast dance for two people. Nobody is sure exactly where polka music originated, but it was already very popular in central Europe by the 1840s. The spirited music written in 2/4 time attracted rural people who would gather and dance to polka tunes played by local musicians. Musicians from central Europe began adapting the polka to their traditional music. The Austrians, Swiss, Czechs, Slovenians, Germans, and others developed their own styles of polka music that sounded quite different from one another.

In the German-speaking parts of Europe, polka music began to be played by military brass bands. Around this time, the now-familiar "oom-pah" sound of German polka music appeared. From then on, bands just couldn't play a polka without a tuba!

German-style polka music was important to the immigrants who wanted to preserve their culture in their new homeland. Many German communities formed music societies and clubs in which to play their music. On Sunday afternoons, people gathered in *beirgartens* (literally, beer gardens) to hear these bands play. Polka bands were also popular at weddings and other celebrations.

Every town with even a small population of

Member of the Jolly Alpine boys singing and playing

Sheet music of "Milwaukee Polka"

weekly radio program hosted by a performer who faked a German accent to sound more authentic. A similar program was broadcast on WKOW in Madison by an announcer who called himself "Uncle Julius."

Musical tastes changed in the 1950s, and as more young people began listening to rock music, German polka music became less common. Yet even today, polka skills get passed along to younger musicians, and polka music continues to be an important part of Wisconsin's current culture. In 1994, the legislature designated the polka as the official state dance.

What polka bands are in your area? Ask your parents and teachers where you might be able to hear one or go to any library or music store to hear polka albums or CDs. If you get the chance to hear polka music from a live band, ask the musicians about how they learned polka music and what particular kinds of polka they like to play.

Germans had polka bands playing in ballrooms, taverns, and fraternal lodges for almost any celebration. These bands were often known as "Dutchman bands" based on the German word *Deutscher* for German. Even when people shunned German culture during World War I, polka music continued to thrive. One of the most famous bands to form was the Alte Kamaraden, or "old comrades," of Freistadt in Ozaukee County. The Alte Kamaraden began playing in the 1840s, and the band still exists today!

The advent of radio and recording technology in the 1920s changed polka music forever. Residents of small towns could now listen to bands from Milwaukee, Sheboygan, Appleton, and even Chicago as well as their local bands. Records turned local bands into performing stars, and polka music became popular even in places where it had never been heard before. In the 1930s, the WTMJ radio station in Milwaukee broadcast "Heinie and His Grenadiers," a popular hour-long

Getting Started on Research

An excellent place to begin researching this topic in Wisconsin is *Germans in Wisconsin* by Richard H. Zeitlin. Another example is "Becoming German American" in *Wisconsin's Past and Present: A Historical Atlas,* pp. 18–19. Your librarian can also direct you to other works. For government census records to research people's place of birth, you can find copies at the Wisconsin Historical Society in Madison. Visit their Web site at http://www.wisconsinhistory.org/.

Wisconsin Blue Books often publish a census summary of Wisconsin in the year after the census results are released (the census is conducted every ten years). For more on polka music, see "Polka Music in a Polka State" by James P. Leary in *Wisconsin Folklore.* You can also hear German-style polka music on the CD *Deep Polka* produced by the Smithsonian Institution. Also, check out your school or local library for other recordings. The Resources section of this book has more details on these sources.

Freedom Ride!
Grant County's African American Pioneers

What does freedom mean to you? Does freedom mean no homework assignments or no more chores to do around the house? Most people in America take many basic freedoms for granted. They can attend the school of their choice, worship whatever and wherever they choose, and live practically anywhere they want. But before the Civil War, not everyone in the United States enjoyed such freedoms.

One family that did not take freedom for granted was John Greene and his daughter, Frances. Both were born into slavery. They had spent all their lives serving James Bross on his farm in Arkansas. Like millions of African and African American slaves living in the South before the Civil War, the Greenes had few rights and even fewer freedoms. Black southerners had no freedom of movement; no freedom of speech; no freedom to worship as they chose; and no freedom to work on their own, vote, or own land.

A crucial Civil War document brought about a major change in American life. It officially bestowed upon Blacks in America the freedoms that all people of the United States deserved

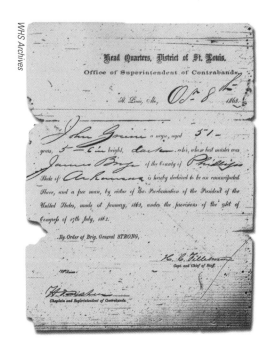

John Greene's Certificate of Emancipation, 1863

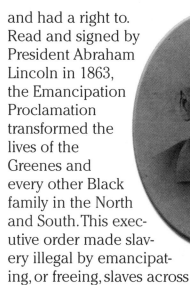

Photo of John Greene

and had a right to. Read and signed by President Abraham Lincoln in 1863, the Emancipation Proclamation transformed the lives of the Greenes and every other Black family in the North and South. This executive order made slavery illegal by emancipating, or freeing, slaves across the United States.

Lincoln wanted to abolish, or eliminate, slavery even as the brutal Civil War was moving with devastating force through Virginia, Maryland, and other Confederate states. Lincoln delivered a preliminary Emancipation Proclamation in September 1862, just before the presidential election. In it, he demanded that the seceding states rejoin the Union or he would outlaw slavery. When the southern states that had seceded, or broken away from the Union, did not stop fighting, Lincoln officially made slavery illegal. On January 1, 1863, he delivered this final version of the Emancipation Proclamation.

But freeing the slaves proved to be a problem in almost every area of American life. While the war was still on, it was a particularly thorny issue for commanders on the battlefield. When Union troops attacked Confederate troops, slaves escaped behind northern lines where they expected not only to win their freedom but to find food and shelter. But providing food, water, and shelter to sometimes hundreds of escaped slaves was extremely difficult. The northern

Getting Started on Research

Excellent source materials on African Americans in Wisconsin, including John Greene, include Zachary Cooper's book, *Black Settlers in Rural Wisconsin* and Barbara J. Shade's article, "Afro-Americans in Early Wisconsin," in *Transactions of the Wisconsin Academy of Sciences, Arts, and Letters.* You can find many more resources on the African American experience in Wisconsin by searching the index of *Wisconsin History: An Annotated Bibliography.* This book contains a lot of valuable tips on finding secondary material.

troops needed these supplies to continue fighting. Consequently, many slaves were sent back to the South and did not gain their freedom in the immediate years after the Emancipation Proclamation.

However, General Benjamin F. Butler found an effective solution to the problem. He decided to call the freed slaves "contrabands," which allowed them to become part of the war effort. Whenever Union victories occurred, thousands of newly freed slaves came along as a result. By becoming contrabands, John Greene and his daughter won their freedom. Each received a Certificate of Emancipation, signed by a military commander for the Office of the Superintendent of Contrabands. After the war, Greene kept his certificate to prove his freedom when he moved to Pleasant Ridge in Grant County, Wisconsin. As a new (and free) Wisconsinite, he started a community for other freed slaves who had followed a similar path to freedom.

In the community of Pleasant Ridge, John Greene soon found he had several new neighbors. Some were other freed slaves who, because they knew the Greenes, made the trip to Wisconsin to find permanent residence. Other neighbors were families from the Grant County area who had purchased land there. Together, white and African American neighbors built a schoolhouse and contributed their taxes to pay for a teacher and to maintain the one-room building. One-room schoolhouses, like the one in Pleasant Ridge, were common across rural Wisconsin.

More and more African Americans moved to Wisconsin after the Civil War to seek a better life. But, when they continued to endure unfair treatment because of the color of their skin, they traveled through the state on the "Underground Railroad" and made their way into Canada.

Can you think of ways in which the Pleasant Ridge community was both different from and similar to other immigrant communities? Where would you start researching the origins and experiences of African American communities in Wisconsin? In what places did newly freed African Americans establish communities in the state? What institutions did they create within their new regions?

WHi (X3) 28262

One-room schoolhouse at Pleasant Ridge

Escape from Laos
The Harrowing Journey of the Hmong to Wisconsin

Map by Carto-Graphics (from the Chipewa Valley Museum Collection)

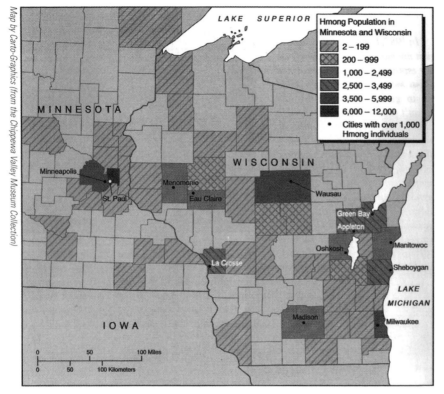

The Hmong population in Wisconsin, from the 1990 U.S. Census

The majority of Wisconsin residents trace their ancestry to northern and central Europe. But events over the past fifty years have transformed our state and made us a much more diverse population. Recent immigration has brought more than 15,000 Hmong people from Southeast Asia to Wisconsin. Many forces influenced in this journey westward.

The Hmong living in Wisconsin today have roots that extend back to the ancient cultures of Eurasia, Siberia, and China. Most of the seven million Hmong living today currently reside in China. But in the early and middle 1800s, approximately a half million moved to Vietnam, Laos, and Thailand. They lived in these southeast Asian mountain regions in self-sufficient agrarian villages.

The story of the Hmong journey to the United States in the late 1900s is closely tied to the Vietnam War, its aftermath, and the politics of the period, especially our government's attempts to stop the global spread of communism during the Cold War era of the 1950s and 1960s. The Hmong settlers in northwestern Laos found themselves, quite literally, in the crossfire in the battle between democracy and communism in the region. When French colonial control of Indochina, including Vietnam, Laos, and Cambodia, collapsed in 1954, the area's inhabitants started to celebrate their liberation. The U.S. government, however, feared that communism might gain a foothold in the region. Because the American political attitude of the day was governed by a policy of "containment," communism had to be prevented on every front "at all costs." This policy was to have far-reaching consequences for the people of Southeast Asia.

In 1961, the U.S. Central Intelligence Agency (CIA) recruited a secret army of Laotian and Vietnamese from the region to assist the United States. By 1964, nearly 30,000 Hmong men and 60% of the Hmong population in Laos had allied itself with the U.S. military. These soldiers ambushed communist supply lines, guarded radar installations, and provided the first line of defense for Laos.

When American troops withdrew from Southeast Asia in 1975, the Vietnam conflict ended. But, it left the Hmong (who had aided the Americans) in the dangerous hands of communists who were coming to power. From 1975 to 1992, thousands of Hmong attempted to rebuild their lives in

Getting Started on Research

Tim Pfaff's *Hmong in America: Journey from a Secret War* and Jane Hamilton-Merritt's *Tragic Mountains: The Hmong, the Americans, and the Secret Wars for Laos, 1942–1992* provide excellent material about the Hmong's escape from Southeast Asia and their experiences in Wisconsin. An outstanding source of primary documents is *The Hmong and Their Stories,* a publication created by the D.C. Everest School District. See the Resources section at the end of this chapter for more details.

Laos, the Hmong faced language, educational, economic, and cultural barriers. Despite these hardships, the Hmong managed to create communities in several states. They tended to regroup near family and clan members, which created concentrations of Hmong in California, Minnesota, and Wisconsin.

Their challenges and resettlement experiences involved trying to preserve traditional Hmong values and a sense of history. These included a deep respect for family and clan relatives, intricate spiritual beliefs, and a strong sense of independence. At the same time, they wanted to accumulate sufficient knowledge of U.S. beliefs, language, and history to survive in their new homeland.

There is limited public knowledge about the "Secret War" that occurred in Laos. As a result, many Hmong veterans have not received the same recognition as American veterans have for serving in the Vietnam War.

their war-torn homeland, but many more thousands fled across the Mekong River to "settlement camps" in Thailand. In these overcrowded refugee camps where they lived sometimes for years, Hmong people had to decide whether to return to Laos or start a new life elsewhere. Any kind of resettlement would be especially difficult for the Hmong, who believe deeply that "To be with family is to be happy; to be without family is to be lost."

Many decided to risk moving away. Some settled in the United States; others traveled to France, Australia, and Canada. The U.S. Catholic Conference, the Lutheran Immigration and Refugee Services, and the Church World Services organizations were among the first agencies to sponsor the Hmong refugees in the United States. These agencies helped the new arrivals deal with the many challenges they faced in making such a long and difficult journey. In addition to dealing with the traumas inflicted by living in war-ravaged

But, the situation has begun to change. In 2000, a monument honoring the Hmong's participation in the war was erected at Arlington National Cemetery, and a federal law was passed waiving the English language requirement for U.S. citizenship for Hmong veterans. In many ways, the Hmong are enjoying the rewards of freedom, independence, and economic vitality that have been and continue to be a vital part of the immigrant experience in Wisconsin.

Science Museum of Minnesota

Hmong storycloth made in the Ban Vinai refugee camp, in northern Thailand (1988). This storycloth depicts the Hmong's journey from their villages, through the jungle, across the Mekong River, and into refugee camps in Thailand. Once there, they applied for resettlement and boarded buses bound for Bangkok. They eventually arrived by airplane in the United States.

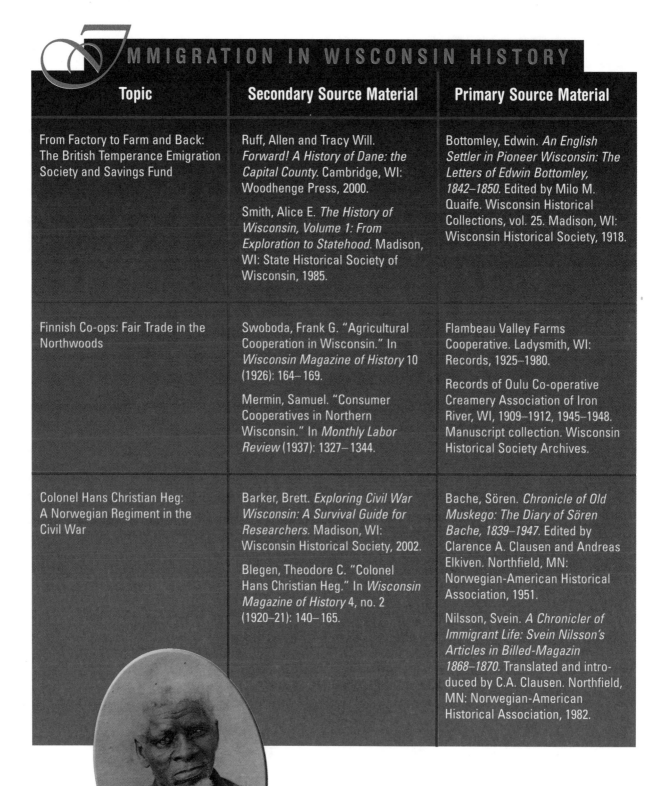

IMMIGRATION IN WISCONSIN HISTORY

Topic	Secondary Source Material	Primary Source Material
From Factory to Farm and Back: The British Temperance Emigration Society and Savings Fund	Ruff, Allen and Tracy Will. *Forward! A History of Dane: the Capital County.* Cambridge, WI: Woodhenge Press, 2000. Smith, Alice E. *The History of Wisconsin, Volume 1: From Exploration to Statehood.* Madison, WI: State Historical Society of Wisconsin, 1985.	Bottomley, Edwin. *An English Settler in Pioneer Wisconsin: The Letters of Edwin Bottomley, 1842–1850.* Edited by Milo M. Quaife. Wisconsin Historical Collections, vol. 25. Madison, WI: Wisconsin Historical Society, 1918.
Finnish Co-ops: Fair Trade in the Northwoods	Swoboda, Frank G. "Agricultural Cooperation in Wisconsin." In *Wisconsin Magazine of History* 10 (1926): 164–169. Mermin, Samuel. "Consumer Cooperatives in Northern Wisconsin." In *Monthly Labor Review* (1937): 1327–1344.	Flambeau Valley Farms Cooperative. Ladysmith, WI: Records, 1925–1980. Records of Oulu Co-operative Creamery Association of Iron River, WI, 1909–1912, 1945–1948. Manuscript collection. Wisconsin Historical Society Archives.
Colonel Hans Christian Heg: A Norwegian Regiment in the Civil War	Barker, Brett. *Exploring Civil War Wisconsin: A Survival Guide for Researchers.* Madison, WI: Wisconsin Historical Society, 2002. Blegen, Theodore C. "Colonel Hans Christian Heg." In *Wisconsin Magazine of History* 4, no. 2 (1920–21): 140–165.	Bache, Sören. *Chronicle of Old Muskego: The Diary of Sören Bache, 1839–1947.* Edited by Clarence A. Clausen and Andreas Elkiven. Northfield, MN: Norwegian-American Historical Association, 1951. Nilsson, Svein. *A Chronicler of Immigrant Life: Svein Nilsson's Articles in Billed-Magazin 1868–1870.* Translated and introduced by C.A. Clausen. Northfield, MN: Norwegian-American Historical Association, 1982.

Topic	Secondary Source Material	Primary Source Material
The *Niagara*: Great Lakes Palace Steamer Fire Kills Hundreds	The Wisconsin Historical Society Archaeology Web site at http://www.wisconsinhistory.org/shipwrecks/index.html Pitz, Herbert. *Lake Michigan Disasters: A Record of the Greatest Ship Wrecks on Lake Michigan Compiled from Various Records and Newspapers of Manitowoc and Sheboygan Counties.* Manitowoc, WI: Manitowoc Maritime Museum, 1925. Jensen, John Odin. "The History and Archaeology of the Great Lakes Steamboat Niagara." In *Wisconsin Magazine of History 82,* no. 3 (1999): 198–230.	*Milwaukee Sentinel* microfilm, 1846. *Evergreen City Times* microfilm, 1856.
Poles in Portage County	*Wisconsin Folklore.* Ed. James P. Leary. Madison, WI: University of Wisconsin Press, 1998. Goc, Michael. *Native Realm: The Polish-American Community, 1857–1992.* Stevens Point, WI: Worzalla Publishing, 1992.	The Wisconsin Historical Society Archives Web site at http://arcat.library.wisc.edu/
Iron Mining and Italian Community Building in Hurley	Magnaghi, Russell. *The Gogebic Iron Range's Italian Immigrants.* Marquett, MI: Belle Fontaine Press, 1984.	The Wisconsin Historical Society Archives Web site at http://arcat.library.wisc.edu/

Topic	Secondary Source Material	Primary Source Material
From Logging to Farming: Selling Northern Wisconsin to Immigrants	Kane, Lucille. "Settling the Wisconsin Cutovers." *Wisconsin Magazine of History* 40, no. 2 (1956–1957): 91–98. Helgenson, Arlan C. *Farms in the Cutovers: Agricultural Settlement in Northern Wisconsin.* Madison, WI: State Historical Society of Wisconsin for the Department of History, University of Wisconsin, 1962. *Wisconsin History: An Annotated Bibliography.* Compiled by Barbara Dotts Paul and Justus F. Paul. Westport, CT: Greenwood Press, 1999.	Henry, William A. *Northern Wisconsin: A Handbook for the Homeseeker.* Madison, WI: Democrat Printing Co., 1896.
Attracting Newcomers to a New State	*Wisconsin History: An Annotated Bibliography.* Compiled by Barbara Dotts Paul and Justus F. Paul. Westport, CT: Greenwood Press, 1999.	Freeman, Samuel. *The Emigrant's Handbook and Guide to Wisconsin.* Milwaukee, WI: Sentinel and Gazette Power Plant Press Print, 1851. (reprint La Crosse, WI: Brookhaven Press, 1998). Wisconsin Commissioner of Immigration. *Annual Report of the Commissioner of Emigration.* Madison, WI: Wisconsin Historical Society Archives, Rare Books collection.
German Music in a German State	Zeitlin, Richard H. *Germans in Wisconsin.* rev. and exp. ed. Madison, WI: Wisconsin Historical Society, 2000. "Becoming German American." In *Wisconsin's Past and Present: A*	*Historical Atlas.* Madison, WI: University of Wisconsin Press, 1998.

Topic	Secondary Source Material	Primary Source Material
	"Polka Music in a Polka State." In *Wisconsin Folklore.* Edited by James P. Leary. Madison, WI: University of Wisconsin Press, 1998. *Deep Polka: Dance Music from the Midwest.* (CD) Released June 16, 1998. Smithsonian Folkways.	Click the Search button at the top of the screen. Then, type in "census" and press the Return key. A listing of census reports for Wisconsin will appear.
Freedom Ride!: Grant County's African American Pioneers	Cooper, Zachary L. *Black Settlers in Rural Wisconsin.* Madison, WI: State Historical Society of Wisconsin, 1994. Shade, Barbara J. "Afro-Americans in Early Wisconsin." In *Transactions of the Wisconsin Academy of Sciences, Arts and Letters,* vol. 69. Madison, WI: The Academy, 1981. *Wisconsin History: An Annotated Bibliography.* Compiled by Barbara Dotts Paul and Justus F. Paul. Westport, CT: Greenwood Press, 1999.	Pleasant Ridge Negro Community documents. Available at Platteville Area Research Center, UW-Platteville Library, Call Number: Platteville, SC 21.
Escape from Laos: The Harrowing Journey of the Hmong to Wisconsin	Pfaff, Tim. *Hmong in America: Journey from a Secret War.* Eau Claire, WI: Chippewa Valley Museum Press, 1995. Hamilton-Merritt, Jane. *Tragic Mountains: The Hmong, the Americans, and the Secret Wars for Laos, 1942–1992.* Bloomington, IN: Indiana University Press, 1993.	*The Hmong and Their Stories.* Weston, WI: D.C. Everest Area Schools, 2001. Project by Wisconsin School District and the Wausau Area Hmong Mutual Assistance Association.

Chapter Three

Environmental History

Fox cleanup dec

Doyle to release details of PCB disposal plan

The Post-Crescent

Gov. Jim Doyle is scheduled to release the final cleanup decision for the PCB-contaminated Fox River at noon today, a blueprint for the largest environmental dredging project attempted anywhere.

Unless the cleanup decision departs dramatically from previously released plans, it will mandate that businesses responsible spend at least $300 million and perhaps as much as $400 million or more to dredge and dispose of 7.25 million cubic yards of contaminated sediments from the lower Fox River.

Polychlorinated biphenyls or PCBs are a

released into the Fo prior to 1971 duri production and recyc carbonless paper.

which the chain contar fish, been li reprod failure birds mamma

Doyle

to developmental pr in the children of n who ate contaminate

The decision be leased by Doyle tod ers what regulators erating units 3.4

The Great Peshtigo Fire
Logging Practices Create Deadly Firestorm

Have you ever heard of the Great Chicago Fire? On the evening of October 8, 1871, flames raced through the city and destroyed much of it. In an odd twist of fate, another devastating fire raged across northern Wisconsin and upper Michigan on the same night. The Peshtigo Fire killed more people and damaged a much larger area, but it is treated today as a mere footnote in American history. The myth of the Chicago fire's origin—Mrs. O'Leary's cow knocking over a lantern—and the fact that Chicago was and is a major city are probably the biggest reasons for the Peshtigo Fire's lack of notoriety. While Mrs. O'Leary's cow is permanently cemented in the national memory, is it

WHi (X3) 96

An engraver's interpretation of the great Peshtigo fire (*Harper's Weekly,* November 25, 1871)

possible that the occurrence of these two fires at the same time was just a coincidence?

The spring and summer of 1871 were unusually hot and dry. It rained only twice between July and September. In northern Wisconsin, several logging practices were creating a potentially volatile situation. Loggers intentionally burned slash—branches and residue, produced by the clearing of virgin pine forests—or left it in huge piles. Unfortunately, the slash made perfect tinder for spreading a fire. Industries, such as sawmills and factories, housed large stockpiles of flammable raw materials (logs), product (lumber, woodenwares), and waste (bark, sawdust). Brush cleared for railroad lines was often left near the newly laid tracks, and sparks from steam engines frequently ignited the dried brush. Finally, almost every home and building on the Midwestern frontier was constructed out of these readily available wood products.

University of Wisconsin Press

Map showing the area burned by the fire.

Although no one has ever determined a specific cause, it is possible that railroad workers clearing land for tracks started the fire in the small village of Peshtigo on Sunday, October 8. The brush fire rapidly transformed into an inferno and scorched more than 1.2 million acres. Huge rising gas clouds combusted when they reached pockets of air where the oxygen had not already been depleted. Many survivors sought refuge in the Peshtigo River, wading in up to their necks and covering themselves with wet blankets. The following quote from Reverend Peter Pernin relates his experience:

> The air was no longer fit to breathe, full as it was of sand, dust, ashes, cinders, sparks, smoke and fire. It was almost impossible to keep one's eyes unclosed, to distinguish the road, or to recognize people, though the way was crowded with pedestrians, as well as vehicles crossing and crashing against each other in the general flight. Some were hastening towards the river, others from it, whilst all were struggling alike in the grasp of the hurricane. A thousand discordant deafening noises rose on the air together.

Damages were estimated at $169 million, roughly the same as the Chicago fire. The swiftly spreading fire affected the surrounding towns in Oconto, Brown,

Peshtigo in ruins

WHi Image ID 2828

Kewaunee, Door, and Menominee counties. But Peshtigo received the worst losses. Within an hour, the fire had decimated the village, and more than 800 Peshtigo residents lost their lives. By the time it was over, the Great Peshtigo Fire had killed 2,200 people, compared to about 250 deaths in the Chicago Fire.

Even at the time, the Chicago disaster eclipsed the Peshtigo Fire in the public imagination. Wisconsin's Governor Lucius Fairchild, state officials, and most of the legislators had collected a trainload of supplies for poor Chicagoans and helped with its distribution. They were in Chicago when they learned about the fate of Peshtigo. By the time the governor returned to Madison, his wife, Frances, had already begun orchestrating relief efforts. She even redirected a Madison relief car slated for Chicago to the north and arranged for others to be sent from Fond du Lac, Watertown, and Oshkosh.

Besides the Peshtigo Fire, what other environmental disasters in Wisconsin spark your interest? Fire was always a threat to the Northwoods. Has there ever been a devastating fire or similar event in your community? How was it handled, how did it end, and what impact did it have on your area?

Getting Started on Research

Father Peter Pernin's vivid narrative in *The Great Peshtigo Fire: An Eyewitness Account* (Wisconsin Historical Society, 1999) provides an outstanding firsthand description, as well as numerous images of the fire and its aftermath. Secondary source material can be found in Denise Gess and William Lutz's *Firestorm at Peshtigo* and in Volume 2 of Richard N. Current's *The History of Wisconsin: The Civil War Era, 1848–1873*. Find more details about these sources in the Resources section at the end of this chapter.

Menominee Tribal Enterprises and Sustained-Yield Forestry

What are some of the things you value? Why are they important to you? To what lengths would you go to protect these significant things? The Menominee people place a high value on their forest, and they have had to fight to maintain it.

As the oldest continuous residents of Wisconsin, the Menominee people originally possessed land holdings of roughly 9.5 million acres. Their territory spanned northern Wisconsin to the Upper Peninsula of Michigan. A series of treaties reduced these holdings to 235,000 acres, which is the size of the Menominee reservation that is currently occupied by the tribe. Created by the Treaty of 1854, the Menominee reservation is located today in northeastern Wisconsin and maintains forest land on 220,000 of its 235,000 acres.

The Menominee have been using sustainable practices since the 1880s, and since 1973, the Menominee Tribal Enterprises (MTE), through the Menominee Forestry Department, has managed the forest. Located in Neopit, MTE works to ensure sustainable-yield production. In other words, the organization makes sure that logging is performed in such a way that it fulfills people's current needs, but does not jeopardize the resources that will sustain future generations. In the Menominee forest, sustainable-yield means the selective harvesting of mature, ailing, or dead trees. Such forest management is consistent with the way the Menominee people respect the natural world. The following is advice that Menominee chiefs gave to the Nation when it was forced to accept a smaller area of land on which to live. This quote, attributed to Chief Oshkosh, epitomizes the philosophy of respect toward natural resources:

> Start with the rising sun, and work toward the setting sun, but take only the mature trees, the sick trees, and the trees that have fallen. When you reach the end of the Reservation, turn and cut from the setting sun to the rising sun and the trees will last forever.

WHi (X3) 26181; Courtesy of Wisconsin Conservation Department

The Menominee forest

Menominee Indian Mills,

WHi (X3) 52114

Neopit sawmill, the Menominee reservation, 1910

In June 1954, the Menominee Termination Act was passed. This act removed the tribe from federal trust protection status, but it was not implemented until April 1961. Previously, the Secretary of the Interior had managed a trust on behalf of the Menominee people, but now the tribe assumed such obligations. The tribe also had to pay taxes on its lands, and the people lost their tribal status as a sovereign nation. All these changes pushed the Menominee into poverty. Hospitals and schools closed, and their lumber business began to operate at a loss.

The idea of sustained-yield is also deeply embedded in Menominee society and culture. Known as the "Keepers of the Forest," the Menominee attempt to balance economic concerns with a cultural respect for all living things and an ecological interest in maintaining a healthy biodiversity in the forest. The Menominee forest is one of the most intensively managed tracts of land in the Great Lakes area. Throughout the last 140 years, the Menominee have removed more than two billion board feet of lumber. Yet, the volume of saw timber exceeds that of 1854!

Historically, the Menominee have had to fight to maintain their forest. In 1887, the U.S. Congress passed the General Allotment Act, in which it urged tribes to divide their reservations into individually-owned segments. The Menominee recognized that other Nations were being divided and destroyed by this act, and they refused to comply. This allowed them to preserve their land base and maintain collective ownership of the forest under the Menominee people.

In response, the Menominee appealed to the federal government to return their tribal status. In 1973, the Menominee Restoration Act did that and more. The Menominee regained their sovereignty and the rights of tribal members, including collective ownership of the forest. Also, the business transferred its assets back to tribal ownership.

How has the Menominee approach to natural resources helped sustain the Nation as well as the forest? What can we learn from their environmental policies? How do other foresters in Wisconsin practice sustainable-yield production?

Getting Started on Research

You can find information about federal policies, congressional legislation, and the history of the Menominee Nation in Patty Loew's *Indian Nations of Wisconsin* and Nancy Lurie's *Wisconsin Indians*. For a more specific study, try Paula Rogers Huff and Marshall Pecore's "Case Study: Menominee Tribal Enterprises." More details about these publications are in the Resources section at the end of this chapter.

Stopping the Lamprey on the Great Lakes

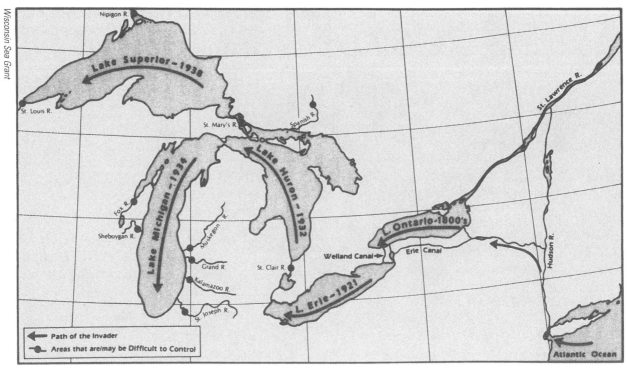

Wisconsin Sea Grant

Map tracing the route of the lamprey invasion in the Great Lakes

Some species of sea life can be very destructive to an ecosystem. This is certainly the case with sea lampreys in the Great Lakes. They have no effective natural predators, and they thrive by pushing out healthy organisms. Fortunately, groups are working to minimize their damage to our waterways.

Native to the Atlantic Ocean, sea lampreys are ocean fish that return to fresh water to spawn, similar to salmon. They have always inhabited Lake Ontario and the St. Lawrence River, which are both open to the Atlantic Ocean. In 1921, lampreys made their first appearance in Lake Erie. They had traveled there through the Welland Canal and eventually spread to all five Great Lakes. Today, major infestations are found in Lake Michigan and Lake Huron.

Sea lampreys are parasitic, eel-like, jawless fish with thorny teeth. A lamprey's mouth is a large disk that it uses for sucking. Very sharp teeth surround its file-like tongue. Lampreys attach to fish and bore a hole into their prey with this tongue. An anticoagulant in their saliva keeps the wound open until the lamprey's hunger is satisfied or the host fish dies. During its adult life span, about 18 months, a single lamprey can kill ten to fifteen pounds of lake trout! It was no surprise that, in the 1940s and 1950s, sea lampreys were responsible for almost wiping out the entire populations of lake trout, white fish, and chub in the Great Lakes.

In 1958, scientists started using the pesticide 3-trifluoromethyl-4-nitrophenol (TFM) to control the lamprey population. They place the substance in low concentrations to attack bottom-dwelling lamprey larvae. Because of these efforts, the lamprey population in Lake Michigan today has dropped to about 10% of its peak in the 1950s. Some scientists worry that lampreys will develop a resistance to the chemicals or learn to spawn on the deltas at stream mouths, which have deeper water that is unsuitable for TFM use.

Several alternatives to the pesticide approach do exist. Barrier dams, which are already used on the Brule and Middle rivers, prevent lampreys from moving upstream to spawn. Lampreys have been considered a delicacy in Europe for centuries, so some people have proposed harvesting and marketing the lamprey as a food product. However, the lamprey's rather unappetizing eel-like appearance has proved to be an unattractive option to American consumers.

In cooperation with the Ojibwe Bad River Tribe, employees of the Great Lakes Indian Fish and Wildlife Commission and interns at Northland College currently catch lamprey five days per week. They freeze the lampreys for the Sea Lamprey Control Program of the U.S. Fish and Wildlife Service in Marquette, Michigan. The lampreys are then scanned for a coated wire tag previously implanted by the Fish and Wildlife Service. The tag identifies where the animals have traveled as adults and helps the Service better control the population.

Lampreys must be removed from the lakes because of their high mercury levels. Lampreys are estimated to have mercury in their systems almost ten times greater than lake trout. The concern is that eagles, the closest thing to a natural predator for

the Lamprey, might consume the deadly toxin and suffer health problems of their own. The problem could then spread beyond the water.

What kinds of dangerous animals or plants have you heard about in your community and in Wisconsin? How has your community dealt with them? What solutions have been proposed to deal with the dangers? What has been the result of these solutions?

Lake trout attacked by lamprey

Great Lakes Fishery Commission

Fish and Game
Aldo Leopold and the Conservation Movement

"There are two spiritual dangers in not owning a farm," Aldo Leopold wrote in *A Sand County Almanac and Sketches Here and There.* "One is the danger of supposing that breakfast comes from the grocery, and the other is that heat comes from the furnace." Leopold never made either mistake. He knew that food came from plants and animals and that heat came from trees. He dedicated his life to cultivating an understanding of the natural world. For years, he quietly went about teaching others how to appreciate the environment and how to interact with it.

Leopold gained much of of his wisdom and insight while spending time at his "shack" on the Wisconsin River near Baraboo. There, he would observe nature and carefully record every detail, such as the arrival of geese every spring and the kind of foods rabbits eat in winter. He recognized how everything in nature was interconnected and how important it was for humans not to neglect the natural environment.

Leopold was born in Iowa in 1887. From an early age, he learned to love the outdoors. Every summer, his family spent six weeks on Marquette Island in northern Lake Huron, where he explored the woods and beaches, learning about the island's animals and plants. Leopold attended Yale University and received a Master of Forestry degree in

Conservationist Aldo Leopold

1909. He then joined the U.S. Forest Service, working in Arizona and New Mexico. During this time, he took a leadership role in soil conservation and wildlife management efforts. In 1924, he became the associate director of the Forest Products Laboratory in Madison. Four years later, he quit the Forest Service to work as an independent researcher and conduct wildlife game surveys. He also published the first textbook on the subject, titled *Game Management.* In 1933, Leopold was appointed professor of game management in the Agricultural Economics Department at the University of Wisconsin, where he not only taught, but directed research efforts at the university's arboretum. Also, he worked with state farmers to continue conservation.

While serving six years on the Wisconsin Conservation Commission, Leopold made his mark on the conservation movement by helping to formulate policy in Wisconsin. His efforts involved firmly establishing the ecological roots of forestry and wildlife ecology. Prior to his work, people believed that land should either be used completely for human needs or to be preserved exactly as it was. Leopold suggested an ecological scenario in which the land could be used for humans and be maintained for wildlife as well. Most of us today appreciate the natural world, but in the 1930s, few knew how

University of Wisconsin Archives

Aldo Leopold's shack on Wisconsin River near Portage, Wisconsin

Getting Started on Research

The best way to understand Aldo Leopold's work is to read *A Sand County Almanac.* What kind of things captured Leopold's attention? You probably know of a place in the countryside where you can sit and observe nature. Make a trip to a spot like this and use a notebook and pencil to write about everything you can observe in one hour. Were any of your sights and descriptions similar to Leopold's? You can learn more about Leopold's life in *Aldo Leopold: His Life and Work,* a book written by Curt Meine. Also, the Aldo Leopold Foundation has a good Web site at http://www.aldoleopold.org/. The site provides photographs of the shack and the region that inspired so much of his work.

to manage it. Leopold emphasized the need for conservation, and he taught people that plants and animals lived in complex ecological systems that had to be treated with respect. He made it clear that small, seemingly insignificant changes made by humans could have unforeseen and unintended consequences. "That land is a community is the basic concept of ecology," he wrote, "but that land is to be loved and respected is an extension of ethics." Forestry meant more than planting trees, and wildlife management meant more than just stocking streams and maintaining large numbers of deer for hunters. Proper management of the natural environment required an understanding of the ecological systems of the land and how plants and animals interacted.

Leopold's most famous book, *A Sand County Almanac,* was published in 1949, a year after his death. The book is a collection of short sketches that describe

a year at his Wisconsin River shack, which he purchased in 1935. The *Almanac* became a major inspiration for twentieth century environmentalism, as people learned to appreciate the wildlife around them and use the land sensibly and sensitively without destroying it.

An excerpt from the original manuscript for *A Sand County Almanac*

UW Archives

Water Policy in Wisconsin
Preserving the St. Croix Riverway

The Mississippi and St. Croix rivers form much of Wisconsin's western boundary. Lakes Superior and Michigan border the state to the north and east. Consequently, Wisconsin has good reason to be concerned about the health of its vast network of waterways. In fact, water policy in Wisconsin has a long history. In 1787, the Northwest Ordinance was adopted to govern the Wisconsin Territory. Since then, the state's navigable waterways have been considered public. In fact, public access was guaranteed in Wisconsin's Constitution. In it, Article IX dictates that all waterways are held in trust and are "forever free."

But Article IX does not, of course, prevent debates about the waterways. Businesses, environmental groups, farmers, tourists, developers, and local residents hold vastly different opinions about the same bodies of water. As Wisconsin's population increased during the 1900s, so did the many functions of the state's water resources and the number of users. In response to the increased activity, the courts and state legislature created a set of laws to protect the rights of both private waterfront property owners and the public. These laws make up the Public Trust Doctrine. Over the years, the Railroad Commission, the Public Service Commission, the Department of

Namekagon River

Natural Resources, and other groups have led the way in defending the public trust in the state's waters. And many controversies involve the St. Croix Riverway. Situated on the Wisconsin and Minnesota border in Wisconsin's northwestern corner, the St. Croix Riverway consists of the Namekagon and St. Croix rivers and runs for 252 miles. The Namekagon section of the Riverway provoked a controversy in the 1950s. The Public Service Commission granted a permit to build a dam on the river. But in its decision to allow the dam, the commission failed to include the recreational value of the river, including its scenic beauty. A conservation group, the Wisconsin division of the Isaak Walton League of America (IWLA), responded by filing suit against the commission. In 1952, the Wisconsin Supreme Court ruled in favor of the IWLA.

The Wild and Scenic Rivers Act of 1968 granted more protection for the St. Croix Riverway. The Lower St. Croix was added in 1972. This act preserved select rivers as free-flowing and protected them from dams and other projects that would impede the natural course of their waters. The Act goes further to classify rivers as wild, scenic, or recreational. It also provides permits to regulate hunting and fishing and authorizes the Secretary of the Interior and the Secretary of Agriculture to study areas and submit proposals to the U.S. President and the Congress. This is not the same, however, as the state park designation. The act did not completely halt development along the river, but established the goal of preserving the "character" of the river.

Getting Started on Research

Primary source material on the Namekagon River case can be found in Walter Scott's *Water Policy Evolution in Wisconsin* and through the Isaak Walton League of America. More information about these sources is listed in the Resources section at the end of this chapter.

Secondary sources can be obtained through the Wisconsin Department of Natural Resources. The Waters of Wisconsin (WOW) Report, which was the product of a three-year initiative on sustainable water use, is available online. Visit the Wisconsin Academy of Sciences, Arts and Letters' Web site at http://www.wisconsinacademy.org/wow/.

Today, the St. Croix Riverway remains controversial. Skyrocketing housing costs and overcrowding have driven many citizens out of the metropolitan Twin Cities area. The population of Chisago County, Minnesota, for example, grew 35% between 1990 and 2000, and 75% of the residents commute to Minneapolis and St. Paul. As urban sprawl encroaches, an increasingly volatile battleground for discussion and debate about the overuse of the St. Croix Riverway is building.

What body of water in your community has been the subject of current or historical controversy? Who was involved, what were their motivations, and what came of it all? What do you think the future holds for water policy in Wisconsin?

Project ELF
The Northwoods' Secret of the Cold War

Between the end of World War II in 1945 and the collapse of European communism in 1991, many people lived in fear of a nuclear war between the United States and the Soviet Union. Although both nations claimed to want peace, each was prepared to attack quickly if the other got too aggressive. To maintain an edge in the number, size, and power of their nuclear bombs and missiles, both nations raced to pile up more weapons than the other. Northern Wisconsin was very far away from Berlin, Cuba, and Vietnam, places where the United States and Soviet Union had a history of confronting one another. But on July 1, 1968, the Cold War came to the Northwoods when the U.S.

Wisconsin Department of Natural Resources

Project ELF transmitter near Clam Lake, Wisconsin

Navy announced it was going to test a new communications facility near Clam Lake.

The facility was called Project ELF. The acronym stands for "extremely low frequency." The idea behind the project was to signal the Navy's nuclear submarines by using low frequency waves transmitted into the earth. Conventional radio waves could not get very far in the ocean's depths, so Project ELF was designed to turn the granite bedrock of the Lake Superior region into a giant antenna capable of sending one-way signals to submarines around the world. It would pump millions of watts of electricity into the earth to create a constant signal deep into any ocean. The facility was constructed in 1969, and the Navy began testing its theories. The Navy also promised to remove the facility once the testing was complete.

In 1982, people were surprised to learn that the facility would become a permanent part of the Navy's communications efforts in the Northwoods. Many were outraged that northern Wisconsin was being used to possibly order submarines to launch a nuclear attack. Many more were worried, too, about the environmental and health risks. The Navy had assured residents a number of times that Project ELF was

MUSIC: TONY BROWN; FOOL'S MOON; BARBARA KOOYMAN; TOM LANGELOH. SPEAKERS: ERWIN KNOLL; JENNIFER SPEICHER & CRAIG KRONSTEDT OF STOP PROJECT ELF; GILAM KERLEY, DRAFT RESISTER; AND MORE...

BRING HOME THE NUCLEAR FREEZE

STOP PROJECT ELF

RALLY * Nov. 16 * Tues.
NOON AT THE CAPITOL
KING ST. SIDE

CONFRONT THE NAVY

1 to 4 pm US Navy Presentation Before the DNR Board
GEF III State Office Bldg. 125 S. Webster Room #11

Wisconsin Department of Natural Resources

A poster for a rally against Project ELF

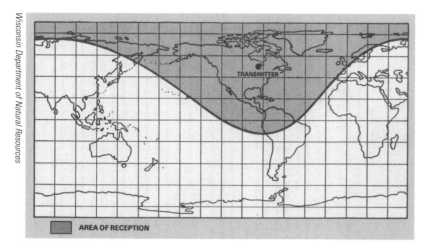

Wiscosin Department of Natural Resources

AREA OF RECEPTION

Technical drawing of the area of reception

safe, but laboratory tests in the 1970s indicated that ELF's radiation could be responsible for altering the behavior and blood chemistry of test subjects. A researcher for the University of Colorado found a link between ELF and higher rates of cancer. In 1984, the State of Wisconsin sued the U.S. Navy to stop the project, and federal judge Barbara Crabb ordered construction halted pending a Supplemental Environmental Impact Statement (SEIS). A federal appeals court, however, overturned the judge's injunction and gave the Navy permission to continue construction.

In the face of this legal defeat, many Northwoods residents refused to back down. From their defiance of the 1850 Fugitive Slave Law to their demonstrations for civil rights and against the Vietnam War, Wisconsinites have a long history of civil disobedience. True to this tendency, several people in northern Wisconsin founded organizations to protest Project ELF and to lobby the U.S. Congress to shut it down permanently. In 1978, fifty people living near Clam Lake formed the Coalition to Stop Project ELF. By 1982, the organization had grown to fifteen hundred members. Some Northwoods activists began a guerrilla war against the facility. In the 1990s, more than 500 arrests were made when citizens protested at Clam

Lake and at a similar site in Marquette, Michigan. Charged with criminal trespassing, those arrested spent nearly two years in jail. In May 2001, eleven people were arrested at a Mothers' Day protest at Clam Lake. All were ready and willing to go to jail.

The public response to Project ELF indicates how much the environment matters to the residents of northern Wisconsin. While there is no clear evidence that the radio waves have ever been a safety threat to the area wildlife or people, the protesters believed it was essential to protect the environment against all potential risks. Stopping the Navy from running its facility continues to be a critical step in that process. Today, Project ELF continues to function in the Northwoods and remains controversial.

Getting Started on Research

Do you find the protesters' arguments for protecting the environment compelling, or do you agree that the U.S. Navy has a right to maintain the Clam Lake facility? Newspapers and Web sites make excellent places to find more about the public reaction to Project ELF. Your teacher or librarian can help you locate newspapers (probably on microfilm) that contain information about the Navy's work in the Northwoods. Of particular interest is the U.S. Navy's announcement of Project ELF in 1969 and when it announced in 1982 that ELF would become permanent. One of several organizations protesting Project ELF was Nukewatch. You can access its Web site at http://www.nukewatch.com/.

For secondary sources about Project ELF, you can begin with *The ELF Odyssey: National Security Versus Environmental Protection* by Lowell L. Klessig and Victor L. Strite. Information to help you find these publications is in the Resources section in this chapter.

The Man from Clear Lake

Gaylord Nelson and Earth Day

WHS Name File

Gaylord Nelson in front of the Wisconsin State Capitol building

Who wants to breathe smoky air or drink dirty water? Today, we take it for granted that factories and other industries have a responsibility to avoid polluting the water and air. But this was not always the case. Throughout the 1940s, 1950s, and 1960s, American industries produced record numbers of goods, but they paid little attention to the damage they were inflicting upon the environment. Wisconsin's Senator Gaylord Nelson had a lot to do with making the care of the environment a major concern for everybody.

Elected governor in 1958, Gaylord Nelson was only the fourth Democrat to be elected to the office in Wisconsin since before the Civil War. He had been an admirer of Robert La Follette, the popular Wisconsin Republican who championed women's suffrage, racial equality, and other progressive causes in the early 1900s. Nelson shared La Follette's belief that industry had a responsibility to make safe products and keep the environment clean, and he was a member of the Progressive Party founded by La Follette's sons, Robert Jr. and Philip. As governor, Nelson developed a plan to expand outdoor recreation facilities. As a U.S. senator, he proposed a constitutional amendment declaring that "Every person has the inalienable right to a decent environment." During the 1960s, Nelson borrowed an idea from the anti–Vietnam War protests: the teach-in. He believed that if only people knew more about the environment, they would take greater care of it and demand that industry do the same. During a speech in Seattle in 1969, Nelson first proposed a full day of teaching and learning about the environment. His efforts led to the first Earth Day on April 22, 1970.

Nelson's idea was met with great enthusiasm, especially among the younger generation. On the first Earth Day, thousands of students in elementary school, high school, and college spent the day learning about pollution and recycling. The day inspired more than talking. People took to the streets to clean up trash. Others held large rallies to demand that big business reform its ways. Every April 22 since then, people take time to consider the environment and try to find ways to make it cleaner.

The federal government responded to Nelson's plea. In the same year that the first Earth Day was celebrated, Congress created the Environmental Protection Agency (EPA). This governmental agency is responsible for keeping the environment safe. Congress also passed the Water Quality Improvement Act and the Air Quality Control Act, both designed to ensure that clean water and air are available to everyone. Some doubted that the federal government could force industries to abide by cleaner standards, but Earth Day and other events have raised people's expectations. Now, everyone expects the environment to be clean and to be kept clean.

Today, school and community initiatives help young children learn how to recycle paper, plastic, and aluminum. Industries today are more aware of their moral and legal responsibilities to monitor what they put into the water and air. If an industry tries to get away with polluting, it must now deal with laws put in place to prosecute that behavior. These and other environmental victories would have happened at some time, but they probably would not have happened as quickly

---

Getting Started on Research

Your local library will have newspapers and magazines from the first Earth Day in 1970. Gaylord Nelson (and others) wrote *Beyond Earth Day: Fulfilling the Promise*, which is an excellent resource on the environmental movement. Interview teachers and administrators who know how your school has celebrated Earth Day in the past. Another excellent resource on environmental issues in Wisconsin is Thomas Huffman's *Protectors of the Land and Water: Environmentalism in Wisconsin, 1961–1968*. Its bibliography is particularly helpful for further research. Online resources include the Envirolink Web site at http://www.earthday.envirolink.org/. Click the History of Earth Day and Site Map links for lots of information and pictures on environmental topics.

---

as they did had Gaylord Nelson not raised the issue before the nation and pushed the government to take action. Although Nelson retired from public life more than twenty years ago, he is still asked to speak about the importance of maintaining a clean environment.

What did your community do on the original Earth Day in 1970? How has Earth Day been celebrated in your community, county, and nation since then? What examples of pollution exist in your community, and are the problems being resolved?

Senate Joint Resolution 169 relating to an environmental agenda for the 1970s

uary 19, 1970   CONGRESSIONAL RECORD — SENATE   81

...an made at the United Nations ... than 20 years ago. It has been ...ng in the Committee on Foreign ...ions for 20 years, and we have failed ... on it. It is entirely up to the Sen-... Presidents since then have asked ... proceed in this regard, and they all favored it without exception. ...s a measure which, of course, in-... no action by the House of Repre-...tives. It is entirely up to the U.S. ...e.

...ond, the Convention on the Aboli-... Forced Labor prohibits any forced ...mpulsory labor for the purpose of, ... political coercion or punishment; ...d, mobilizing labor for economic de-...ment; third, labor discipline; ..., punishing participation in ..., or fifth, racial, social, national, or ...us discrimination.

...re is another convention which was ... us by President Kennedy in 1963. ...entirely within the province of the ...te to act. It is long overdue. It should ...acted.

...rd, the Convention on Political ... for Women provides that women ... be entitled to vote in all elections ...ual terms with men. It also provides ...women shall be eligible for election ...publicly elected bodies, to hold pub-...ice, and to exercise public functions ...lished by national law, all on equal ... with men.

...ce again, this was sent to us by ...dent Kennedy 7 years ago, and we ...yet to act on it.

... validity and justification for these ...ntions is acknowledged by a major-... nations throughout the world. We ...ne of the very few nations that has ... on none of these treaties. This Na-...however, which affirms these rights ...gh its laws and traditions for its ...

ORDER FOR RECESS

Mr. BYRD of West Virginia. Mr. President, I ask unanimous consent that, when the Senate completes its business today, it stand in recess until 12 o'clock noon tomorrow.

The PRESIDING OFFICER. Without objection, it is so ordered.

SENATE JOINT RESOLUTION 169— INTRODUCTION OF A JOINT RESOLUTION RELATING TO AN ENVIRONMENTAL AGENDA FOR THE 1970'S

Mr. NELSON. Mr. President, in the nearly 40 years since Franklin D. Roosevelt said in his first inaugural address that "this great Nation will endure as it has endured, will revive and will prosper," our economy has soared to levels that no one in the 1930's could have imagined. In these past four decades we have become the wealthiest nation on earth by almost any measure of production and consumption.

As the economic boom and the post-war population explosion continued to break all records, a national legend developed: With science and technology as its tools, the private enterprise system could accomplish anything.

We assumed that, if private enterprise could turn out more automobiles, airplanes, and TV sets than all the rest of the world combined, somehow it could create a transportation system that would work. If we were the greatest builders in the world, we need not worry about our poor and about the planning and building of our cities. Private enterprise with enough technology and enough profit would manage that just fine.

In short, we assumed that, if private enterprise could be such a spectacular...

We have not. For, in addition to the other traumatic national and international events, the 1960's have produced another kind of "top of the decade" list. It has been a decade when the darkening cloud of pollution seriously began degrading the thin envelope of air surrounding the globe; when pesticides and unrestricted waste disposal threatened the productivity of all the oceans of the world; when virtually every lake, river, and watershed in America began to show the distressing symptoms of being overloaded with polluting materials.

These pivotal events have begun to warn the Nation of a disturbing new paradox: The mindless pursuit of quantity is destroying—not enhancing—the opportunity to achieve quality in our lives. In the words of the American balladeer, Pete Seeger, we have found ourselves "standing knee deep in garbage, throwing rockets at the moon."

Cumulatively, "progress—American style" adds up each year to 200 million tons of smoke and fumes, 7 million junked cars, 20 million tons of paper, 48 billion cans, and 28 billion bottles.

It also means bulldozers gnawing away at the landscape to make room for more unplanned expansion, more leisure time but less open space in which to spend it, and so much reckless progress that we face even now a hostile environment.

As one measure of the rate of consumption that demands our resources and creates our vast wastes, it has been estimated that all the American children born in just one year will use up 200 million pounds of steel, 9.1 billion gallons of gasoline, and 25 billion pounds of beef during their lifetimes.

To provide the electricity for our air conditioners, a Kentucky hillside is stripmined. To provide the gasoline for our...

Recreation and Employment
The New Deal and Wisconsin Parks

Everyone appreciates natural beauty. Who doesn't enjoy lush forests, gleaming streams, flowing rivers, and tumbling waterfalls? Wisconsin has more than forty beautiful state parks that attract visitors from all over the country. You may have already visited Devil's Lake, Copper Falls, Roche-A-Cri, Rib Mountain, and others. But there is more to these parks than just hiking trails, fishing holes, and camping grounds. Many were created or expanded in the 1930s by the

federal government in an effort not only to develop recreational areas but to provide work for those who had lost their jobs during the Great Depression.

Like other states, Wisconsin was hit hard by the high unemployment that resulted from the stock market crash in 1929. Thousands of Wisconsinites were out of work, and no one was sure what to do about it. In response to the crisis, state and national governments implemented various programs to put citizens to work on useful projects in their states. President Franklin D. Roosevelt instituted these programs, which were part of the New Deal. Some of the most successful New Deal programs established outdoor recreation areas and improved state and national parks. These included the Civilian Conservation Corps (CCC) and the Works Progress Administration (WPA).

The CCC was founded in 1933 and brought unemployed young men to camps where they worked on conservation projects. Workers for the CCC stocked rivers with fish, planted trees, constructed nature trails, fought forest fires, and planted trees. The camps provided them with a place to live and eat, and each worker received $30 per month ($25 was sent to his family each month). It was a meager amount of money, even in the 1930s, but it was a wage when wages were hard to come by. Between 1933 and 1942, approximately 92,000 Wisconsin men worked for the CCC. They constructed 500 bridges and more than 4,000 miles of fire lanes, trails, roads, and telephone lines. The WPA was established in 1935 and became the largest public works program ever created by the federal government. Workers for the WPA built hospitals, schools, and playgrounds,

Wisconsin Conservation Department

COPPER FALLS STATE PARK

Park Boundaries
Roads
Parking Area
Trail
Foot Bridge
Shelter
Camp Grounds
Observation

WPA-era map of Copper Falls, 1936

Getting Started on Research

Which parks in your area were developed by the CCC or the WPA? Many people in your community may remember these programs and may have even participated in them. These people might be government employees, school administrators, park officials, or retired workers. Interview them to learn more about their role in making or improving local parks. Your librarian can help you find microfilm of newspapers and magazines from the 1930s that describe the conservation and environmental work going on in Wisconsin.

The governor during much of this period was Philip F. La Follette. His papers are located at the Wisconsin Historical Society in Madison, and many of these primary sources address the state's work programs. You can also consult the fourth volume of *History of Wisconsin: War, a New Era, and Depression, 1914–1940* by Paul Glad. Look up CCC and WPA in the book's index to see what programs were active in Wisconsin. The National New Deal Preservation Association Web site provides a link to the history of the New Deal (including WPA and CCC programs) at http://www .newdeallegacy.org/.

and see the magnificent waterfalls. Other state parks were improved so people could see more of their natural beauty and explore them more safely. Decades after the last CCC and WPA worker left, people still come from miles away to enjoy the fruits of their labors.

In April 1935, the Wisconsin WPA administrator Ralph Immell described the reasons for investing so much time and money into the state's natural resources when he said, "Responsible government plans in terms of centuries. We who live today are but temporary tenants of the resources of the state or nation." There is no doubt that these programs helped teach generations that conservation and reforestation are ways to restore and maintain the environment. But the WPA and CCC were also a means of providing work for the unemployed and creating an environment to be enjoyed not only by tourists to the state but by the residents who live here.

as well as outdoor recreation areas, parks, and campgrounds throughout the state.

This emphasis on conservation, construction, and recreation made a lasting impression on the northern part of our state. Copper Falls State Park near Mellen, for example, is a major outdoor recreation spot because of the CCC. The park was established in 1929, but in 1936, the CCC enlarged it and constructed a network of trails and bridges along the Bad River. This allowed visitors to walk among the old-growth trees

WPA-built rustic bridge at Copper Falls

WHi Image ID 5751

Wisconsin's First State Park

Interstate Park at the St. Croix Dalles

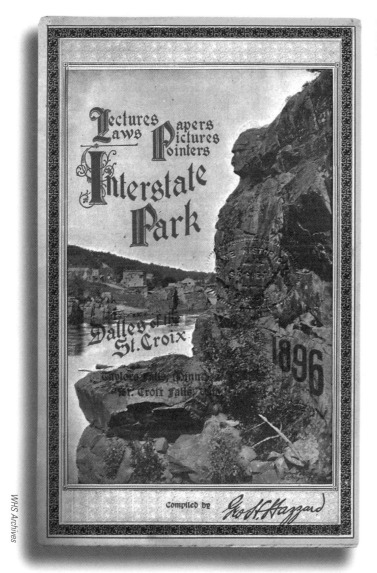

Cover of George Hazzard's book on the St. Croix Dalles

WHS Archives

In the late 1860s when George Hazzard heard that St. Paul street builders were planning to use crushed rock from the St. Croix Dalles for making city roads, he took action. Hazzard had fallen in love with the Dalles as a boy. He later worked as a general agent for railroads and steamboat lines out of St. Paul, which furthered his appreciation of the area. When he heard that developers might damage this unique natural resource, he organized a preservation movement to protect it. He worked to designate the Dalles as a state park, which would ensure its protection.

In 1895, Minnesota legislators proclaimed the west bank of the St. Croix Riverway to be a state park, even though the funds for maintaining it had not been fully appropriated. Wisconsin had no state parks at the time, and legislators were unwilling to commit funds to the project because they knew little about that part of the state. By 1899, however, legislators were convinced that such a designation was worthwhile, and the Wisconsin segment of Interstate State Park formally came into existence.

But, that was only the beginning of the story. The land first had to be acquired from its current owners. Obtaining it could turn into years of lobbying to purchase, claim, or even condemn the land so it could be bought cheaply and made into the park. Between 1901 and 1911, Madison citizen Harry D. Baker took on the task of

Developers, private property owners, businesses, and residents seem to have completely different visions about how to use their parcels of land. They and others in our nation's urban centers constantly argue about "green space." The story of the origin of Wisconsin's first state park highlights these never-ending debates about land usage. It also hints that the arguing may not stop anytime soon.

Getting Started on Research

George Hazzard's *Interstate Park: Lectures, Laws, Papers, Pictures, Pointers* is filled with relevant primary source material. For a detailed secondary source about the park's history, consult chapter 4 of McMahon and Karamanski's *Time and the River: A History of the Saint Croix*. The National Park Service Web site provides links to many of the people and places in our nation's national park history. Begin your search online at http://www.nps.gov/.

diplomatically bartering with several of the land owners. Eventually, the efforts of Hazzard, Baker, and others paid off. Wisconsin contributed more resources than Minnesota, and today, only 292 acres of dalles parklands are in Minnesota, while 1,734 acres are situated in Wisconsin.

Even before the St. Croix Dalles became a state park, people were drawn to the area's majestic beauty and plentiful flora and fauna. About 6,000 years ago, different groups of Native Americans made their homes in the area. Beginning with the trapping of beaver and other fur-bearing animals in the 1600s, European and European American settlers began to tap the area's natural resources. Logging was especially popular because the St. Croix Valley's white pine lumber was highly valued. Then early tourism began to exploit the region in a different way. In 1838, steamboat service brought visitors to Taylors Falls, a perfect example of the natural beauty of the St. Croix Dalles region. Even more tourists flowed in when the railroad arrived in 1880.

The geological history of the area contributes mightily to its natural magnificence. About 1.1 billion years ago, a rift formed along a line from Lake Superior to Iowa. Flows of lava erupted from the cracks and solidified into a hard, rocky substance called basalt. Interstate State Park's dalles are made of this strong, dark gray rock. Some 500 to 600 million years ago, a sea covered the entire area. Compressed and hardened over time, the sand and silt deposited by the sea formed sandstone and shale. The warming of global temperatures caused glaciers to move across Wisconsin. When the last glacier melted 10,000 years ago, its water rushed south, carving out the St. Croix Valley and leaving the resistant basalt cliffs behind. Massive whirlpools in the rushing river also gouged out large holes in the bedrock, creating the area's now famous potholes.

The push to establish Wisconsin's first state park highlights broader historical debates about natural beauty, land usage, and ownership that still have meaning in our own time. The next time you visit a state park, read the literature about the area and think about its history and the issues that helped or hindered the quest to protect it. What is the history behind the state parks in your region of Wisconsin? What are the benefits and drawbacks of state parks? Consider the people who helped make Interstate Park what it is today. What impact did they have on the intersection of natural history and human history?

WHS Archives

Brochure published in 1900 to promote Interstate Park.

Pesticide on Trial

Wisconsin's Role in Banning DDT

Scientific progress can sometimes have unforeseen results, as in the case of the once-common pesticide DDT. In the 1940s, the chemical dichloro-diphenyl-trichloroethane (DDT) was being sprayed over swamps that bred disease-carrying mosquitoes and over crops that needed to be rid of damaging insects and other pests. Allied troops used DDT to kill mosquitoes that carried malaria and a variety of other tropical diseases during World War II. In Milwaukee, DDT was being sprayed on trees to control Dutch elm disease. The pesticide was cheap and effective, and by 1945, factories were producing two million pounds of it every single month.

In 1948, the chemist responsible for discovering DDT was awarded the Nobel Prize in medicine. A few years later, however, a number of scientists expressed concerns about the widespread use of DDT in the United States. They realized that the chemical remained in the environment long after it was sprayed. Tests revealed that DDT could accumulate in the fat cells of animal and human bodies! Wildlife biologists linked DDT to the declining populations of several species of birds, including the bald eagle. Over time, animals at the top of the food chain that consumed smaller animals gradually built up dangerous levels in their systems. Alarmed environmentalists, scientists, and citizens began advocating the banning of DDT.

In 1968, Wisconsin became the center of the DDT debate. Opponents of the chemical's usage took advantage of a provision

The Capital Times

Historic Conference on DDT's Impact on Nature Opens Today

IF MANKIND SHOULD survive his own poisons—nuclear chemical and social—it may be recorded that the light generated in Madison in December of 1968 is responsible.

The eyes of the nation — at least the eyes of ecologists and the chemical industry — are focussed on Madison today where historic hearings begin on one of the most troublesome and significant issues of today.

Scientists from across the nation are gathering here to discuss and debate the controversial question of what DDT is doing to the balance of nature. It is seldom that such outstanding authorities in their fields will get together on a more important issue.

Today's conference, which may continue for a fortnight or more, has been called by the State Department of Natural Resources at the request of the Citizens Natural Resources Association and the Wisconsin Division of the Izaak Walton League of America who have requested a declaratory judgment on the use of DDT in this state. If Wisconsin restricts or bans DDT it could start a nationwide movement.

Some of the most careful and conservative scientists in the country will present testimony about the imbalance that has already been created that will shock thoughtful people. And scientists with other views will respond.

In the long run the decision on this vital issue will be made by the public. The conference starting today may well be the most important one of its kind and inestimably valuable in its education impact.

The public will do well to follow it.

Article from the *Capital Times*, Madison, Wisconsin, December 2, 1968

in Wisconsin law that allowed any group of citizens to request that a state agency make decisions on questions of law. In this case, a group called the Citizens Natural Resources Association asked the Wisconsin Department of Natural Resources (DNR) to rule on whether or not DDT was a water pollutant. The hearings took place between December 1968 and April 1969 and provided the environmental group a forum to make its case. Anti-DDT arguments were presented in an orderly and compelling fashion, not just to the DNR but to the nation as a whole. Newspapers across the country followed the hearings and published daily updates.

Hundreds of people lined up to sit in on the hearings that opened in December. To

Getting Started on Research

One of the best places to begin gathering information about DDT and Wisconsin's role in banning it is the article "DDT on Trial: The Wisconsin Hearing, 1968–1969" by Thomas R. Dunlap in the *Wisconsin Magazine of History*. Look at the footnotes for information on newspaper accounts and government records of the hearings.

Newspapers all over the country followed the Wisconsin DDT hearing. What did local newspapers say about the event? Your librarian can help you find microfilm copies of newspapers that covered the story. Other primary sources can be found by serarching the Wisconsin Historical Society Archive's online catalog using the keyword "DDT."

accommodate the size of the crowd, the hearings had to be moved to the State Assembly chamber. Senator Gaylord Nelson, already famous as a protector of the environment, offered testimony just as he had done in Congress. The Citizens Natural Resources Association called professors from the University of Wisconsin to explain how DDT builds up in an environment and affects the food chain. The most dramatic example, and consequently the one that captured the public's imagination, was the case of large birds of prey. The environmentalists demonstrated how concentrations of DDT caused the birds' eggs to be thin-shelled and easily damaged. They insisted that DDT could effectively wipe out whole populations of birds, including the bald eagle.

The hearings continued through the middle of January and then halted to allow the makers of DDT the opportunity to prepare a response. When the hearings resumed in April, it became clear that the chemical industry had not done enough testing to be able to show that DDT was safe. As a result of the hearings, the DNR ruled that DDT was, in fact, a water pollutant. Several states, including Wisconsin, almost immediately began action to ban DDT. Soon afterward, DDT was banned nationally. It was a stunning victory for the environment, for the Citizens Natural Resources Association and those who testified, and for citizens everywhere.

Document showing the Wisconsin DNR ruling on DDT.

Wisconsin Department of Natural Resources

Ruling

DDT, including one or more of its metabolites in any concentration or in combination with other chemicals at any level, within any tolerances, or in any amounts, is harmful to humans and found to be of public health significance. No concentrations, levels, tolerances or amounts can be established. Chemical properties and characteristics of DDT enable it to be stored or accumulated in the human body and in each trophic level of various food chains, particularly the aquatic, which provides food for human consumption. Its ingestion and dosage therefore cannot be controlled and consequently its storage is uncontrolled. Minute amounts of the chemical, while not producing observable clinical effects, do have biochemical, pharmacological, and neurophysiological effects of public health significance.

No acute or chronic levels of DDT which are harmful to animal or aquatic life can be established. For the reasons above set forth a chronic level may become an acute level. Feeding tests, laboratory experiments and environmental studies establish that DDT or one or more of its analogs is harmful to raptors and waterfowl by interfering with their reproductive process and in other birds by having a direct neurophysiological effect.

Feeding tests or experiments and environmental studies establish that DDT at chronic low levels is harmful to fish by reducing their resistance to stress.

Let the Waters Flow
Dam Removal Projects

Wisconsin has a network of rivers running through it. This network contains hundred of miles of waterways that link virtually every part of the state. Native people and early European explorers learned that the Fox, Wisconsin, Black, and St. Croix rivers,

Waterworks Dam on the Baraboo River before its removal

River Alliance of Wisconsin

These structures created huge ponds to store logs that were floated down from logging centers. Groups in Milwaukee, Wisconsin Dells, and other locales constructed dams for industry and for generating electricity. In other areas of the state, dams created recreation areas like Mondeaux Flowage in Taylor County. By the late 1900s, nearly 1,000 dams blocked Wisconsin rivers.

Many of these dams had grown old and no longer served their original purpose. Many were dangerous. Company owners and residents had to decide whether to repair the dams or remove them. Faced with the high cost of repairs, many decided simply to remove the dams and let the river flow freely. Between 1960 and 2000, approximately eighty dams were removed.

Removing dams often improved the environment. Canoes and kayaks could travel along the river with ease. Land that had

among others, were natural highways that could be easily traveled by canoes. The Euro-American settlers who arrived began to manipulate the flow of this network. First, they built a series of locks on the lower Fox River to accommodate steamboats. Then, they began to build a canal at Portage to connect the Fox and Wisconsin rivers. They planned more canal projects, but railways made the rivers less essential for transporting passengers and goods. The rivers maintained their importance as major resource corridors, however, and people found other reasons to control water flow.

Throughout northern Wisconsin in the late 1800s and early 1900s, lumber companies started building dams on the rivers.

River Alliance of Wisconsin

Removing the Waterworks Dam on the Baraboo River

been underwater became available for recreation spots and park areas. Along the Kickapoo and a few other rivers, trout fishing became popular once the fish were reintroduced into the flowing waters. As rivers were restored to their original state, natural wildlife and plants returned, aiding conservation efforts. People could once again experience the environment as it had been in the 1800s.

One of the best success stories of dam removal is the Baraboo River project. The Baraboo flows for more than 100 miles from Monroe County to Columbia County. Just northwest of Portage, it joins the Wisconsin River. The Baraboo Rapids, a five-mile stretch of the river, drops 45 feet. Early settlers saw this drop as a good place to construct dams because it seemed able to generate a useful amount of mechanical energy. Three dams were built to energize grist mills, lumber mills, and the city's waterworks. But, the dams slowed the river, making it uninhabitable for many species of fish. Among the species affected was the sturgeon for which the river was named (*barbeau* is French for "sturgeon"). By the 1990s, these dams were unsafe and were no longer serving their intended purpose. When the Department of Natural Resources ordered the city of Baraboo to repair or remove the Waterworks Dam, the city chose to tear it down.

Former site of the Waterworks Dam on the Baraboo River at Circus World

Three other dams on the Baraboo River were also removed between 1999 and 2001. Two were in the city, and one was approximately 30 miles upstream. The removal of these dams allowed the Baraboo River to flow freely for the first time in a century. This provided many benefits to city residents, including several new parks and walking paths. It also spurred a revitalization effort aimed at making the city's waterfront more beautiful and practical. The rapids became a popular destination for canoeists. The number of fish species more than doubled, attracting more sport fishing.

Many other communities throughout the state that had been hobbled by century-old dams have seen economic revitalization and environmental improvement as they brought the rivers back to life. Is your hometown built on or near a river? Were dams constructed near your community for hydroelectric power, lumber mills, or other purposes? Do any still function, or do plans exist to remove or repair them? Search your library or the Internet for old newspapers that document the construction of these dams, how they were removed, and what they look like now. What benefits might your community receive if its dams were removed or repaired?

Getting Started on Research

Much of the financial and educational support for dam removal comes from the River Alliance of Wisconsin, based in Madison. Visit its Web site at http://www.wisconsinrivers.org/. For more information about the Baraboo River and other dam removal projects around the state, ask your librarian for help with sources from the Gaylord Nelson Institute for Environmental Studies in Madison. The organization helps communities decide when and how to repair or to remove aging dams. Visit the Institute's Web site at http://www.ies.wisc.edu/. Interview environmental specialists, civil engineers, and community leaders for different perspectives on the process of dam removal and river restoration.

Cleaning the Fox River

The Battle over PCB Removal

Environmental issues often inspire debate. These debates can occur locally, at the state level, or on a national scale. Disputes usually involve attempts to assign responsibility or to place blame on others for past negligence. Such debates also tend to assign a value to things that are difficult to quantify, such as clean air or water and issues or objects that may have potential value in the future. Examples include rainforest plants used for medical purposes.

During the 1950s, 1960s, and 1970s, seven Fox River Valley paper companies released polychlorinated biphenyls, or PCBs, into the Fox River. These industrial chemicals are by-products resulting from the manufacture of carbonless copy paper and are known to cause cancer in animals. In humans, exposure to PCBs can cause acne-like skin conditions, liver damage in adults, and neurobehavioral and immunological abnormalities in children. PCBs also pose a threat to fish and the small organisms they consume. Like DDT, PCBs can accumulate in highly concentrated amounts in the fatty tissues of water-dwelling animals. When humans and animals consume PCB-contaminated fish, they can ingest chemical levels thousands of times higher than those in the water.

In 1977, the U.S. government banned the manufacture of PCBs. Its decision was based upon evidence showing that PCB accumulation in the environment causes harmful heath problems. But, the legislation was too little too late. PCBs do not just disappear from the environment or dissolve into the soil. In fact, they bind strongly to soils in the ground and at the bottom of rivers and lakes. This is why high levels of the toxic chemicals remain in the sediments of the Fox River. Approximately 35 tons can be found there. Some of it stays, but a lot of it gets carried along in the flow of the river. Thirty-five more tons of PCBs have been found at the extreme southern end of Green Bay, and 70% of all PCBs entering Lake Michigan can be traced back to the Fox River!

But, cleanup efforts have sparked controversy. The Wisconsin Department of Natural Resources (DNR) and the U.S. Environmental Protection Agency (EPA) have forged a partnership to develop a solution. Whatever is decided, the cleanup promises to be costly and lengthy. Estimates range from $400 million to $1.2 billion, and the effort is expected to take several decades or more. Environmental activists

Article from the *Fox River Valley Post Crescent,* July 28, 2003

Fox cleanup decision made

Doyle to release details of PCB disposal plan

The Post-Crescent

Gov. James Doyle is scheduled to release the final cleanup decision for the PCB-contaminated Fox River at noon today, a blueprint for the largest environmental dredging project attempted anywhere.

Unless the cleanup decision departs dramatically from previously released plans, it will mandate that six paper companies spend at least $300 million and perhaps as much as $400 million or more to dredge and dispose of 7.25 million cubic yards of contaminated sediments from the lower Fox River.

Polychlorinated biphenyls or PCBs are a class of industrial solvents

released into the Fox River prior to 1971 during the production and recycling of carbonless paper. PCBs, which enter the food chain and contaminate fish, have been linked to reproductive failure in birds and mammals and to developmental problems in the children of mothers who ate contaminated fish.

Doyle

The decision being released by Doyle today covers what regulators call operating units 3, 4 and 5. Unit 3 is the stretch of river

in Brown County between the dam at Little Rapids and the dam at De Pere. Unit 4 is the seven-mile stretch between the dam and the mouth of the river.

Unit 5 is the bay of Green Bay, added to the state-led cleanup study after environmentalists lobbied for its inclusion and the U.S. Environmental Protection Agency backed them up. State and federal officials have given no hint that they plan any direct action in the bay, however.

Regulators previously released a formal Record of Decision for operating units 1 and 2. Unit 1 encompasses Little Lake Butte des Morts. Unit 2 is the 20-mile section of river between the uppermost dam in Appleton, below the Memorial Drive

See **PCB, A-5**

Getting Started on Research

Source material can be collected from area newspapers, such as the *Fox River Valley Post-Crescent*, the *Green Bay News-Chronicle*, and the *Green Bay Press Gazette*, which include first-hand testimony from local residents, activists, and paper company representatives. State agencies (Wisconsin Department of Natural Resources) and environmental groups on both sides of the issue produce newsletters, newspaper articles, and Web site content to review as well.

contend that the seven companies should pay for the cleanup, but the companies argue that taxpayers should shoulder at least some of the burden.

The goal of the cleanup itself has also fueled debate. The Record of Decision, which released the finalized cleanup plan in July 2003, proposed a set of goals and procedures that environmental groups argue is inadequate. At the grass-roots level, some contend that the best approach to the cleanup is "natural recovery," the belief that untouched areas will improve themselves. Others argue that dredging, or scraping the PCB-laden sediment from the water, is the most viable solution. Still others believe that "capping," or covering the sediments with sand or rock, would be the most effective way.

The cleanup issue also brings up complicated economic and social questions. These

are not only about who will cover the costs, but about who and what will be hurt and who and what will be helped. The good news is that Wisconsin's history of placing a passionate priority on environmental health and safety has ensured that the decision-making process will include the needs of the land every bit as much as the needs of those who live on it.

The Fox River is certainly not the only place in our state where an environmental controversy has raged. What similar problems have occurred in your community, city, or county? What issues were at stake? Who was involved: an environmental group versus the government, community versus another community, or something else? Who were the groups or individuals, and how did they work to resolve the problem?

Map of problem areas along the Fox River Valley

PCB removal from the Fox River

The second part of the cleanup decision for the Fox River was announced Monday. Cost estimates for dredging sections 3 and 4 are based on pumping contaminated sediment through a temporary pipeline.

Section 4
From the De Pere dam to Green Bay
- Cleanup method: Hydraulic dredging
- Cubic yards removed: 5.88 million
- Cost estimate: $257.5 million

Section 3
From Little Rapids to De Pere dam
- Cleanup method: Hydraulic dredging
- Cubic yards removed: 586,800
- Cost estimate: $27.5 million

Section 5
Green Bay
- Cleanup method: Monitored natural recovery
- Cost estimate: $39.6 million

Paper mill locations
1. Georgia-Pacific
2. U.S. Paper Mills Corp.

Section 2
From Appleton to Little Rapids
- Recovery estimate: at least 40 years
- Cost estimate: $10 million

Section 1
From Little Lake Butte des Morts to Appleton
- Cleanup estimate: 6 years
- Cost estimate: $58 million
- Cubic yards to be removed: 780,000

The Fox River Mills
The federal government has named these seven paper companies as potentially responsible parties for PCB damage to the lower Fox River.
1. Georgia-Pacific
2. U.S. Paper Mills Corp.
3. NCR
4. Appleton Papers
5. Riverside Paper Corp.
6. WTM1*
7. P.H. Glatfelter
* Formerly Wisconsin Tissue Mills

Section 5
Green Bay
- Recovery estimate: at least 40 years
- Cost estimate: $40 million

Section 4
From the De Pere Dam to Green Bay
- Cleanup estimate: 7 years
- Cost estimate: $170 million
- Cubic yards removed: 5.88 million

Section 3
From Little Rapids to the De Pere Dam
- Cleanup estimate: 5 years
- Cost estimate: $31 million
- Cubic yards removed: 590,000

Cleaning up the Fox River
A state Department of Natural Resources analysis found that dredging and disposal of contaminated sediment from sections 1, 3 and 4 would provide maximum permanent benefit to human health and the environment.

Sediments containing more than 1 part per million PCBs will be targeted for dredging in those sections. The agency determined that dredging in Section 2 could be difficult and cost prohibitive due to the physical characteristics of that part of the river, which includes seven locks and dams.

Section 5, the bay of Green Bay, now contains about 70 percent of all PCBs released into the river. But the agency determined PCB concentrations in the bay are low because the chemicals are spread over a wide area.

The agency expects ecologically safe levels of PCBs in most areas of the dredged sections in 20-40 years. Natural recovery in Section 2 could take as long as 70 years to return that portion of the river to ecologically safe PCB levels, and as long as 100 years or more in the bay of Green Bay.

Source: Wisconsin Department of Natural Resources, EPA

Daniel Higgins/Press-Gazette

The Green Bay Press Gazette

ENVIRONMENTAL HISTORY

Topic	Secondary Source Material	Primary Source Material
The Great Peshtigo Fire: Logging Practices Create Deadly Firestorm	Gess, Denise and William Lutz. *Firestorm at Peshtigo: A Town, Its People, and the Deadliest Fire in American History.* New York: Henry Holt and Company LLC, 2002. Current, Richard N. *The History of Wisconsin: The Civil War Era, 1848–1873,* vol. II. Madison, WI: State Historical Society of Wisconsin , 1976.	Pernin, Peter. *The Great Peshtigo Fire: An Eyewitness Account,* 2nd ed. Madison, WI: Wisconsin Historical Society, 1999.
Menominee Tribal Enterprises and Sustained-Yield Forestry	Loew, Patty. *Indian Nations of Wisconsin: Histories of Endurance and Renewal.* Madison, WI: Wisconsin Historical Society, 2001. Lurie, Nancy. *Wisconsin Indians.* rev. and exp. ed. Madison, WI: Wisconsin Historical Society, 2002.	Huff, Paula R. and Marshall Pecore. "Case Study: Menominee Tribal Enterprises." Produced for the Wisconsin Institute for Environmental Studies and the Land Tenure Center, January 1995.
Fish Story: Stopping the Lamprey on the Great Lakes	The University of Wisconsin Sea Grant Web site at http://www.seagrant.wisc.edu/ Bogue, Margaret Beattie. *Fishing the Great Lakes: An Environmental History, 1783–1933.* Madison, WI: University of Wisconsin Press, 2000.	The *Ashland Daily Press* and other local newspapers The United States Geological Survey Web site at http://www.usgs.gov/ The Wisconsin Department of Natural Resources Web site at http://www.dnr.state.wi.us/
Fish and Game: Aldo Leopold and the Conservation Movement	Meine, Curt. *Aldo Leopold: His Life and Work.* Madison, WI: University of Wisconsin Press, 1988. The Aldo Leopold Foundation Web site at http://www.aldoleopold.org/	Leopold, Aldo. *A Sand County Almanac and Sketches Here and There.* New York: Oxford University Press, 1989.

Topic	Secondary Source Material	Primary Source Material
Water Policy in Wisconsin: Preserving the St. Croix Riverway	The Wisconsin Department of Natural Resources Web site at http://www.dnr.wi.us/ WASAL. 2003. "Waters of Wisconsin: The Future of Our Aquatic Ecosystems and Resources." Madison, WI: Wisconsin Academy of Sciences, Arts and Letters, 2003. The WASAL Web site at http://www.wisconsinacademy.org/wow/	Scott, Walter. "Water Policy Evolution in Wisconsin: Protection of the Public Trust." Madison: Wisconsin Academy of Sciences, Arts, and Letters, 1965. The Isaak Walton League of America Web site at http://IWLA.org/
Project ELF: The Northwoods' Cold War Secret	Klessig, Lowell L. and Victor L. Strite. *The ELF Odyssey: National Security Versus Environmental Protection*. Boulder, CO: Westview Press, 1980.	The Nukewatch Web site at http://www.nukewatch.com/
The Man from Clear Lake: Gaylord Nelson and Earth Day	Nelson, Gaylord, Susan Campbell, and Paul Wozniak. *Beyond Earth Day: Fulfilling the Promise*. Madison, WI: University of Wisconsin Press, 2002. Huffman, Thomas. *Protectors of the Land and Water: Environment-alism in Wisconsin, 1961–1968*. Chapel Hill, NC: University of North Carolina Press, 1994.	Wisconsin Historical Society Archives http://arcat.library. wisc.edu/ keyword: Gaylord Nelson
Recreation and Employment: The New Deal and Wisconsin Parks	Glad, Paul. *History of Wisconsin: War, a New Era, and Depression, 1914–1940*, vol. 5. Madison, WI: State Historical Society of Wisconsin, 1990.	La Follette, Philip F. Papers. Wisconsin Historical Society Archives, Madison, Wisconsin. The National New Deal Preservation Association Web site at http://www.newdeallegacy.org/

Topic	Secondary Source Material	Primary Source Material
Wisconsin's First State Park: Interstate Park at the St. Croix Dalles	Eileen M. McMahon and Theodore J. Karamanski. *Time and the River: A History of the Saint Croix.* Omaha, NE: Midwest Regional Office, National Park Service, United States Department of the Interior, 2002. The National Park Service Web site at http://www.nps.gov/	Hazzard, George H. *Interstate Park: Lectures, Laws, Papers, Pictures, Pointers.* St. Paul, MN: Pioneer Press, 1896.
Pesticide on Trial: Wisconsin's Role in Banning DDT	Dunlap, Thomas R. "DDT on Trial: The Wisconsin Hearing, 1968–1969." *Wisconsin Magazine of History* 62, no.1 (1978): 2–24.	Wisconsin Historical Society Archives http://arcat.library. wisc.edu keyword: DDT

Historic Conference on DDT's Impact on Nature Opens Today

IF MANKIND SHOULD survive his own poisons—nuclear chemical and social—it may be recorded that the light generated in Madison in December of 1968 is responsible.

The eyes of the nation — at least the eyes of ecologists and the chemical industry — are focussed on Madison today where historic hearings begin on one of the most troublesome and significant issues of today.

Scientists from across the nation are gathering here to discuss and debate the controversial question of what DDT is doing to the balance of nature. It is seldom that such outstanding authorities in their fields will get together on a more important issue.

Today's conference, which may continue for a fortnight or more, has been called by the State Department of Natural Resources at the request of the Citizens Natural Resources Association and the Wisconsin Division of the Izaak Walton League of America who have requested a declaratory judgment on the use of DDT in this state. If Wisconsin restricts or bans DDT it could start a nationwide movement.

Some of the most careful and conservative scientists in the country will present testimony about the imbalance that has already been created that will shock thoughtful people. And scientists with other views will respond.

In the long run the decision on this vital issue will be made by the public. The conference starting today may well be the most important one of its kind and inestimably valuable in its education impact.

The public will do well to follow it.

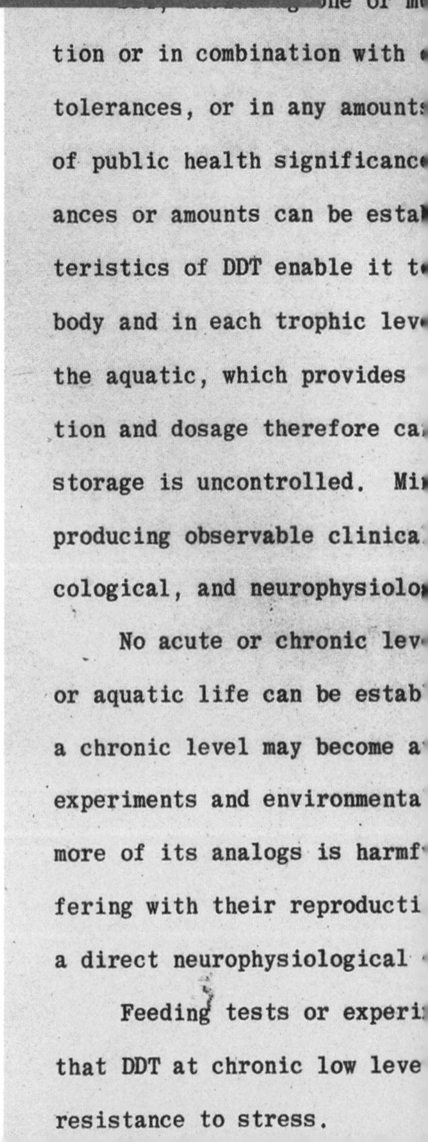
one or m
tion or in combination with
tolerances, or in any amount
of public health significanc
ances or amounts can be esta
teristics of DDT enable it t
body and in each trophic lev
the aquatic, which provides
tion and dosage therefore ca
storage is uncontrolled. Mi
producing observable clinica
cological, and neurophysiolo

No acute or chronic lev
or aquatic life can be estab
a chronic level may become a
experiments and environmenta
more of its analogs is harmf
fering with their reproducti
a direct neurophysiological

Feeding tests or experi
that DDT at chronic low leve
resistance to stress.

Topic	Secondary Source Material	Primary Source Material
Let the Waters Flow: Dam Removal Projects	The Institute for Environmental Studies at the University of Wisconsin–Madison Web site at http://www.ies.wisc.edu/	The River Alliance of Wisconsin Web site at http://www.wisconsinrivers.org/
Cleaning the Fox River: The Battle over PCB Removal	The Wisconsin Department of Natural Resources Web site at http://www.dnr.wi.us/ The River Alliance of Wisconsin Web site at http://www.wisconsinrivers.org/ The Gaylord Nelson Institute for Environmental Studies Web site at http://www.ies.wisc.edu/	*Fox River Valley Post-Crescent* *Green Bay News-Chronicle*

tabolite

ls at any level, within any

to humans and found to be

trations, levels, toler-

mical properties and charac-

r accumulated in the human

food chains, particularly

n consumption. Its inges-

olled and consequently its

of the chemical, while not

have biochemical, pharma-

of public health significance.

ich are harmful to animal

the reasons above set forth

. Feeding tests, laboratory

tablish that DDT or one or

and waterfowl by inter-

d in other birds by having

vironmental studies establish

l to fish by reducing their

Fox cleanup decision made

Doyle to release details of PCB disposal plan

The Post-Crescent

Gov. James Doyle is scheduled to release the final cleanup decision for the PCB-contaminated Fox River at noon today, a blueprint for the largest environmental dredging project attempted anywhere.

Unless the cleanup decision departs dramatically from previously released plans, it will mandate that six paper companies spend at least $300 million and perhaps as much as $400 million or more to dredge and dispose of 7.25 million cubic yards of contaminated sediments from the lower Fox River.

Polychlorinated biphenyls or PCBs are a class of industrial solvents released into the Fox River prior to 1971 during the production and recycling of carbonless paper. PCBs, which enter the food chain and contaminate fish, have been linked to reproductive failure in birds and mammals and to developmental problems in the children of mothers who ate contaminated fish.

The decision being released by Doyle today covers what regulators call operating units 3, 4 and 5. Unit 3 is the stretch of river in Brown County between the dam at Little Rapids and the dam at De Pere. Unit 4 is the seven-mile stretch between the dam and the mouth of the river.

Unit 5 is the bay of Green Bay, added to the state-led cleanup study after environmentalists lobbied for its inclusion and the U.S. Environmental Protection Agency backed them up. State and federal officials have given no hint that they plan any direct action in the bay, however.

Regulators previously released a formal Record of Decision for operating units 1 and 2. Unit 1 encompasses Little Lake Butte des Morts. Unit 2 is the 20-mile section of river between the uppermost dam in Appleton, below the Memorial Drive

See **PCB**, A-5

Chapter Four

Tourism

- **Lucky 13: Automobile Tourism to Northern Wisconsin**
- **Back to Nature: Wilderness Tourism in the Northwoods**
- **Electrifying Tourism: The Bayfield Electric Cooperative**
- **Calvin Coolidge Vacations on the Brule River**
- **Bringing Main Streets Back to Life: Saving Wisconsin's Downtowns**
- **The Yellowstone Trail: Wisconsin's First National Tourist Highway**
- **Governor Warren Knowles: Promoting Tourism and Protecting Water**
- **H.H. Bennett: Inventing the Wisconsin Dells**

Summer AND
FISHING
Resorts
IN
THE
LAKE
REGION
OF
...ERN WISCONSIN
.D MICHIGAN
..WAUKEE, LAKE SHORE & WESTERN ...

STATE HISTORIC SOCIETY

NATION'S CH...
IS THOROUGH...
ENJOYING RES...

President Finds Plenty
of Relaxation and
Sport.

...LS TO VISIT DESK

...nce From Office Is
...id to Charm of
...sland Eden.

...A. D. KAPPLIN,
...erald Staff Writer.
...t Coolidge is thor-
...joying himself
...d lodge ...
...ber ...

YELLOWSTONE TRAIL

Lucky 13
Automobile Tourism to Northern Wisconsin

When was the last time you went on a long car trip? Car trips can sometimes be long and dull, but they can also be fun. You can see new sites, stop at interesting places, and stay in a spot as long as you like.

Lucky 13 brochure cover

In the 1920s, automobile tourism was a new and exciting experience. When Henry Ford began mass-producing affordable cars, many people started driving them on vacations. Instead of taking the train, entire families would pack their bags, climb into their car, and drive off to fish, camp, or sightsee. People no longer had to arrange their trips around erratic train schedules. Vacationers in vehicles could simply pull onto the side of the road, set up a tent, and go to sleep! It was a liberating experience.

Throughout the 1920s, more and more people traveled by car to vacation in northern Wisconsin. The many rivers, parks, and forests made excellent vacation spots. Resorts began attracting large numbers of visitors. Residents in every small town energetically welcomed tourists, encouraging them to eat at their restaurants and shop in their stores. In 1928, one newspaper reported that, in the previous summer, around 11,000 people entered the state in automobiles every single day and spent a total of $124,152,505. Such tourist activity motivated state and county governments to improve roads and highways to make leisure driving more attractive for tourists.

One of the most popular vacation routes for motorists was Highway 13, which ran from the Illinois border near Beloit all the way up to Ashland and around the Bayfield Peninsula. Resort owners promoted the highway as "Lucky 13" and promised that tourists could find almost anything they wanted on it.

Brochures and pamphlets were sent out to encourage travel along the highway. These brochures promised all kinds of interesting sites. In Madison, for example, visitors could tour the state capitol and university. A few miles up the road, they could

Getting Started on Research

For contextual background on the development of highways and early twentieth century tourism in Wisconsin, Paul Glad's *The History of Wisconsin, Volume V,* pages 155–164 and 211–220, is a good place to begin. The footnotes and bibliography will also be helpful. M.G. Davis' *A History of Wisconsin Highway Development, 1835–1945,* a joint project of the State Highway Commission of Wisconsin and the Public Roads Administration, is also a useful overview of the history of highways in the state. Contact local business and tourist resorts to find out how long they've been in business, how many people visit them annually, and how they try to attract tourists. Many newspapers have published advertisements over the years about tourism to Wisconsin. Their publications can be found on microfilm or microfiche at your local library or on the Internet. Ask your librarian to help you start a search.

along Lucky 13, and tourism has remained a major industry ever since. In 1941, the federal government published *Wisconsin: A Guide to the Badger State,* which highlighted the fun of driving Highway 13. It also described the history and industry of every spot along the way and listed all the people and events visitors might encounter.

What role has automobile tourism played in your area? How does your city or town try to attract visitors? In the 1920s and 1930s, what did local businesses do to encourage tourism to their city? In what ways can local businesses use brochures, guidebooks, videos, or Web sites to attract tourists? What were the prime tourist attractions in the 1920s that brought visitors to Wisconsin? What are the major attractions today?

take an excursion boat to the Dells of the Wisconsin River. Every little town along the highway, including Friendship, Wisconsin Rapids, Nekoosa, Marshfield, Colby, Abbotsford, Medford, Park Falls, Mellen, and Ashland, had something interesting to offer. Highway 13 extended all the way into the Northwoods, which had already become a popular fishing and vacation destination. Copper Falls State Park and the Apostle Islands were other tourist attractions situated just a few miles off the road.

"Would it thrill you," one brochure asked, "to take your family and friends with you, out on this great friendly road, up through Wisconsin, famous for her health and beauty, to show them a trail of natural wonders, to let them enjoy boating, bathing, fishing, golf, and all the kindred summer sports and pastimes, giving them a wonderful vacation the pleasures and places of which they will never forget?" Many vacationers did choose to drive

Interior of Lucky 13 brochure listing some of the route's attractions.

WHS Archives

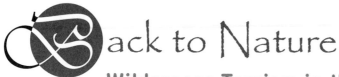

Back to Nature

Wilderness Tourism in the Northwoods

The word *tourist* appeared in print as early as 1800 in the United States. By the end of that century, advancements in transportation, a romantic view of the North American continent, and the desire to see inspiring landscapes in popular photography were major factors encouraging tourism. People traveled for many reasons. Some sought spiritual renewal and physical regeneration, while others sought freedom from social restraints.

Middle- and upper-class people in urban centers who sought to escape from the hustle and bustle of city life found tranquility in the peaceful locales of the countryside. The Grand American Tour (a new version of the Grand Tour across southern Europe) developed at this time and included visits to the Hudson River, Niagara Falls, the Catskills, Yellowstone, and Yosemite. These tours combined visits to areas of natural beauty and sites of historic or symbolic significance, including rural settings.

Northern Wisconsin, like other regions of natural beauty, was perceived positively during the "Back to Nature" movement. It attracted those who enjoyed pristine wilderness and were awed by uncluttered landscapes. For some, such interaction with nature helped them spiritually connect with God.

The attitude that problems with modern city life could be cured by experienc-

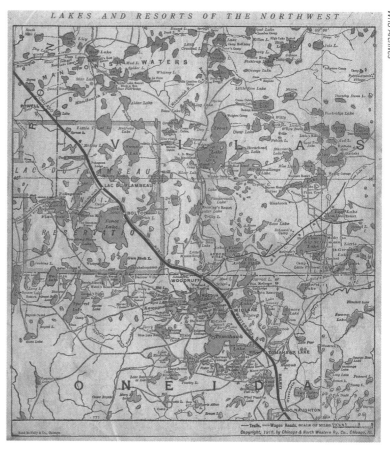

Map to Northwoods summer resorts in a tourist guide published by the Chicago and Northwestern railway line

ing the simplicity of nature was growing in popularity. This notion of the natural world was tightly connected to the idea of the "rugged individual." Being rugged also implied the ability to experience nature directly.

People also viewed places like northern Wisconsin, or the Northwoods, as the region was later designated, as the last vestiges of America's vanishing "pure" frontier. By the 1890s, writers and historians (such as Frederick Jackson Turner) had started to tie American national identity to the frontier spirit.

The Northwoods became a vacation haven for wealthy people from cities all

92

across the Midwest. The Chicago and Northwestern Railway lines, among others, carried passengers to northern Wisconsin for fishing, hunting, and camping. Resorts sprang up in the region to cater to the needs of visitors. In 1896, Charles Bent bought some property for sport fishing on Lake Mamie in Vilas County near the Michigan border. He created Bent's Camp, which consisted of several log cabins designed exclusively for anglers.

Those who traveled to Bent's Camp were drawn to the area by the abundance of bass and other fish in the Cisco Chain of Lakes, which form the headwaters of the Ontonagon River, which flows into

WHS Archives

Lake Superior. In the years before World War I, Bent logged and built more cabins. In wartime, tourism slowed considerably, but in the 1920s, the resort saw a resurgence. Before good roads were built from the railroad landing at Cisco to the resort, boats and launches would greet guests at the train and transport them to Bent's Camp. In the early 1900s, those who could afford vacations in the Northwoods came for the entire summer, not just a weekend, and they brought enough supplies to last through the entire season!

Where do people in your community go for their vacations? Why do they go there? Think of a few reasons why a tourist would want to come to the area and then create a promotional piece that entices them. What destinations would you display in your travel brochure? What feelings would you try to inspire and how would you use images? How and why has tourism changed in our state since the late 1800s?

Getting Started on Research

For secondary source material, William Cronon's essay, "The Trouble with Wilderness, or Getting Back to the Wrong Nature" in *Out of the Woods: Essays in Environmental History* is extremely helpful, as is Timothy Bawden's "The Northwoods: Back to Nature?" in *Wisconsin Land and Life*. Primary sources about Bent's Camp can be found on the Wisconsin Pioneer Experience Web site at http://libtext.library.wisc.edu/wipionexp/. *The Cisco Chain of Lakes from History and Memory* by Waube Kanish is in the pamphlet collection of the Wisconsin Historical Society.

Brochure which lists summer and fishing resorts in northern Wisconsin's lake region, published in 1891.

Electrifying Tourism
The Bayfield Electric Cooperative

Wisconsin Electric Cooperative News (Madison, WI)

Serving Our Recreation Industry

Just as modern highways and the automobile have shortened the path between the hot cities and our beautiful lakes and streams, the introduction of electricity to our northern vacationland is making cottage and resort life more attractive to our many city friends. These factors have all combined to provide our area with an industry redounding to the benefit of all of us.

It was primarily with this thought in mind that the summer cottage rate established by the cooperative is considerably less than that of any other utility serving the area for we all know that all segments of the local economy benefit when our recreation business is fully developed.

Under our present rates schedule our cottage members pay a service charge of $15 per year plus seven cents per kw for the first 400 each year and three cents per kwhr after that. This charge is fairly low in considering the relatively few cottage members who are normally located on a mile of line and the fact that usually such service is built through wooded areas where the chances of storm damage cause a much higher maintenance cost to repair damage causing service interruption.

In recent years marked progress has been made in the development of cottage occupancy. Our resorts too, have in many cases realized considerable saving in money and bother by being able to replace home electric plants with central station highline service. This has made it possible for many resorts to introduce modern new electric operated appliances, hot water and better lighting conditions which have gone far toward improving the attractiveness of our area to the distant vacationist.

A relatively new development, but one which promises to contribute materially to the stability of the vacation business in this area is the year around resort. On this page you will see a view of beautiful Mount Telemark near Cable, which has become increasingly popular to winter vacationists. This skiing haven served by your co-op, has attracted business to many resorts in the immediate area as well as to its genial manager, Tony Wise. Wise has been sufficiently encouraged by the promise of this development that he has opened a second such center near Superior.

The resort facilities of Bayfield, Ashland, Iron, Sawyer and Douglas counties are perhaps unmatched in natural assets by any similar area in the world. It is the extra hospitality our local people can offer the vacationer through such developments as good roads, good fishing and modern electric facilities which will make the vacation business of the area unmatched anywhere.

Your electric cooperative knows its policy of encouraging our vacationland business bears the endorsement of every member.

Pictured at the left is a typical cottage home in our area which has been "winterized" to provide comfortable living on a year around basis. It is one of many hundred cottages owned by our members.

* * *

Above is a picture taken at beautiful Mount Telemark, near Cable, served by the Bayfield Electric Co-op. This recreation center is leading the way in making the recreation business in this section of the state a full year program.

HEADQUARTERS DEDICATION   25

Page from a 1952 pamphlet about the Bayfield Electric Cooperative, Inc. of Iron River, Wisconsin

Most of us today take electricity for granted, but until the 1930s, very few farms had much electrical capability. Constructing the poles, running the lines, connecting the wires, and generating energy to power them were all costly and difficult things to do. Few farmers in the 1920s and 1930s could afford electrical equipment, much less use it. For-profit power companies were therefore reluctant to spend a lot of money to run electricity to farmhouses, especially to those that were so few and far between. The power companies preferred to find their customers in cities, where large numbers of consumers were located close together. Wisconsin, like many other states, was divided into two worlds: electrified cities and non-electrified rural areas.

In 1935, President Franklin Roosevelt established the Rural Electrification Administration (REA) as a way to help farmers meet their growing needs for electricity. The agency provided low-interest loans to organizations of farmers, known as cooperatives. These loans helped farmers build their own lines and provide their own electricity. The agency was a great success. Within 15 years, 90% of American farms had electricity and could take advantage of the same conveniences as city dwellers. Many farmers were now able to plug in or flip a switch to use washing machines, refrigerators, lights, radios, televisions, and new electric-powered farm equipment.

On September 12, 1940, several farmers met in Iron River to establish the Bayfield Electric Cooperative, Inc. They elected the new co-op's board of directors and sent volunteers door-to-door to ask other farmers to join. The board of directors negotiated a loan with the REA and worked out a deal with the power companies to purchase electricity. These efforts resulted in the founding of the Bayfield Electric Cooperative in the northwest part of the state, one of the largest cooperatives in

Wisconsin. Electricity generated by this organization went to parts of Bayfield, Ashland, Douglas, Iron, and Sawyer counties. Because this region was sparsely populated, the cooperative handled electricity needs that the private power companies refused to address.

In April 1941, the REA granted a $202,000 loan to build 246 miles of electric line to serve 619 Bayfield Electric Cooperative members. The first pole was erected on November 25, 1941. When World War II broke out soon after, construction was delayed until 1945. Once the war was over, the cooperative grew quickly. In 1947, it had 1,000 members, and by 1950, it was serving a diverse membership of 2,367, with more than 1,000 miles of functioning power line.

Although rural electrification began primarily to help farmers, it quickly contributed to the growth of northwest Wisconsin as one of the state's most popular tourist destinations in both summer and winter. Resort and cottage owners benefited from the low-cost electricity as well. They realized that electricity,

The men involved in setting the first pole rested from their labor, as soon as it was tamped in to place, for the above picture. From left to right the principals are: Director Ole Anderson, Attorney Walter Norlin, Director Tony Radosevich, County Agent Roy Hovenstat, William Ziemer, on whose property the pole had been erected; Directors Russell Rowley, Emil Aho, Andrew Mihalak, and Gerald Grubisic. On the right of the pole appears President Earl Anderson, Manager Arvid Wentela, Director John Shykes, a crewman, Director Herman Hanson, with two crewmen on the extreme right.

11

Bayfield Electric Cooperative Annual Report, 1964–1965

just like automobiles, would make the area more attractive to tourists. To encourage the electrification of resorts, the Bayfield cooperative established a "summer cottage rate," a much lower rate than it charged business and homeowners. With affordable electricity, the resort industry boomed as tourists grew more willing to vacation where they could get hot water and good lighting! Electricity also attracted tourists during the winter skiing period, which meant year-round income for many businesses. All of this was made possible by people working together for the common purpose of improving their region.

What it would be like to live without electricity? Many rural people in the 1930s had to do just that. Ask your parents or grandparents about living without electricity. The next time you are in a rural area, such as a farm or vacation resort, imagine how different life would be without basic electricity. What kinds of things do you do now that can only be done with electricity? How would you do them if you didn't have electricity?

Getting Started on Research

Cooperatives, such as Bayfield Electric, are proud of their accomplishments, and they often keep good records of their past and current work, especially the ones with a long history. Look at Bayfield Electric's Web site at http://www.bayfieldelectric.com/ or examine their pamphlets in the Wisconsin Historical Society (WHS) collection at http://www.wisconsinhistory.org/. Relevant background information can be found in WHS' archives catalog, ArCat, under Rural Electrification Administration; Lemont K. Richardson's *Wisconsin REA: The Struggle to Extend Electricity to Rural Wisconsin, 1935–1955,* and Forrest McDonald's *Let There Be Light: The Electric Utility Industry in Wisconsin, 1881–1955.* For primary sources, call a local cooperative, farm, or vacation resort and interview the owner or a longtime employee about when and how rural electrification happened for their business.

Calvin Coolidge Vacations on the Brule River

What do you like to do on your summer vacation? President Calvin Coolidge liked to fish. After he decided not to run for another term as president, he chose to take a long vacation away from the sweltering heat of Washington, DC. That summer of 1928, he vacationed in northern Wisconsin.

"Silent Cal" was famous for being a quiet man, even taciturn, and he enjoyed a rather relaxed presidency. The 1920s were a time of relative peace and prosperity, so there was little need for an active, outspoken leader in the White House. But when he went on a trip, he was no ordinary vacationer. Special arrangements were always made weeks before his arrival to ensure that he could be in touch with the White House, and vice versa. Highway 2 in the Northwoods was repaved and new telephone lines were set up to accommodate his needs. Secret Service agents scoured the area to make sure the president would be safe. Superior High School served as the "Summer White House" where the president could work. Even though he visited his office only occasionally, a crowd always gathered to greet him when he arrived, and Coolidge always smiled and waved politely in return.

Coolidge was one of many vacationers who came to northern Wisconsin in the 1920s. During the 1890s and early 1900s, lumber companies heavily logged much of the region. The resulting

WHS Archives, President Coolidge Brule River Scrapbook

This cartoon illustrates how Calvin Coolidge influenced the tourism economy in northern Wisconsin.

Getting Started on Research

Several newspapers reported on President Coolidge's visit to northern Wisconsin. Your library can help you find copies of the *Superior Evening Telegram,* the *Ashland Daily Press,* and the *Duluth News-Tribune.* Infamous people have vacationed in northern Wisconsin as well, including Al Capone and John Dillinger. You can learn about them in *Gangster Holidays* by Tom Hollatz. Historian Paul W. Glad writes about tourism in northern Wisconsin in *The History of Wisconsin: War, a New Era, and Depression 1914–1940* (Volume 4, pages 211–220).

"cutover" had been settled by farmers who owned small farms, usually 40 acres in size. But they found much of the land rocky, sandy, and not very good for farming. In the 1920s, when automobiles became more common, many parts of northern Wisconsin began to promote tourism. Promoters as well as locals promised weary visitors beautiful lakes, streams full of fish, and hiking trails. Many people began to vacation in places like Minocqua, Hayward, and the Apostle Islands.

Coolidge arrived with his wife Grace on June 15, and they stayed near the Brule River at a lodge on Cedar Island. During the vacation, they toured the Apostle Islands and even ate a picnic lunch on Devil's

Island. They also visited Duluth and Wausau. Mostly, though, Coolidge fished. Almost every day, he went into the Brule River wearing a business suit beneath his hip-waders and fished for hours. But Coolidge had his Secret Service agent unhook his fish for him! Coolidge even skipped the Republican National Convention, where his successor, Herbert Hoover, was nominated. Hoover was an energetic man whom Coolidge sarcastically called "the wundah boy."

The Coolidges left Wisconsin on September 10, eighty-eight days after they had arrived. Both felt rested and refreshed.

Although he never returned even after his presidency, Coolidge told reporters that the fishing in northern Wisconsin was excellent. "I think this is going to be a coming region for those who are seeking recreation." He added, "The fishing around here, I can testify, is fine. The climate is wonderful. It has been a great benefit to Mrs. Coolidge and myself, and we are returning to Washington refreshed and invigorated." Soon afterward, the area became a popular vacation destination. People began driving up from Chicago and Milwaukee to spend their weekends and summers fishing, hiking, and hunting. Tourism has been important to the Northwoods' economy ever since.

Has anyone famous ever visited your community? What activities and sights could the President enjoy today? How do you think a presidential visit would affect your community?

One newspaper account of President Coolidge's visit

Bringing Main Streets Back to Life

Saving Wisconsin's Downtowns

We live in an age of shopping malls and megastores. But, in the 1960s, most communities depended solely upon the businesses and shops along a town's main street for their livelihood. Back then, settlers establishing communities throughout the state lined their "Main Street" with bakeries, cafés, butcher shops, dry-goods stores, pharmacies, clothing stores, banks, doctors' and dentists' offices, and virtually any other business that local residents wanted. In most every community, these two- and three-story brick buildings were the centers of town life. People came not only to shop, but to conduct business and socialize.

But by the time the 1960s rolled around, many new and larger stores began opening up on the outskirts of these towns. These new "chain" stores had several advantages over the more established ones in town. Land was cheaper; they could offer a wider variety of goods in newer, brightly lit stores; and parking was more convenient and plentiful. Instead of going downtown to buy groceries or hardware, people began driving to the edge of town for less expensive products. Even doctors, dentists, lawyers, and other professionals who built new office complexes away from downtown saw positive results. In time, "Main Street" stores began closing their doors.

More and more of Wisconsin's Main Streets were lined with empty buildings.

The decline of Main Street Wisconsin meant an end to small-town life. People no longer knew everyone in town or could expect to meet friends and neighbors in old, familiar places. In 1977, the National Main Street Program began efforts to revitalize Wisconsin's Main Streets into more attractive businesses and shops. The program hoped to return small-town main streets back to the social centers they once were, in part, by restoring historic buildings to their original glory. Beautification of the surrounding landscape was an important part of the plan as well. Making old buildings fit new needs meant renovations for fitness centers and apartments. Small towns throughout Wisconsin participated in this program, and in the

Chippewa Falls Union Block before the restoration

1980s, Main Streets became vibrant and important centers of life once again.

Chippewa Falls is a good example of this kind of rejuvenation. Between 1989 and 1998, more than $48 million in public and private funds were invested in the downtown district. Construction crews renovated approximately 142 old buildings there. They removed unsightly alterations and non-historic additions, and repaired and restored buildings to their original appearance. Fortunately, photographs of many downtown buildings from earlier years still existed and were immensely helpful in capturing the way the old buildings used to look. The economic and aesthetic reconstruction projects helped open 140 new businesses in town and created more than 800 new jobs. In 1996, Chippewa Falls became one of five communities in the nation to receive the Great American Main Street Award, presented annually by the National Trust for Historic Preservation.

Now that we've successfully entered the twenty-first century, it is more important

Getting Started on Research

What is Main Street like in your community? What old buildings are there? Are they still being used, and if so, what are they used for? Find a photograph of an old main street building and list the things that are different from the way they are now. Your town's historical society, tourist information center, chamber of commerce, library, or newspaper can help you find old photographs of many of these buildings.

The Wisconsin Main Street Program sponsors downtown restoration efforts. Its Web site can be accessed at http://www.commerce.state.wi.us/ CD/CD-bdd.html. Main Street Chippewa Falls also has a Web site at http://www .chippewafallsmainst.org/.

How could your community benefit from a Main Street Program renovation? What kinds of businesses and activities could become part of your downtown area? Perhaps some buildings in your town have already been restored. Contact the marketing or public relations departments of these businesses and ask about the specific restoration done to their building. The librarian at your school or local public library can show you where valuable materials for your research may be found.

Union Block after the restoration

Chippewa Falls Main Street, Inc.

than ever to remember our past. The Main Street Program has proved that history is more than just paper. It has brought real change to real people and has shown the benefits of economic and social improvement that cooperation can bring. The restoration of Main Streets all over Wisconsin helps every one of us touch a part of our past and enjoy a greater sense of community.

The Yellowstone Trail

Wisconsin's First National Tourist Highway

Have you ever wondered about when, how, or why the modern interstate system began? As vacationers in their automobiles drove across Wisconsin and other states, it became more important than ever for states to provide clean and easy ways to travel. As one of the first transcontinental highways to meet this need, the Yellowstone Trail served as an inspiration for what has become our modern interstate system. Anyone could now travel from one side of the United States to the other.

In the early 1900s, going cross-country by automobile was a complicated thing to do. Railroads, once the dominant form of transportation, were losing their popularity, in part because unreliable schedules often caused delays. Rising ticket prices also made vacationing less affordable. The automobile, on the other hand, allowed for privacy, flexibility, and independence, and it rapidly became a popular way to travel. But many cities and towns had only dirt roads that were not able to handle the demand. In rain and other bad weather, automobile travelers might experience delays, distractions, and dangers. The road signs that existed were crude or not even posted and offered little help to travelers who were unfamiliar with the area. A routine trip over one of these unpaved roads could quickly turn into a nightmare.

With the growing need for safe and reliable roads in mind, J. W. Parmley of Ipswich, South Dakota, proposed an idea for the first intercontinental automobile highway. Originally conceived as a 25-mile road inside South Dakota that stretched from Ipswich to Aberdeen, the route was expanded to link the northwestern states around Washington to the northeastern ones around Massachusetts. The route became known as the Yellowstone Trail because Yellowstone National Park was a major tourist destination along the route.

Formed in October 1912, the Yellowstone Trail Association primarily consisted of business people and chamber of commerce members. They were interested in boosting their local economies by increasing traffic on their roads. They lobbied for improved streets, encouraged local support for new roads, and promoted cross-country automobile tourism. They also marked the Yellowstone Trail's routes and provided maps. These efforts made the Trail unique as a grassroots effort. It was started by ordinary citizens who lived and drove in the cities and towns through which it ran. In contrast, other routes, such as the Lincoln Highway, were spearheaded by wealthy business people with financial interests at stake.

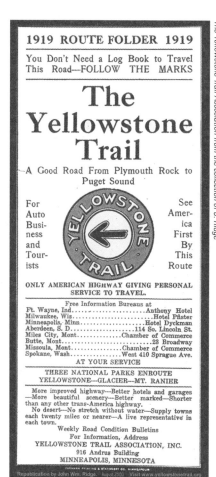

The Yellowstone Trail Association from the collection of J. Ridge

Cover of the Yellowstone route folder, 1919

The Yellowstone Trail Association offered memberships to the towns it served and provided support for local delegates to raise money. These funds went, in part, to mark the route with either yellow stones or the YTA's official yellow circle and arrow. Today, remnants of these markings can still be seen along many back roads of the four-county Yellowstone Trail Corridor Project, which spans Portage, Wood, Clark, and Chippewa counties.

In 1918, Wisconsin became the first state to number its highways, but in 1926, the federal agency known as the American Association of State Highway Officials (AASHO) established a different interstate numbering policy. This new system rendered the Yellowstone Trails' efforts obsolete. The onset of the Great Depression in 1929 further eroded the significance of the

Information about Wisconsin in a Yellowstone Trail brochure

The Yellowstone Trail Association from the collection of J. Ridge

Getting Started on Research

To find out more about the Yellowstone Trail, visit http://www.yellowstonetrail.org/. For other resources on the Internet, go to any search engine and type the words "Yellowstone Trail." Click the Enter key and choose from the many options listed. Additional information can be found in Harold Meeks's *On the Road to Yellowstone: The Yellowstone Trail and American Highways, 1900–1930* and John and Alice Ridge's *Introducing the Yellowstone Trail: A Good Road from Plymouth Rock to Puget Sound, 1912–1930.* The Resources section at the end of this chapter contains more information about these publications.

Yellowstone Trail Association. Merchants could no longer afford to pay dues, and tourism began to trickle in the face of an ailing economy. In 1930, the association officially disbanded.

What can you investigate about the economic, environmental, social, and political impact of the Yellowstone Trail? How has automobile travel to scenic destinations along the Yellowstone Trail helped shape our state's economy and identity? In what ways does the federal interstate system help tourism in Wisconsin?

Governor Warren Knowles
Promoting Tourism and Protecting Water

From 1965 to 1971, Governor Warren Knowles ran the state from the capitol building in Madison. But, there were few things he enjoyed more than trout fishing. When he saw a photo of four brown trout caught by a man in Luxemburg, he sent his congratulations to the fisherman, a man by the name of Urban Dorner. Knowles added enviously, "Some time when I am up in Kewaunee area, I would like to have the opportunity to meet you personally and learn your fishing secrets." To Knowles, loving the sport of fishing also meant having an appreciation for the habitat in which fishing takes place—fresh water!

If we stand still, we can lose our billion dollar tourism economy to other states. Minnesota and Michigan will sell those licenses to Illinois fishermen. The parks of Ontario will fill up with visitors who tire of our cramped and overused camping and picnic grounds. Our boaters will tow their cruisers elsewhere to avoid tainted lakes and ruined rivers.

To my mind, failure to pass ORAP 200 would be standing still. It would, in fact, be a backward step.

Text of a speech that Governor Knowles gave to the state assembly and senate conservation committees on March 19, 1969

Conservation was a hot issue in Wisconsin in the 1960s. People were becoming increasingly aware of the dangerous effects of pollution on land, water, and wildlife. Many worried that clean land where people could fish, watch birds, and hunt could soon disappear. In 1965, Governor Knowles signed the Water Resources Act to protect the state's water

resources. Two years later, the state legislature created the Department of Natural Resources (DNR) to ensure that one state agency had the responsibility to ensure air and water quality. But simply protecting the land from pollution through legislation was not enough. Suburban development was threatening to swallow up much of the land that had been used for recreation. In response, the state began to purchase land to protect and preserve environments from too much development and pollution.

Governor Knowles recognized the need for urban and industrial growth, but he also wanted the state to remember its commitment to maintaining a clean environment and preserving its parks and forests. Tourism was, and is, a major industry in Wisconsin. Knowles understood the long-term value both of preserving the rivers and forests for Wisconsinites. He also wanted to ensure that out-of-state visitors would continue to recognize Wisconsin as a great place to vacation.

In 1969, Knowles spoke to the state assembly and senate conservation committees. He urged them to allocate more funds for the purchase of land on which to create state parks. "We have a state park system that compares well with any in the land," he told them. "Our residents and our visitors enjoy superb boating on some waters not yet blighted by sewage, scum, and slime." Knowles strongly urged the legislature to continue its efforts to purchase and maintain park lands, but always to be mindful that tourists would go elsewhere if Wisconsin stopped providing outstanding lakes and forests. Land prices were increasing, but he asked the legislature

Getting Started on Research

Warren Knowles's papers provide valuable glimpses into his life, work, and personality. They are housed in the Wisconsin Historical Society (WHS) Archives in Madison. The collection includes 14 boxes of correspondence, 19 reels of microfilm, and several boxes of newspaper clippings and photographs. Libraries and research centers around the state can provide you with portions of the Knowles collection for research. Also, you can learn more about Knowles and his papers on the WHS Archives Web site at http://arcat .library.wisc.edu/.

The *2003–2004 Wisconsin Blue Book* contains lists of state parks and the dates they were opened. Your librarian can help you find newspaper accounts of the history of these parks, or you can find several versions of the *Blue Book* on the Wisconsin State Legislature Web site at http://www.legis.state.wi.us/. Just click *Wisconsin Blue Book* in the menu on the left side of the screen to view the documents or download them (free of charge).

In 1970, Knowles signed legislation establishing the St. Croix River State Forest in Burnett County. In 1981, the forest was renamed Governor Warren P. Knowles State Forest to recognize Knowles' efforts in conservation. It was a suitable honor for a man who loved Wisconsin fishing so much!

How many state parks or recreation areas are in or near your community? Your teacher or librarian can help you find out when they were established. You can research newspapers from the time to find out the history of these areas and how they became state facilities. What kinds of activities can people do there? Are there other Wisconsin parks that you would like to visit? Why do you believe people feel so strongly about protecting lands and conserving natural resources?

for additional appropriations and mentioned the timeliness of his request by warning them that: "As years go by, as potential parks and open spaces disappear, as lakes and rivers deteriorate, as the state slips from leadership … growth [will] slow and progress [will] stagnate." Because of Governor Knowles's strong support for ongoing efforts, the legislature agreed that the state could incur a debt up to $56 million to buy land for recreation. Since then, the state has purchased thousands of acres of land to use for this purpose.

Knowles (eighth person from left) and friends with their catch, May 1966

WHI (x3) 48594

H.H. Bennett
Inventing the Wisconsin Dells

Most people know the Wisconsin Dells as the state's most popular vacation spot. Every summer, visitors flock there to enjoy its water parks, ski shows, miniature golf, and wax museums. Today, several Dells resorts try to appeal to families year-round by featuring indoor water parks and other comfortable amenities. But long before the amusement parks and t-shirt shops, the Dells of the Wisconsin River were already famous. The Dells owe their initial popularity largely to the efforts of one man: Henry Hamilton Bennett. His photographs of the eerily beautiful rock formations that line the Wisconsin River helped Bennett create a vision of nature that brought hundreds of thousands of people from all over the country. Those eager to escape the industrial cities of Chicago, Milwaukee, Cleveland, Pittsburgh, and others came to see these idyllic wonders for themselves.

Before Bennett's photographs were widely circulated, the dells had already captured imaginations. Increase Lapham, a natural scientist from Milwaukee, heard stories of the curious features of the river and led an expedition there in 1849. His diary of the trip describes the vegetation and geological formations in detail. Other travelers followed when the railroad arrived in 1856, and Kilbourn City, as Wisconsin Dells was called then, became easily accessible from many places outside the state. At first, the lack of hotels and difficulties in finding river guides prevented tourism from becoming a major industry. Then in 1873, the steamboats arrived. These vessels were capable of carrying hundreds of passengers at a time. But, even then, tourism to the area did not bring significantly large numbers.

H.H. Bennett and his images transformed the situation. In the late 1860s, Bennett worked as a portrait photographer in the big city. But in his spare time, he photographed the landscapes in the dells. He rowed himself around on the river on a tiny boat, lugging cumbersome cameras and the heavy equipment he needed to develop the glass plates on the spot. To further engage people's interest, Bennett gave many of the rock formations fanciful names such as Witches' Gulch, Fat Man's Misery, and

"Leaping the Chasm," arguably Bennett's most famous photograph

WHi image ID 2101

WHI Image ID 8069

The Bennett family on the Dell Queen steamboat

plans to get to the Dells to see the images personally.

Bennett's photographs quickly drew large numbers of tourists to the Kilbourn City area. While new hotels, parks, and other attractions began popping up at a record pace, the strange landscapes along the Wisconsin River remained the principal destination. Many stopped first at Bennett's studio to purchase copies of his photographs before embarking on a tour of the river on boats that regularly ferried tourists.

the Sugar Bowl. Bennett was a perfectionist, and he often took photographs of the same view again and again until he got the shot he wanted. People all over the nation caught a glimpse of The Dells in national magazines that displayed his photographs.

Bennett not only developed the photos on site, but he produced three-dimensional, stereoscopic views in which the same object is photographed from two slightly different angles. When viewed through special lenses, the landscape makes the viewer feel as if he or she is actually there. Soon, people all over the country were enjoying Bennett's stereoscopic photos and making

Bennett died in 1908, but his family continued to sell his photographs to visitors. Even today, Bennett's images still captivate visitors eager to come to the scenic haven. In the 1930s, residents decided to rename Kilbourn City the Wisconsin Dells as a more fitting tribute to the scenic location made famous by Bennett's photographs.

Bennett's business card

WHS H. H. Bennett Papers

How do tourist destinations in your county promote themselves as vacation spots to people living in Milwaukee, Chicago, or even farther? Have you ever seen historic photographs of your hometown? Who took them and what do you think the photographer was intending to communicate in the images? How were these photographs used to encourage people to come and visit?

Getting Started on Research

Two excellent books displaying Bennett's stunning photography of the Wisconsin Dells are *Others Before You: A History of the Wisconsin Dells Country* (edited by Michael Goc) and *Pioneer Photographer: Wisconsin's H.H. Bennett* by Sara Rath. In 1997, the H.H. Bennett studio became one of the historic sites operated by the Wisconsin Historical Society. Many of Bennett's images can be viewed on the Historical Society's Web site at http://www.wisconsinhistory.org/.

TOURISM

Topic	Secondary Source Material	Primary Source Material
Lucky 13: Automobile Tourism to Northern Wisconsin	*Wisconsin: A Guide to the Badger State*. Compiled by Writers' Program of the Work Projects Administration. 2nd Ed. New York : Duell, Sloan. 1941. For a map of Lucky 13, with phone numbers and addresses of resorts and businesses, visit the Wisconsin Indian Head Country Web site at http://www.wisconsinindianhead.org/area2.htm/ Davis, M.G. *A History of Wisconsin Highway Development, 1835–1945*. Madison, WI: Department of Transportation, 1989.	Wisconsin Historical Society Archives http://arcat.library.wisc.edu/
Back to Nature: Wilderness Tourism in the Northwoods	Cronon, William. "The Trouble with Wilderness, or Getting Back to the Wrong Nature." In *Out of the Woods: Essays in Environmental History*. Edited by Char Miller and Hal Rothman. Pittsburgh, PA: University of Pittsburgh Press, 1997. Bawden, Timothy. "The Northwoods: Back to Nature?" In *Wisconsin Land and Life*. Edited by Robert C. Ostergren and Thomas R. Vale. Madison, WI: University of Wisconsin Press, 1997.	The Wisconsin Pioneer Experience Web site at http://libtext.library.wisc.edu/wipionexp/ Kanish, Waube and Dunny Bent. *The Cisco Chain of Lakes from History and Memory*. Doylestown, PA: Arthur J. Bent, 1987

Topic	Secondary Source Material	Primary Source Material
Electrifying Tourism: The Bayfield Electric Cooperative	Richardson, Lemont K. *Wisconsin REA: The Struggle to Extend Electricity to Rural Wisconsin, 1935–1955.* Madison, WI: University of Wisconsin Experiment Station, College of Agriculture, 1961. McDonald, Forrest. *Let There Be Light: The Electric Utility Industry in Wisconsin, 1881–1955.* Madison, WI: American History Research Center, 1957. Bayfield Electronics web site at http://www.bayfieldelectric.com/	Wisconsin Historical Society Archives http://arcat.library.wisc.edu/
Calvin Coolidge Vacations on the Brule River	Hollatz, Tom. *Gangster Holiday: The Lore and Legends of the Bad Guys.* St. Cloud, MN: North Star Press of St. Cloud, 1989. Glad, Paul, et al. *The History of Wisconsin, War, a New Era, and Depression 1914–1940,* vol.4. Madison, WI: State Historical Society of Wisconsin, 1997, p. 211–220.	The Superior *Evening Telegram* The Ashland *Daily Press* The Duluth *News-Tribune*

Topic	Secondary Source Material	Primary Source Material
Bringing Main Streets to Life: Saving Wisconsin's Downtowns	*Downtowns: Revitalizing the Centers of Small Urban Communities.* Edited by Michael A. Burayidi. New York: Routtedge, 2001.	The Bureau of Downtown Development's Wisconsin Main Street Program Web site at http://www.commerce.state.wi.us/ CD/CD-bdd.html The Chippewa Falls Main Street Web site at http://www .chippewafallsmainst.org/
The Yellowstone Trail: Wisconsin's First National Tourist Highway	Meeks, Harold A. *On the Road to Yellowstone: The Yellowstone Trail and American Highways, 1900–1930.* Missoula, MT: Pictorial Histories Publishing Company, 2000. Ridge, John and Alice. *Introducing the Yellowstone Trail: A Good Road from Plymouth Rock to Puget Sound, 1912–1930.* Altoona, WI: Yellowstone Trail Publishers, 2000.	The Yellowstone Trail Web site at http://www.yellowstonetrail.org/

1919 ROUTE FOLDER 1919

You Don't Need a Log Book to Travel This Road—FOLLOW THE MARKS

The Yellowstone Trail

—A Good Road From Plymouth Rock to Puget Sound

For Auto Business and Tourists

See America First By This Route

ONLY AMERICAN HIGHWAY GIVING PERSONAL SERVICE TO TRAVEL.

Free Information Bureaus at
Ft. Wayne, Ind. . . . . .Anthony Hotel
Milwaukee, Wis. . . . . .Hotel Pfister
Minneapolis, Minn. .Hotel Dyckman
Aberdeen, S. D. . . . . .114 So. Lincoln St.
Miles City, Mont. . . . . .Chamber of Commerce
Butte, Mont. . . . . .West 410 Broadway
Missoula, Mont. .23 Broadway
Spokane, Wash. . . . . .West 410 Sprague Ave.

AT YOUR SERVICE

THREE NATIONAL PARKS ENROUTE
YELLOWSTONE—GLACIER—MT. RANIER
More improved highway—Better hotels and garages than any other trans-America highway.
More beautiful scenery—Better marked—Shorter No desert—No stretch without water—Supply towns each twenty miles or nearer—A live representative in each town.

Weekly Road Condition Bulletins
For Information, Address
YELLOWSTONE TRAIL ASSOCIATION, INC.
916 Andrus Building
MINNEAPOLIS, MINNESOTA

Republication by John Wm. Ridge.

Topic	Secondary Source Material	Primary Source Material
Governor Warren Knowles: Promoting Tourism and Protecting Water	*2003–2004 Wisconsin Blue Book.* Compiled by Wisconsin Legislative Reference Bureau. Download the *Blue Book* free of charge from the Wisconsin State Legislature Web site at http://www.legis.state.wi.us/ Also, copies may be purchased from Document Sales Unit, Department of Administration, 202 S. Thornton Avenue, Madison (P.O. Box 7840, Madison 53707-7840).	Knowles, Warren. Papers. Madison, WI: Wisconsin Historical Society Archives. Visit the WHS Archives Web site at http://arcat.library.wisc.edu/
H.H. Bennett: Inventing the Wisconsin Dells	Dells Country Historical Society. *Others Before You: A History of the Wisconsin Dells Country.* Edited by Michael Goc. Friendship, WI: New Past Press, 1995. Rath, Sara. *Pioneer Photographer: Wisconsin's H.H. Bennett.* Madison, WI: Tamarack Press, 1979.	Find the H.H. Bennett studio on the Wisconsin Historical Society Web site at http://www.wisconsinhistory.org/ Type "Bennett Studio" in the search box.

Chapter Five

Industry

THE

BROWNSTONE CO.

IS PREPARED

TO FILL LARGE OR SMALL ORDERS

ON SHORT NOTICE.

Quarries at Houghton, Bayfield County, Wis.

BRANCH OFFICES:

AT THE QUARRIES.

NEW YORK, 44 BROADWAY.

CHICAGO, 714 TACOMA BLDG.

MAIN OFFICE:

ASHLAND, WIS.,

Room 311-313, Knight Block.

Cold Hard Profit
Ice Harvesting in Wisconsin

Men poling blocks to the hoist, undated.

Have you ever wondered how people kept food cold before refrigerators were invented? Maybe you've heard somebody say "ice box" when referring to a refrigerator. "Ice box" is a term that came from the days when people kept meat, milk, and other perishables in wooden (sometimes metal) cabinets. These boxes contained large blocks of ice, which kept the food cold. But now you might be asking yourself: Where did the ice for the ice boxes come from in the first place?

Some families, particularly in rural areas, cut their own ice from ponds or lakes in winter, packed it tightly with sawdust for insulation, and stored it in small buildings where it remained frozen even on hot summer days. People in the cities had no ponds and, therefore, needed ice to be delivered regularly. Every day, an iceman in a horse-drawn cart brought new blocks of ice to homes and businesses.

By the 1880s, ice harvesting was a thriving industry in Wisconsin. The industrial growth in Milwaukee and Chicago, and the resulting water pollution, greatly increased the demand for ice from fresh, non-polluted water. So, every winter, when the ice was deep enough to "harvest"—usually from the middle of January until the middle of March—crews moved onto frozen lakes to cut large blocks of ice. Then, they hauled the blocks away for storage. Because farmers had little to do in the winter, they were often employed by the ice companies to do the cutting and hauling. It was hard and dangerous work to cut most of the five-hundred-pound blocks by

Ice harvesting on the Mississippi River near Alma, Wisconsin

Getting Started on Research

For information about Madison's ice-harvesting industry, see *Madison: A History of the Formative Years* by David Mollenhoff. For more on the Miller-Rasmussen Company of Green Bay, see "Harvest of Ice: The Miller-Rasmussen Ice Company" by James P. Krudwig in *Voyageur.*

Your teacher or librarian can help you find local histories and early newspapers that describe the ice-harvesting industry in your community. Search the Wisconsin Historical Society Archives (ArCat) Web site and type the keywords "ice harvesting" and "Wisconsin" to locate several primary documents relating to ice companies.

hand. But, it was work, and winter work helped pay bills.

As the twentieth century began, about a dozen ice houses in Madison stored ice. The largest was owned by Conklin & Sons. It stood on the shore of Lake Mendota just a few blocks north of the capitol. Local brewers, butchers, and railroad executives owned smaller ice houses around Madison's lakes. The most highly prized ice in the state, however, came from northern Wisconsin. In Green Bay, the largest ice company was the Miller-Rassmussen Company, which delivered ice to a number of breweries. It also provided ice for refrigerated railroad cars shipping cheese, Door County cherries, and carp.

Several industries depended upon ice. Breweries used a million tons of it every year for distributing beer to taverns. Milwaukee's Best Brewery was the largest consumer of ice in the city. As the meatpacking industry developed in Chicago, meat was shipped across the country in refrigerated railroad cars. With Chicago's weather too unreliable for

safe ice harvesting and its waters too polluted, Wisconsin became a major supplier of ice for the trains shipping meat. Families, too, depended upon ice to keep their milk and produce cold, and icemen delivered hundred-pound blocks to individual homes several times a week.

But around 1910, businesses began to rely upon mechanical refrigeration. Within a decade, the ice harvesting industries were dealt a devastating blow when Prohibition, which outlawed the production of alcoholic beverages, took effect. Prohibition wiped out the demand for ice from brewers. By the mid-1920s, technology and Prohibition combined to end large-scale ice harvesting. When Prohibition ended in the 1930s, people were enjoying their drinks with ice made by electric freezers. By the 1940s, ice delivery faded as an industry. But, even today, people still call electric refrigerators "iceboxes."

How or where did people in your community get their ice in the early 1900s? What businesses in your community then and now rely heavily upon clean, unpolluted ice?

Ice wagon, Madison, undated

Hogs on Wheels

The Evolution of the Harley-Davidson Motor Company

Walter Davidson and the Harley-Davidson motorcycle he drove to victory in the two-day endurance run on June 28 and 29, 1908. The race went from Catskill, New York, to Brooklyn and around Long Island.

It was 1903 in Milwaukee, when 21-year-old William S. Harley and 20-year-old Arthur Davidson sold their first Harley-Davidson motorcycle. They designed and built their cycle in a 10 x 15-foot wooden shed with Harley-Davidson Motor Co. scrawled crudely on the door. The founders soon discovered a demand for their product, and the company was incorporated in 1907. Four years later, the trademark V-twin engine, which gives the cycle its classic sound, was born. The "V" refers to the shape of the engine, and it became a standard design for the firm. In the 1920s, the motorcycle obtained its nickname "hog" when a Harley-Davidson racing team won a race and carried its mascot—a pig—on a victory lap around the track.

Several factors have contributed to the firm's success through the years. Harley-Davidson motorcycles are known for their longevity and reliability. These attributes reflect the ingenuity and hard work the founders put into their design. Riders also appreciate the way newer Harley models can be repaired easily with older model Harley-Davidson parts.

The Harley-Davidson Motor Company has weathered a changing industry, economic downturns, and competition from lighter-weight European models. After being criticized for the heavier V-twin style, the company diversified its line, but it still manufactures its standard "classic" model. Buyer loyalty, as well as savvy business sense on the part of the owners, has contributed to the lasting success of the "Cadillac" of motorcycles.

Harley-Davidson motorcycles first captured the nation's imagination in 1947. An event occurred that solidified the "bad" image that is still attached to Harley bikes

Harry McDaniel's motorcycle and bicycle shop, Madison, 1912

WHi (x3) 24022. © Harley-Davidson

World War II Harley-Davidson models mounted by ever-alert military police (MPs).

and their riders. *Life* magazine reported that, on July 4, a gang of bikers called the Boozefighters terrorized the small California town of Hollister. The magazine published a photograph of an alleged Boozefighter member astride a Harley-Davidson motorcycle. He was drunk and surrounded by empty beer bottles. Despite the fact that most firsthand accounts agree that the photograph was staged and the event was exaggerated by *Time,* the image of the Harley-Davidson "bad boy" on his mean machine endures.

Biker James Cameron was present in Hollister that day and comments: "All that mess never happened." He points out that acting in such a way would have drawn the ire of local police. He does acknowledge, however, that members of the gang were fond of carousing, but he insists that "nothing happened that didn't happen at other [motorcycle] meets. We drank a lot, maybe someone rode their motorcycle into a bar, stuff like that." The supposed incident became so popular that it was later made into the movie *The Wild One* starring Marlon Brando, further establishing the image of the rebellious Harley rider in popular culture.

The Harley-Davidson Motor Company and the "hog" remain successful to this day. Back in 1983, the Harley Owners' Group (affectionately called HOG) was the largest factory-sponsored motorcycle club in the world. Within six years, membership soared to 90,000, and by the year 2000, it had exceeded 500,000. In the summer of 2003, the Harley-Davidson Motor Company marked its one-hundredth anniversary with a massive celebration in Milwaukee.

The Harley-Davidson Motor Company stands today as one of the most successful and enduring businesses in Wisconsin. What companies in your community, city, or country have been in business for 50 years or more? What kinds of products do they design, build, and/or sell? Why do you think they have endured?

Getting Started on Research

Excellent secondary sources include Tom Bolfert's *The Big Book of Harley-Davidson,* Peter Reed's *Well Made In America,* and Rich Teerlink and Lee Ozley's *More Than A Motorcycle: The Leadership Journey at Harley-Davidson.* Information on the early years of the Harley-Davidson Motor Company can be found in Herbert Wagner's *At the Creation: Myth, Reality, and the Origin of the Harley-Davidson Motorcycle, 1901–1909.*

Primary source material about the Harley-Davidson motorcycle and the company and men who built it can be found in *Life* magazine, as well as newspapers and other publications from the 1940s to the 1970s. The Wisconsin Historical Society houses a collection that can be accessed from their Web site (type the keyword Harley-Davidson).

The Harley-Davidson Motor Company maintains its own Web site at http://www.harleydavidson.com/. The site includes a history of the company and early and modern images of their popular machines.

Superior Shipbuilding
Quintuplets and the War!

At the outbreak of World War II, the United States suddenly needed ships. The city of Superior, nestled in one of the world's best natural harbors, already had a significant shipping and shipbuilding industry. The city boasted the largest coal docks, ore docks, and grain elevators in the world. After Pearl Harbor, the shipyards quickly increased production to keep up with the war demand for cargo vessels. In 1942, the port shipped more than 31 million tons of iron ore. That year, the Walter Butler shipyards employed 4,200 workers. Every single week, the company had to bring in nearly a half million dollars just to pay them—and every single week, the money was there. In one year alone, the firm built 18 ocean freighters and started building an additional 12 escort vessels. This rate of production was typical of wartime industry, and Superior's shipbuilding ranked among the best at what it did.

The most famous example of Superior's shipbuilding success occurred in May 1943. The Butler Shipyards had just finished building five coastal cargo vessels.

The Dionne Quintuplets

This was not unusual, but because the company had boasted that it could produce four ships a month, such boldness had created an opportunity for a grand publicity stunt. On Mothers' Day, May 9, 1943, the five ships were christened by the (then) world-famous Dionne quintuplets.

The Dionne quintuplets—Annette, Cecile, Emelie, Marie, and Yvonne—had been born in 1935 near Callendar, Ontario, in Canada. Five sisters born on the same day would be an unusual event at any time, but in their day, it was unprecedented! Newspapers all over the world carried the story and chronicled the critical early days after their births. Day after day, millions of people awaited the news, hoping that, against all odds, all five girls would survive. They not only made it through, but they thrived. The girls were celebrities even before they could crawl. During World War II, the Canadian government capitalized on the quintuplets' celebrity to promote the Canadian war effort. The girls were photographed purchasing war bonds, knitting clothing for British troops, and contributing money and supplies for Chinese and French relief.

By 1943, the war was not going very well for the Allies. Nazi Germany controlled almost all of Europe, except for Great Britain. Allied efforts had begun liberating North Africa, but only at great cost. Meanwhile, Japan had won several significant battles in the Pacific. The quints' cheerful optimism gave people on the homefront a much-needed a boost.

At home, Americans aided the war effort by collecting scrap metal and rubber to be recycled into materials for building airplanes and tanks. People purchased "liberty bonds" from the U.S. government to

Douglas County Historical Society

Page from *News and Views,* February 1943, published by Walter Butler Shipbuilders, Inc. of Superior, Wisconsin

help pay for the war. The government rationed gasoline, as well as sugar, oil, and many other essential goods—goods that Americans had always seemed to take for granted. Civilians were important in the war effort, too. But, the longer the war went on, the more people grew weary of rationing and dealing with the shortages. Nagging fears of the next German or Japanese attack were wearing down the nation. In the midst of this national anxiety, events like the Dionne quintuplets' visit to Superior served to cheer everybody up. These events also help inspire the spirit and drive to continue the war effort.

The quintuplets' arrival in Superior for the ceremony was witnessed by more than 20,000 people on hand and by countless others who were listening to the live radio broadcast. This was the girls' first visit to the United States. In fact, people were more interested in the sisters than in the five ships they came to launch!

One by one, the girls broke a bottle across each ship's bow and watched the structure slowly slide into the harbor. Traditionally, champagne was used. But for this ceremony, five bottles of water from Niagara Falls, which symbolized American and Canadian friendship, were used instead. Behind the Dionne girls stood their parents and Robert Butler, the president of the firm. Butler was proud of his firm and its work. The girls' mother called it "the happiest Mother's Day I have ever known."

The launching of the five ships was national news. Newspapers in your community likely covered the story. How did your local newspapers, magazines, or other publications describe the event? World War II radically changed Wisconsin industry throughout the war. How was your community affected by the war and by the businesses that were committed to the war effort? What local companies produced materials for the war? How did your community, city, or county in general promote the war effort?

Getting Started on Research

To learn more about Wisconsin during World War II, see *The History of Wisconsin, Volume VI: Continuity and Change, 1940–1965* by William F. Thompson. Your public library will have a variety of resources, such as local newspapers and documentaries from that period. A search using the keyword "shipbuilding" at the Wisconsin Historical Society"s Archives (ArCat) Web site will yield several primary documents relating to Superior shipbuilders.

$\mathcal{B}$oom to $\mathcal{B}$ust

The Brownstone Industry of Chequamegon Bay

Photograph of the "MONOLITH" from the PRENTICE BROWNSTONE QUARRY, Washburn, Wis. Taken Nov. 18, 1892, when it was loosened from its bed. Height, when set up at the World's Fair, 115 feet; base 10 ft. square.
J. E. Powell, Ashland, Wis.

Men working at Prentice Brownstone Quarry, Washburn, 1892.

Most people who hear about the Apostle Islands probably think of tourism. After all, the islands have been a popular vacation destination since the late 1800s. Prior to tourism, though, there was a period when the islands' most valuable resource wasn't spectacular scenery or clear water, but a dark-colored variety of sandstone known as brownstone. In the late nineteenth century, brownstone was a popular building material in cities all over the United States. And the rock that had lined the Chequamegon region for 600 million years promised a fortune for anyone who could quarry it and ship it.

Quarries in the area were pits cut into the ground. The rock was carved out in huge blocks with the aid of steam-powered cutting equipment.

THE
PRENTICE BROWNSTONE CO.

IS PREPARED
TO FILL LARGE OR SMALL ORDERS
ON SHORT NOTICE.

Quarries at Houghton, Bayfield County, Wis.

BRANCH OFFICES:
AT THE QUARRIES.
NEW YORK, 44 BROADWAY
CHICAGO, 714 TACOMA BLDG.

MAIN OFFICE
ASHLAND, WIS.
Room 311-313, Knight Block.

Promotional materials from Prentice Brownstone Company, 1890

Although no one is exactly sure who opened the islands' first quarry, one possibility is a man named Frederick Prentice. He worked as an agent for the American Fur Company in the 1850s and claimed to have discovered the Chequamegon brownstone when he noticed similarities between it and the stone widely used in New York City buildings. Another possibility is Alanson Sweet, a land speculator who spent 15 months searching for a quarry site in the mid-1800s. In 1867, both men opened quarries on the south end of Basswood Island. From there, the brownstone industry quickly boomed.

Within a few years, 10 quarries were operating on the islands and the Bayfield peninsula. Stone from these quarries was used extensively in the eastern and midwestern parts of the country. The Milwaukee County Courthouse, for example, was constructed in 1870 with stone from Basswood Island. The largest quarry, at Houghton Point on the Bayfield Peninsula, provided stone for buildings in 10 states and 40 cities. In 1892, the quarry operators conceived a huge publicity stunt. They donated a gigantic, 105-foot obelisk shaped like the Washington Monument. It was cut from a single piece of stone for the World's Fair in Chicago. State officials were initially delighted to show off this marvel from Wisconsin. However, when they learned that transporting it from Bayfield to Chicago would cost

Getting Started on Research

An excellent account of the Chequamegon region can be found in *Madeline Island and the Chequamegon Region* by John O. Holzhueter. The history of the Apostle Islands is also discussed on the Web at http://www.nps.gov/apis/. The bibliography of Kathryn Bishop Eckert's *The Sandstone Architecture of the Lake Superior Region* provides a number of primary sources. Also, the Northern Great Lakes History Center and Archives has several primary documents relating to the brownstone industry of Chequamegon Bay.

$40,000, they abandoned the idea. Smaller brownstone pillars eventually made it to Chicago as part of Wisconsin's exhibit.

The Prentice Brownstone Company, crowed one promotional brochure, "is prepared to fill large or small orders on short notice." It had little trouble providing plenty of stone. Photographs of the quarries show many beds of stone waiting to be lifted out.

But a large supply alone does not keep a company in business. Profitability depends upon demand and, in this case, the aesthetic tastes of city dwellers. In the 1890s, the popularity of the stone began to decline. More and more people simply chose to build more and more structures with wood, brick, or lighter-shaded stone. The American novelist Edith Wharton captured the growing distaste for the once-popular stone in *The Age of Innocence:* "This little, low-studded rectangular New York, cursed with its universal chocolate-coloured coating of the most hideous stone ever quarried, this cramped horizontal gridiron of a town without towers, porticoes, fountains or perspectives, hidebound in its deadly uniformity of mean ugliness." With this bleak

assessment, brownstone went out of fashion. By 1910, the once-bustling Wisconsin island quarries had closed.

Life, however, went on for those who lived in the Chequamegon region. Prentice achieved even greater business success elsewhere, and the lumbering and mining industries stayed around a little longer. Throughout the brownstone heyday, the biggest draw to the area remained its scenic beauty. Visitors would come from hundreds of miles to paddle among the islands and sit along the relaxing shores. Today, the same location that produced the "ugly" brownstone remains one of the state's great examples of natural beauty.

What do you think life was like for people in the area and for worker in the quarries in the 1890s? How do you think people reacted to the decline in popularity of their major source of income? Compare and contrast these feelings to today's employees who find themselves out of work. Ask your librarian or teacher for help locating primary and secondary sources for your research.

Brownstone quarry workers, Bayfield Peninsula, 1890

From Lead to Zinc

The Mining Heyday in Southwest Wisconsin

In 1836, the government of the newly established Wisconsin Territory was in need of an official seal. This seal was to be used to certify documents and legal papers, and it needed to depict something that symbolized the territory. Judging from today's most famous Wisconsin icon, you might guess that the seal was fashioned in the shape of a wedge of cheese. But neither cheese, nor a cow, nor even a farm scene was chosen. Instead, the official seal bore the image of an arm holding a pickaxe over a pile of ore.

At that time, lead ore made Wisconsin's economy tick. Between 1822 and 1836, most of Wisconsin's settlers came not to farm but to mine lead in southwest Wisconsin, particularly in the counties of Grant, Crawford, Iowa, and Lafayette. By 1829, more than 4,000 miners worked in the region, and 52 smelting works produced 13 million pounds of lead a year.

Lead-mining was not new to the area. For hundreds of years before the French arrived, the Ho-Chunk, Mesquakie, Sauk,

Map of Wisconsin lead mining district, 1829

and other Indian nations had been mining the region's easily accessible lead. Two French explorers, Nicolas Perrot in the 1680s and Julien Dubuque a century later, began mining lead in the area as well.

One of the earliest American miners in Wisconsin was John Bonner. He moved to Hard Scrabble, in what is now Grant County, in 1824. While digging a shaft, he found lead ore after only four feet. Within a day, he had removed 17,000 pounds—nearly nine tons! Lead was then worth $80 a ton, so a miner like Bonner could make a lot of money very quickly.

Once the surface lead had disappeared, miners sunk shafts deep into the earth; often up to 60 feet. Then, they descended into the shafts on ropes to dig for galena, or lead sulfide, the purest form of lead ore. From the depths, they hoisted the ore to the surface in buckets. Once at the surface, the ore was transformed by

Zinc mine in Iowa County, undated

smelters into 70-pound rectangular blocks called "pigs." At first, lead pigs were shipped down the Mississippi River to Missouri. Later, they traveled by horse cart and rail to Milwaukee.

Miners who moved into the area in the 1820s and 1830s wasted no time building shelters. While some constructed crude log houses, others simply dug holes into a hillside. These simple burrows quickly earned miners the nickname "badgers." Rough-and-tumble settlements sprang up around the mines. Their names were Hard Scrabble, Work's Digs, Hamilton Digs, Miners Grove, New Diggings, and Mineral Point. The growth of such communities reflected the economic boom. Many miners came from Missouri, which had experienced a lead boom a few years earlier. In the 1830s, a growing population of experienced miners arrived from Cornwall in southwestern England. The Cornish settlers came to Mineral Point and constructed small houses of buff-colored limestone, some of which are still visible and standing today at the state historic site, Pendarvis.

Lead mining peaked in the 1840s. Production reached 18 million pounds a year, more than half the national output.

Getting Started on Research

In chapter 6 of *The History of Wisconsin, Volume I: From Exploration to Statehood,* Alice Smith does an excellent job describing the Lead District and the mining boom. You can find another fine description of lead mining and miners in "The European Settling and Transformation of the Upper Mississippi Valley Lead Mining Region," by Michael P. Conzen in *Wisconsin Land and Life.* To learn more about Mineral Point and its Cornish settlers, read *Mineral Point: A History* by George Fiedler. You can find archival information or learn out about Pendarvis on the Wisconsin Historical Society Web site. If your community has a local historical society, you can find information on mining (especially if you live near the old mining regions). Also, visit the Badger Mine and Museum in Shullsburg or the Mining Museum in Platteville.

But, demand was declining. Miners, who had exhausted the easily obtained ore near the surface, could only reach the deeper ore with expensive equipment. Those looking for quicker money moved on. In 1844, almost one-third of the lead district residents left for the copper mines of Upper Michigan. By 1849, most of the remaining headed for the gold fields of California.

Those who stayed turned largely to farming to make a living. Some men continued to mine lead, but they also mined for zinc. For a few years in the late 1800s, Mineral Point had the largest zinc smeltery in the world. During World War I and II, zinc mining increased, but it too, soon faded. By the time the mining era ended in the 1970s, southwest Wisconsin had operated the longest continuously operated mining effort in North America.

What do you think life was like for the miners and their families? What was the impact on the environment from all the mining? What pysical evidence of the mining era remains today?

WHi Image ID 3785

Miners in lead mine at Platteville, 1930

Allis-Chalmers
Manufacturing for Manufacturers

Manufacturing produces items large and small—from computers and cars to appliances, furniture, and any goods you can buy in a store or online. But who fabricates the equipment used by the factories in order manufacture all of these material possessions? One of Wisconsin's leading companies was one that constructed industrial machinery for manufacturers—the Allis-Chalmers Company. The company was founded in Milwaukee by Edward P. Allis. Allis was born in Cazevonia, New York in 1824, and at the age of 22, he moved to Milwaukee and opened a leather shop.

In May 1861, Allis purchased a bankrupt factory called the Reliance Works, which made flour-milling equipment and millstones. Allis employed around 40 men who worked six days a week, making machinery for mills. But Allis wanted a larger factory that could produce more products. So, in 1868, he moved his workers to a new and much bigger plant.

Allis won the contract for a new city water main the following year, and realized that the project offered him an excellent opportunity to expand even further. Because pumps were required to feed the water system, Allis started building them, investing $100,000 in a new pipe foundry. When he won the contract to construct the complicated water system for Milwaukee, Allis proved what his factory could do.

Allis himself was not an inventor, but he had the ability to foresee the needs of industrialists and to find talented, innovative partners. In 1873, he hired George Hinkley to head the sawmill machinery division of the company. Within a few years, Hinkley and Allis revolutionized the lumber industry. They started the first successful bandsaw mill and exhibited at the Jump River Lumber Company in Dorchester. The timing was perfect. Just as lumber mills were starting up all over northern Wisconsin, the Allis Company was developing the most advanced sawmill equipment in the world!

A similar advance was made in flour-milling. In 1877, William Gray began work as the superintendent of Allis' milling machine department. At the time, flour was produced by grinding whole grain between two

WHi (x3) 37408. Courtesy of Allis-Chalmers, A-C Industrial Press, Milwaukee, Wisconsin.

Allis-Chalmers workers building machinery for the Utah Copper Company.

huge stones. Gray had learned new milling techniques in Europe, and the next year, he installed the first roller mill at the Eagle Mill in Milwaukee. In the roller mill, steel rollers more efficiently reduced the grains to flour. By the 1880s, the major milling firms in the Midwest, including the Washburn and Pillsbury mills in Minnesota, converted to roller-mill technology. This approach soon became the national standard.

In 1877, Allis hired another engineer, Edwin Reynolds, to work at his plant. Reynolds had been working for the Corliss Steam Engine Company of Providence, Rhode Island. But he wanted more independence in developing a superior steam engine. Soon, Reynolds developed a faster, stronger, and more efficient steam engine. This technology also became the national standard. In fact, Reynolds designed the engine that powered the 1893 World's Fair in Chicago, which was built by Allis' Reliance Works.

Edward Allis died in 1889, but he left his company in good hands. The Reliance Works continued to manufacture new machinery and develop new technologies. In 1901, the firm merged with a Chicago company headed by William J. Chalmers.

WHi (x3) 50223, Courtesy of Allis-Chalmers, A-C Industrial Press, Milwaukee, Wisconsin.

Industrial workers atop large machinery built by Allis-Chalmers

His firm specialized in making mining equipment. Allis-Chalmers produced machinery for manufacturers, as well as a host of other products, until it was bought out by a German-based company in the the late 1980's. During its over 120-year history, Allis Chalmers stood as a major industrial leader and innovator and remains one of the state's greatest business success stories.

What manufacturing companies are in or near your community or county? Pick a company in your area to research. Describe its history—its beginnings, its founders, and its main products or services. Your teacher or librarian can help you find more information about Wisconsin's industrial giants. Local newspapers can be very helpful.

Getting Started on Research

The history of the Allis-Chalmers company is described in the third volume of the *History of Wisconsin* series, titled *Urbanization and Industrialization: 1873–1893* by Robert C. Nesbit. Many primary sources from the Allis-Chalmers Company can be found in the archives at the Wisconsin Historical Society in Madison (or from their Web site).

D.C. Everest

Building Wisconsin's Paper Industries

WHS Archives

Autographed photo of D.C. Everest, 1948

The history of the paper industry in Wisconsin is older than Wisconsin's statehood! The first paper—with pulp made from rags—was produced in Milwaukee on March 7, 1848. It was only three months prior to the signing of legislation formally recognizing Wisconsin as a state. Although Milwaukee was the site of the state's first paper production, the paper industry's requirements for supplies of fresh water and wood pulp shifted focus to sites along the state's major rivers, including the Fox, Wisconsin, Chippewa, Menominee, Peshtigo, Eau Claire, Flambeau, and others. In 1872, the introduction

of the Keller groundwood process to the Fox River Valley moved papermaking from a rag-based enterprise to one centered on wood pulp.

Papermaking was, and is, a significant part of Wisconsin's economy. Although perhaps more famous for its dairy production, and cheese in particular, Wisconsin's papermaking ranks among the leaders in the industry. Paper companies experienced their most rapid growth between 1900 and 1930. Paper moved from eighteenth place in output of state industries in 1880 to fourth place in 1925. In the 1950s, Wisconsin led the United States in the amount of paper and board produced. Today, Wisconsin stands as the primary paper-manufacturing state. Pulp, paper, and related businesses employ more than 52,000 people, according to the Wisconsin Paper Council. This trade association represents the pulp, paper, and allied industries.

Born in Pine Grove, Michigan, in 1882, David Clark Everest was at the forefront of the paper industry just as it was beginning. At age 16, his father's factory burned down. Soon after, his father died. To support his mother and sister, Everest worked as a

> While the progress of Marathon Corporation may not have been dramatized as much as some others, we now seem to be coming into the limelight and people realize that it was more than a "one-man concern," as some of our financial friends always tried to indicate. It has been the teamwork of all concerned which has made the success possible.
>
> As I review it now, I think perhaps my main role in the whole performance was in having a little imagination and then the courage to get the Board of Directors to back up my opinion with money. I know that at times I have skated on thin ice and have made some mistakes, but as an overall picture I think the organization has done a mighty fine job.

WHS Archives

Copy of unsigned letter from D.C. Everest to colleague Allen Abrams, March 3, 1950

Getting Started on Research

Secondary source material can be obtained from Steven Burton Karges' dissertation titled *David Clark Everest and Marathon Paper Mills Company: A Study of a Wisconsin Entrepreneur 1909–1931*. Excellent secondary source materials on the state's paper industry can be found in *Wisconsin History: An Annotated Bibliography*. D.C. Everest's papers are housed in the Wisconsin Historical Society Archives.

bookkeeper and office boy. In 1899, while working these jobs, Everest completed his high school education. A decade later, Everest, at 27, joined the Marathon Paper Mills Corporation as a general manager. The financial backers were originally intent upon producing newsprint, but Everest convinced them to invest in the paper specialty field. This proved to be a wise business move because a stable demand existed, and was in fact growing, for specialty paper.

Despite his lack of formal technical education, Everest enacted changes that greatly influenced the paper industry. He was one of the original founders of the Institute of Paper Chemistry in Appleton (now the Institute of Paper Science and Technology in Atlanta, Georgia). He also was the first person without a technical education to receive a Gold Medal from TAPPI, the Technical Association for the Pulp and Paper Industry.

Everest was always involved in conservation efforts, which were partially to the industry's benefit. Papermakers' investments were much greater than were the lumber companies', and conservation efforts, such as reforestation, protected that investment. As early as 1925, Everest promoted a statewide system of fire protection and state tree nurseries. He also supported the legislation in 1927 to create the Forest Crop Law, which allowed landowners to pay taxes only after they harvested. The law encouraged long-term investment, as well as proper forestry management.

Everest was also a charter member of the Wisconsin Conservation Commission's forestry advisory committee. In this role, he assisted in developing and expanding the state forest program. In 1991, he was inducted into the Wisconsin Conservation Hall of Fame. Despite his efforts, papermaking left Wisconsin with a legacy of polluted water. PCBs, which are toxic chemicals used in paper production, have been dumped into waterways, where they remain in large, and sometimes harmful, quantities. Cleanup efforts are still a major problem, with no major success in sight.

Are there paper industries in your community? If so, how do they fit into the state's papermaking chronology? What industries in your community have flourished over the past several years?

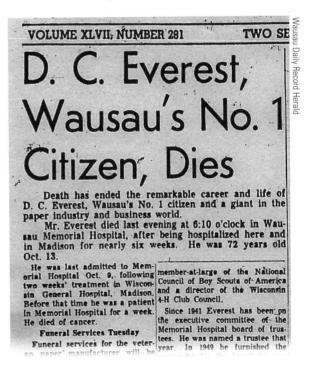

VOLUME XLVII; NUMBER 281   TWO SE

D. C. Everest, Wausau's No. 1 Citizen, Dies

Death has ended the remarkable career and life of D. C. Everest, Wausau's No. 1 citizen and a giant in the paper industry and business world.

Mr. Everest died last evening at 6:10 o'clock in Wausau Memorial Hospital, after being hospitalized here and in Madison for nearly six weeks. He was 72 years old Oct. 13.

He was last admitted to Memorial Hospital Oct. 9, following two weeks' treatment in Wisconsin General Hospital, Madison. Before that time he was a patient in Memorial Hospital for a week. He died of cancer.

Funeral Services Tuesday

Funeral services for the veteran paper manufacturer will be

member-at-large of the National Council of Boy Scouts of America and a director of the Wisconsin 4-H Club Council.

Since 1941 Everest has been on the executive committee of the Memorial Hospital board of trustees. He was named a trustee that year. In 1949 he furnished the

Wausau Daily Record Herald

D.C. Everest's obituary in the *Wausau Daily Record Herald*, October 29, 1955

$\mathcal{S}$ilent $\mathcal{S}$ervice

Manitowoc's Submarine Industry in World War II

Manitowoc Herald Times

In 1939, Charles C. West, president of the Manitowoc Shipbuilding Company, attempted to secure a Navy shipbuilding contract. Government contracts for shipbuilding had evaporated during the Great Depression, but now with a war in Europe, contracts were available. West presented his proposal to build destroyers. But Navy representatives suggested that West's company build submarines instead, an unusual request for a Midwest firm whose employees had never built anything like a submarine before!

Despite the company's inexperience, on September 9, 1940, the Manitowoc Shipbuilding Company received a Navy contract to build 10 underwater

MANITOWOC, WIS., THURSDAY, APRIL 30, 1942   Price Four Cents   NO. 163

First Sub To Be Built On Great Lakes Launched Here

Headline in *Manitowoc Herald Times,* April 30, 1942

submarines. Later, the contract was extended to 47 subs, but the war's end terminated the contract after just 28 had been built.

In addition to the fact that they had never produced a sub, the Manitowoc Shipbuilding Company faced several other obstacles. None of the workforce of 500 employees had any applicable training. Supplies and other materials to build a submarine were located on the east and west coasts. The company's shipbuilding yard on the narrow, shallow Manitowoc River made launching a submarine a very dangerous, if not impossible, task. Then, should a submarine be completed and successfully launched, there remained the problem of transporting the cumbersome object all the way down the Mississippi River to New Orleans!

There were, however, some advantages to having the Wisconsin-based company do the job. The employees were experienced in building quality ships, and a large labor force would be no problem to assemble, given the size of the local population. Also, Manitowoc's location—some 1,800

Wisconsin Maritime Museum

Side-launching of the *Peto* in Manitowoc, April 30, 1942

miles from open sea—made enemy sabotage highly unlikely. And finally, the deepest part of Lake Michigan was directly north, which could provide a great proving ground for the submarine.

For the launch of the first Manitowoc-built sub—the *Peto*—on April 30, 1942, the company developed an innovative side launch technique to accommodate the Manitowoc River's narrow, shallow channel. The *Peto* was significant for two reasons. It was the first sub to be built on the Great Lakes for the U.S. Navy, and it was the first sub anywhere ever to be side-launched. The Manitowoc company also adapted new construction and assembly techniques. The company became renowned for its efficiency and craftsmanship. In fact, in the time the Navy normally allotted to build 10 submarines, Manitowoc Shipbuilding produced 28. At the peak of production, the workforce consisted of 7,000 people. A floating dry dock towed by a tug transported the subs down the Mississippi River to New Orleans.

Some historians partially attribute the Japanese army's defeat in the war to attrition. The Japanese economy possessed

The *Raton* in the dry dock, Manitowoc

industrial strength, but lacked resources. It relied upon its merchant fleet to deliver goods to and from the island nation. The Allied naval powers interfered with these transactions. The U.S. Pacific submarine force sank 1,392 enemy merchant vessels, boats, and warships. This represented 55% of all Japanese vessels lost. Manitowoc subs were partly responsible for this success. Twenty-five of the 28 subs engaged in battle in the Pacific sank more than 125 vessels. These vessels represented 9.8% of the total tonnage sunk by American submarines in the Pacific theatre. In a real way, Manitowoc subs helped win many battles and contributed to the ultimate victory in the war.

What industries in your community contributed to the war effort in WWII, the Korean War, or the Vietnam War? How did they contribute? How do companies today handle employees who are also veterans, reservists, or in the National Guard?

Getting Started on Research

William T. Nelson's pamphlet "Fresh Water Submarines: the Manitowoc Story," Robert L. Lyman's "The Momentous Moment: The Submarine Building Program at the Manitowoc Shipyards in World War II," and Steven R. Milquet's "A Lakeshore Legacy: Manitowoc Submarines" all give excellent secondary information. For primary resources, consult your local librarian or the Maritime Museum in Manitowoc.

Wisconsin Maritime Museum

Soldiers without Guns
Milwaukee Women during World War II

Enola O'Connell, the only woman welder at Heil Company, at work in Milwaukee, February 1943.

On December 7, 1941, Japanese forces attacked U.S. naval forces at Pearl Harbor, Hawaii. Within a few days, the United States had joined the Allies of Great Britain and France in war against Germany, Italy, and Japan. Ordinary Americans rallied to the cause. More than 330,000 men and women from Wisconsin served in the armed forces during the war in Europe, the Pacific, and Africa. Approximately 8,000 died and another 13,000 were wounded in combat. But winning World War II depended upon more than just providing large numbers of troops to serve in the armed forces. The home front had to play a crucial role.

World War II was a total war, which meant that civilians actively participated in the war effort. Thousands collected scrap metal and rubber to be remanufactured into tanks and airplanes. They bought war bonds and submitted to the rationing of gasoline and a variety of other necessities. The war lasted until August 1945, so for four years, daily challenges were a part of everyone's life.

Industrial employment provided one of the most valuable ways for civilians to aid the war effort. In the years prior to the war, many people had lost their jobs due to the economic difficulties of the Great Depression. Fewer people could afford to purchase cars, washing machines, or even new clothes and shoes, so industrial production had slowed greatly. When the United States entered the war, suddenly the government needed American factories to build airplanes, jeeps, uniforms, boots, and virtually everything else American soldiers needed. As a result, America went back to work since the country's industries dedicated themselves to helping the United States win the war.

But many of the men who normally would have worked in these factories were also needed to fight. More than 16 million Americans served in uniform, and many of them were industrial workers. When the men left to fight overseas, women took their place in many industries. Images of active, dedicated women, such as "Rosie the Riveter," grew popular. This fictional character worked in a factory that built airplanes. Rosie symbolized the millions of women who entered the industrial workforce during the war. Nationwide, the number of women working in factories leaped from 13 million to 19 million in a relatively short time.

Manufacturing in Milwaukee is a good example of the way the war changed many lives in America, especially those of women. According to the U.S. War Production Board, manufacturing jobs in Milwaukee increased from around 110,000 in 1940 to almost 200,000 in 1943. In 1937, the Allis-Chalmers Manufacturing Company, one of the largest factories in the region, employed only 144 women—about 3% of a total workforce that exceeded 4,700. But by December 1941, the factory had more than doubled its workforce to 11,250, with 750 women (about 6%). When the war ended in August 1944, women working at the main plant totaled nearly 25% of the entire workforce. In other Allis-Chalmers plants, the proportion was even higher!

But women moving into factory jobs encountered difficulties that had not been problems faced by men. Many women were mothers with children who needed daycare. They also faced economic inequality—often being paid far less than male workers with the same or less experience. This inequality was evident in both unskilled and skilled positions.

One Milwaukee woman who dealt with all these challenges was Rose

Getting Started on Research

To learn more about Wisconsin during World War II, start with chapter 3 in *The History of Wisconsin, Volume VI: Continuity and Change, 1940–1965* by William Thompson. Rose Kaminiski's story and those of many other Wisconsin women can be found in *Voices of the Wisconsin Past: Women Remember the War, 1941–1945,* a collection of oral history interviews and an excellent primary source (edited by Michael E. Stevens and available through the Wisconsin Historical Society). Another way to find excellent primary source materials is to interview a great-grandparent or other adults who recall the war years. Ask them to describe how the war affected their lives and the lives of their family members.

Kaminski. Her husband John was drafted in 1944. Even before he left, Rose Kaminiski would take her daughter to an older neighbor and go to work at jobs normally held by men. First, she worked in the General Electric Supercharger machine shop. A few months later, she became a crane operator for the Rex Chain Belt Company. Then, she took a similar position with the Harnischfeger Corporation. While her work experience necessarily expanded her skills, the transition was very hard on her and her family. And when it was all over—after aiding the war effort for almost three years—she did what most women like her did: She left her job, her new skills, and her economic livelihood behind to return to homemaking, all to make room for a returning veteran.

How did the war effort affect the lives of women and families in your community? In what ways did companies in your community participate in the war effort? Local public libraries have resources, such as newspapers and other documents from the 1940s, to help you learn more about your community's involvement in this important period in American history.

WHi (X3) 32696

President Franklin Roosevelt (near window) and other officials visiting women working at the Allis-Chalmers factory in Milwaukee, September 19, 1942.

Sawdust Cities
How Lumber Mills Created Towns

Look closely at a map of northern Wisconsin and you will quickly see that most major cities in the area are built on rivers. Nekoosa, Wisconsin Rapids, Stevens Point, Wausau, Merill, and Tomahawk are situated on the Wisconsin River. Green Bay, Kaukauna, Appleton, Neenah, and Menasha are on the Fox River. Chippewa Falls and Eau Claire are on the Chippewa River. This is not a coincidence. All these cities had their origins as mill towns. They were places where sawmills were opened in the late 1800s to process logs from the great pine forests.

At that time, rivers were important for several reasons. Before paved roads and railroads were built in northern Wisconsin, rivers provided a convenient way to transport the pine logs from the forests to the mills—one of the great virtues of pine is its ability to float! Lumberjacks cut trees all winter, and in the spring the melting snow made rivers run fast and deep. Not every lumber camp was on a major river, of course, but most were near small creeks or

Home (no longer standing) of lumberman O.H. Ingram, Eau Claire

on a river that eventually joined a major waterway, such as the Wisconsin, Chippewa, or Black. This network of waterways created a liquid highway system to move heavy logs from one place to another.

The mills themselves depended upon water for power. In cities like Eau Claire and Mosinee, logs piled up in mill ponds to be sawed into boards. Most cities had more than one mill, and many smaller towns had mills, as well. Each mill used huge saws, powered by waterwheels, to cut the logs into boards. Water flowing over the wheels created the mechanical energy needed to drive the machinery. Every spring, these "sawdust cities" would be flooded with lumberjacks floating their logs down the river and then spending their income in local saloons and stores. Whole cities sprang up around the mills, providing general stores, warehouses, machine shops, butchers, grocers, tailors, bankers, and many other business needed to support a growing population. Soon, many of these cities became thriving commercial centers.

Eau Claire is a good example of how quickly a mill can create a city.

Bird's eye view of Eau Claire in 1880

The city is located where the Eau Claire and Chippewa rivers join, making it an easy destination for lumber camps farther north. Two large ponds provided ideal holding areas for the logs after they arrived and were ready to be cut. In 1860, five companies in Eau Claire County were in the lumber business. The largest, Chapman & Thorp, ran three sawmills and one flour mill. The firm also operated a large store and boardinghouse to meet the needs of its workers.

Once the sawmills were established, people quickly followed. In 1855, the area's population was about 100. But the rapidly growing mill operations attracted newcomers and businesses. The following year, the first hotel, school, and bank were built. By 1870, Eau Claire's population was up to 2,000. Soon afterward, the lumber boom really hit. Ten years later, more than 10,000 people had come, and the numbers continued to increase rapidly. Another decade later, 17,000 citizens resided in the thriving metropolis of Eau Claire.

Despite the output, the pine forests were not inexhaustible resources of lumber, however. As vast stretches of the

Getting Started on Research

To learn more about Wisconsin's lumber industry, read chapter 2 of *The History of Wisconsin, Volume III: Urbanization and Industrialization, 1873–1893* by Robert Nesbit. A good general work on the Chippewa Valley is *Settlement and Survival: Building Towns in the Chippewa Valley, 1850–1925.* For primary documents, search the Wisconsin Historical Society online archives. Use the keywords "sawdust cities," "water," "power," and "mills."

Chippewa Valley were logged off, the lumber industry declined. But the city outlasted the lumber boom. By the twentieth century, new industries had come to Eau Claire, including shoe and tire manufacturing. Today, Eau Claire—like other "sawdust cities" in Wisconsin's north—is still a major economic, cultural, and political center, having lived through the lumber boom that brought it into existence.

What are the names of any sawmills in your community? Did they begin in the 1880s? How important has the lumber industry been to your town? Your teacher or librarian can help you find out more about the history of Wisconsin's "sawdust cities."

Photo of lumber operations of the Stevens and Jarvis Lumber Company, Eau Claire, 1907

WHi (x3) 33025, courtesy of Eau Claire Public Library

Badger Ordnance
How Wisconsin Helped Win World War II

When Japanese planes attacked Pearl Harbor on December 7, 1941, the United States entered World War II. The enormous needs for equipment overseas meant that production had to be stepped up on the home front. Factories across the nation switched from producing consumer goods to building planes, tanks, and other military equipment.

In 1941, the war came home to the residents of Sauk County. The federal government had just announced plans to construct a new munitions factory there. It would be called the Badger Ordnance Works and would be built on prairie land just south of Baraboo. Converting this prairie into a major industrial complex permanently affected the area.

A new factory was good news to business owners in Baraboo and in nearby Sauk City and Prairie du Sac. The factory's many workers—more than 12,000 in 1942 and about 7,500 over the next three years—earned high wages. They shopped in local stores, ate in local restaurants, and patronized local business, associations, and services. After the Great Depression, the business community welcomed the influx of new workers and the boost to the area's economy.

But not everyone in the area was pleased to see the Badger Ordnance Works constructed. More than 100 families lost their homes and farms to the construction that took upwards of 10,000 acres of land. Most of the displaced families moved to new farms elsewhere, and many others had to go to court to get a fair payment for the land the government had condemned in order to gain rights to the area.

The Badger Ordnance Works operated throughout

WHS Archives

Woman working in the Badger Ordnance Works in 1954 or 1955.

Page from a promotional brochure about Badger Ordnance Works

the war. But once the war was over, the economic boom ended with it. The army no longer needed the munitions plant or its workers. And nobody knew what to do with the huge complex, which could not be easily converted to civilian use. Workers who had moved across the highway to Badger Village now found themselves out of work with few employment opportunities in the immediate area. The economic hardship caused by the shutdown and huge unemployment rippled through the entire region. Businesses saw their best customers lose jobs and move away.

The facility reopened briefly during the Korean War and again during the Vietnam War. During the 1960s, it was renamed the Badger Army Ammunition Plant, and it produced explosives for the war in Vietnam. Because of its association with the Vietnam War, the facility became a popular staging site for anti-war protests.

By the 1980s, residents of Sauk county generally regarded the plant as an aging eyesore. Badger Ordnance had also become an environmental hazard. Pollution from the plant had contaminated underground water supplies. In 1997, the U.S. Army finally decided to sell the facility. But once again, no one was sure what to do with the 7,000-acre site. After much public debate among farmers, developers, environmentalists, and the Ho-Chunk Nation, the plant was divided up in 2003. Some of the land was to be used for prairie restoration. Ironically, the site that produced ammunition and explosives for war would now be used for growing wildflowers.

In what additional ways do you think the army facility changed everyday life in Sauk County? If you were in the community at the time, what ideas would you have for using such a large site?

Article about scrap drives in the *Badger Ordnance News*, October 9, 1942

Getting Started on Research

William Fletcher Thompson thoroughly discusses the Badger Ordnance Works plant and Wisconsin's response to World War II in *The History of Wisconsin, Volume VI: Continuity and Change, 1940–1965*. A search for Badger Ordnance in the Wisconsin Historical Society Archives will yield primary documents abut the history of the munitions plant.

Contact your local historical society to find oral histories from the war period. Do your own research project in which you create an oral history (interviews, anecdotes, etc.). Your librarian can help you find old newspapers that describe the war's impact on your area.

Fairlawn

From Millionaire's Mansion to Orphan's Home

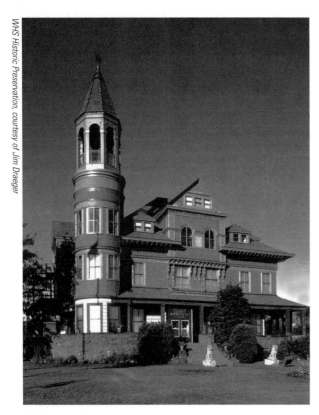

WHS Historic Preservation, courtesy of Jim Draeger

Fairlawn exterior

In 1890, Martin and Grace Pattison of Superior, Wisconsin, set out to build a house. They did not intend to build just any home, but the largest and most splendid house anyone in the city had ever seen. The result was a 42-room, Queen Anne-style mansion that sat in the middle of its own city block and held a commanding view across Lake Superior.

The Pattisons spared no expense, and their builder used lavish imported woods, polished stone, and stained glass. The basement had a bowling alley and a swimming pool! An awestruck reporter for the *Superior Evening Telegram* toured the house, and in May 16, 1891, called it "the most perfect of any house within some hundred miles." Fairlawn cost $150,000 to build at a time when an expensive house

would cost as much as $20,000. But the Pattisons could afford it, and the self-made man wanted a home that suited his business success. The majestic house became more than just one family's proud statement, however. The same house that was home to the city's richest residents would become a home for the city's poorest orphans.

Martin Pattison was born in Ontario, Canada, to American parents. The family moved to Michigan when Martin was 11. At 17, he went to work at a lumber camp and, by the age of 25, he became a partner in a successful firm. In 1872, Pattison abruptly moved to the upper peninsula of Michigan and began a lumber and mining firm with his brother William. But, Martin Pattison thought that the upper peninsula had limited potential, and so he and his brother headed west. They reestablished their firm in Superior, at the head of Lake Superior.

The firm logged along the Black River, just south of the city. But, Pattison became interested in the mining potential of northern Minnesota. So, he personally trekked through the region, first assessing the land and its mineral wealth, then purchasing desirable parcels. Within a few years, he was one of the largest shareholders in a profitable iron mine in the Vermillion Range. By the 1880s, he was a very, very wealthy man.

Pattison decided to enter politics in 1884 and was elected sheriff of Douglas County. At a time when vice and corruption were common in politics, Pattison remained scrupulously honest. He served only one term as sheriff, then in 1890 he was elected mayor of Superior. He served two terms during a time when Superior

Getting Started on Research

Ask your librarian for help finding county histories and newspaper accounts of life in Superior (or your own community) at the beginning of the twentieth century. Your local library or historical society can provide sources for research so you can answer some of the questions presented in this story.

Visit the Fairlawn museum and learn more about the Pattison family and the place they called home. For Fairlawn history, photos, a virtual tour of the museum, and other links, go to the Superior Public Museum's official Web site at http://www.superiorpublicmuseums.org/.

To learn more about the early history of Superior, read *Frontier Village: The Birth of Superior, Wisconsin* by Ronald Mershart.

underwent rapid development into an industrial center with improved, modernized streets and utilities. "During his regime," the *Inland Ocean* proclaimed in its April 2, 1893 issue, "the city made the most rapid strides toward industrial and commercial supremacy that it has in its history."

Soon, Superior was Wisconsin's second-largest city with the largest grain and ore docks in the world. In his later life, Pattison got involved in the banking business and became president of the United States National Bank of Superior.

In 1918, Pattison fell ill and died in his sleep. He left behind his wife Grace and six grown children. Two years later, Grace decided to leave Fairlawn and move to California. She donated the huge mansion to the Superior Children's Home and Refuge Association in 1920, specifying that the house could be used for a Protestant home for children and unwed mothers. Soon, the lush interiors were converted to meet the needs of rambunctious children. In 42 years, more than two thousand orphans lived in the house. In 1962, changes in the state's child welfare law made the orphanage obsolete. Once again, the great house was vacant.

Just as it was about to be demolished the following year, the city of Superior acquired the property and converted Fairlawn into a historical museum. Between 1996 and 1998, a vast community effort restored the building to its original appearance. The structure—home to millionaires and orphans—became a showplace of art and craftsmanship.

What would it have been like to live in such a large and luxurious home? What kind of life would you lead had you been one of the Pattison children in the early 1890s? Likewise, what would life have been like for an orphan in the same time period?

Douglas County Historical Society

Orphans at Fairlawn

INDUSTRY

Topic	Secondary Source Materials	Primary Source Material
Cold Hard Profit: Ice Harvesting in Wisconsin	Mollenhoff, David. *Madison: A History of the Formative Years*. 2nd ed. Madison, WI: University of Wisconsin Press, 2003. Krudwig, James. "Harvest of Ice: The Miller-Rasmussen Ice Company." *Voyageur* 1 (December 1984): 20–25.	The Wisconsin Historical Society Archives Web site at http://arcat.library.wisc.edu/
Hogs on Wheels: The Evolution of the Harley-Davidson Motor Company	Bolfert, Thomas C. *The Big Book of Harley-Davidson*. Milwaukee, WI: Motorbooks, 1989. Reed, Peter. *Well Made In America: Lessons from Harley-Davidson on Being the Best*. New York: McGraw-Hill, 1990. Teerlink, Rich and Lee Ozley. *More Than a Motorcycle: The Leadership Journey at Harley-Davidson*. Boston, MA: Harvard Business School Press, 2000. Wagner, Herbert. *At the Creation: Myth, Reality, and the Origin of the Harley-Davidson Motorcycle, 1901–1909*. Madison, WI: Wisconsin Historical Society Press, 2003.	The Wisconsin Historical Society Archives Web site at http://arcat.library.wisc.edu/ The Harley-Davidson Company Web site at http://www.harleydavidson.com/
Superior Shipbuilding: Quintuplets and the War!	Thompson, William. *The History of Wisconsin, Volume VI: Continuity and Change, 1940–1965*. Madison, WI: State Historical Society of Wisconsin, 1988.	The Wisconsin Historical Society Archives Web site at http://arcat.library.wisc.edu/

Topic	Secondary Source Materials	Primary Source Material
Boom to Bust: The Brownstone Industry of Chequamegon Bay	The National Park Service's Apostle Islands Web site at http://www.nps.gov/apis/ Holzhueter, John. *Madeline Island and the Chequamegon Region.* Madison, WI: State Historical Society of Wisconsin, 1986.	Eckert, Kathryn Bishop. *The Sandstone Architecture of the Lake Superior Region.* Detroit, MI: Wayne State University Press, 2000. See the bibliography section for sources. Northern Great Lakes History Center and Archives: 715-685-2647.
From Lead to Zinc: The Mining Heyday in Southwest Wisconsin	Smith, Alice. *The History of Wisconsin, Volume I: From Exploration to Statehood.* Madison, WI: State Historical Society of Wisconsin, 1985. Conzen, Michael. "The European Settling and Transformation of the Upper Mississippi Valley Lead Mining Region." In *Wisconsin Land and Life.* Madison, WI: University of Wisconsin Press, 1997. Fiedler, George. *Mineral Point: A History,* 3rd ed. Mineral Point, WI: Memorial Pendarvis Endowment Trust Fund, 1986.	The Shullsburg Historic District (Badger Mine and Museum) Web site at http://wicip.uwplatt.edu/lafayette/ci/shullsburg/ The Mining Museum Web site at http://www.platteville.com/mining_museum.htm The Pendarvis Web site at http://www.wisconsinhistory.org/pendarvis The Wisconsin Historical Society Archives Catalog Web site at http://arcat.library.wisc.edu/ keywords: lead mining
Allis-Chalmers: Manufacturing for Manufacturers	Nesbit, Robert C. *The History of Wisconsin, Volume III: Urbanization and Industrialization, 1873–1893.* Madison, WI: State Historical Society of Wisconsin, 1985.	The Wisconsin Historical Society Archives Catalog at http://arcat.library.wisc.edu/ keywords: Allis-Chalmers

Topic	Secondary Source Material	Primary Source Material
D.C. Everest: Building Wisconsin's Paper Industries	Karge, Steven Burton. "David Clark Everest and Marathon Paper Mills Company: A Study of a Wisconsin Entrepreneur 1909–1931." PhD diss. University of Wisconsin-Madison, 1968. *Wisconsin History: An Annotated Bibliography.* Compiled by Barbara Dotts Paul and Justus Paul. Westport, CT: Greenwood Press, 1999. *Mapping Wisconsin History.* Wisconsin Cartographers Guild and Bobbie Malone, eds. Madison, WI: State Historical Society of Wisconsin, 2000. Wisconsin Cartographers Guild. *Wisconsin's Past and Present.* Madison, WI: University of Wisconsin Press, 1998. *Cultural Resource Management in Wisconsin.* Madison, WI: Historical Preservation Division, State Historical Society of Wisconsin, 1986. Malone, Bobbie and Jefferson Gray. *Working with Water: Wisconsin Waterways.* Madison, WI: Wisconsin Historical Society Press, 2001.	The Wisconsin Historical Society Archives Catalog Web site at http://arcat.library.wisc.edu/ keyword: D.C. Everest
Badger Ordnance: How Wisconsin Helped Win World War II	Thompson, William F. *The History of Wisconsin, Volume VI: Continuity and Change, 1940–1965.* Madison, WI: State Historical Society of Wisconsin, 1988.	The Wisconsin Historical Society Archives Catalog Web site at http://arcat.library.wisc.edu/ keywords: Badger Ordnance

Topic	Secondary Source	Primary Source Material
Silent Service: Manitowoc's Submarine Industry in World War II	Nelson, William T. *Fresh Water Submarines: the Manitowoc Story*. Alexandria, VA: W.T. Nelson, 1986. Lyman, Robert L. "The Momentous Moment: The Submarine Building Program at the Manitowoc Shipyards in World War II." Manitowoc: Manitowoc Historical Society (Occupational Monograph 37), 1979. Steven R. Milquet. "A Lakeshore Legacy: Manitowoc Submarines." *Voyageur* 6, no. 1, 1989.	The Wisconsin Maritime Museum Web site at http://www.wimaritimemuseum.org/
Soldiers without Guns: Milwaukee Women during World War II	Thompson, William. *The History of Wisconsin, Volume VI: Continuity and Change, 1940–1965*. Madison, WI: State Historical Society of Wisconsin, 1988.	*Voices of the Wisconsin Past: Women Remember the War, 1941–1945*. Michael E. Stevens, ed. Madison, WI: Center for Documentary History, State Historical Society of Wisconsin, 1993.
Sawdust Cities: How Lumber Mills Created Towns	Nesbit, Robert C. *The History of Wisconsin, Vol. III: Urbanization and Industrialization, 1873–1893*. Madison, WI: State Historical Society of Wisconsin, 1985. Pfaff, Tim. *Settlement and Survival: Building Towns in the Chippewa Valley, 1850–1925*. Eau Claire, WI: Chippewa Valley Museum Press, 1994.	The Wisconsin Historical Society Archives Web site at http://arcat.library.wisc.edu/ keywords: Eau Claire, water, power, and mills
Fairlawn: From Millionaire's Mansion to Orphan's Home	Mershart, Ronald. *Frontier Village: The Birth of Superior, Wisconsin*. Superior, WI: Douglas County Historical Society, 2003.	The Superior Public Museum (Fairlawn) Web site at http://www.superiorpublicmuseums.org/

Chapter Six

Agriculture

Prisoner
To Work
Hands in

Branch Camp Is
Established at
Tri-City Airport

A branch prisoner of war camp
was opened here Sunday at the Tri-
City Airport to provide agriculture
and food processing labor and to
meet the extreme shortage in seasonal field workers in this immediate area. The announcement was
authorized by Colonel George J.
Sheridan, Ill. The prisoners started
their jobs today with the first
going to a number

CHARLES KOSS,
HERM. T. KOSS.

Chas. Koss & Bro.

IMPORTED
AND
DOMESTIC

HOPS

BREWERS' & BOTTLERS'
SUPPLIES.
85
WEST-WATER ST.
MILWAUKEE.

J.I. Case
Industry for Agriculture

In the 1800s, wheat harvesting could be a complicated venture. Wheat fetched a high price, but harvesting it often proved problematic. Wheat ripens all at once, so a farmer has to cut and gather it within days before the wheat shatters. Traditional techniques and tools for harvesting grain limited farmers. They could harvest only two or three acres in a day. But, farms frequently consisted of many acres, and labor was scarce. Jerome Increase Case's agricultural innovations changed much of this picture by increasing efficiency and productivity.

Born in 1816 in Oswego County, New York, Case had ambitions at a young age. In 1842, at age 23, he left New York for Rochester in the Wisconsin Territory. A newspaper account had declared the area surrounding Rochester to be the Midwest's wheat center. This convinced Case that it was the perfect region for him to create and market his threshers.

Before leaving New York, Case purchased six "ground hog" threshers on credit. He sold five of them before reaching Wisconsin Territory and used the sixth to make a living. While in Rochester, Case made an improvement to the simple "ground hog" thresher. He made the new machine beat out and separate the wheat kernels from the straw.

Case planned to build a shop in Rochester and

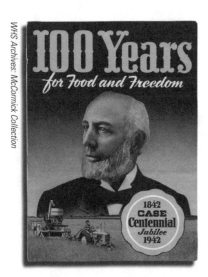

100 Years for Food and Freedom

1842 CASE Centennial Jubilee 1942

Case promotional brochure from 1942

Case logo on a piece of machinery

manufacture his improved machines there. However, the owners of the water power rights to the Fox River dam denied him permission to install yet another mill-race and wheel. Undeterred, Case moved east to Racine, where he used the water power from Lake Michigan for his operations. He rented a small shop and began to build his threshers. In 1847, Case built a three-story brick shop in Racine, which became the core of his farm implements business.

With three partners, Case created J.I. Case and Company in 1863. He and the others—Massena Erskine, Robert Baker, and Stephen Bull—became known as the Big Four. In the 1860s, Case recognized the need for a new power source for his threshers. Until that time, the machines had run on treadmill horsepower. In 1869, Case produced his first steam engine. It was the first engine used for agriculture, and the actual engine is now housed in the Smithsonian Institution in Washington, DC. Eventually, Case and Company became the world's larger producer of steam engines.

In 1880, the Big Four partnership was dissolved, and the J.I. Case Threshing Machine Company was incorporated. Throughout the decade, Case continued to make his presence known to farmers in meaningful ways. Case died on December 22, 1891, and was buried in Mound Cemetery in Racine, but his company and the agriculture legacy he created lives on.

Thirty years after his death, Case's company announced plans to build a $200,000 foundry in Mt. Pleasant, south of Racine. Three years later, in 1913, the new J. I. Case South Works consisted of a foundry, a power plant, a two-story machine shop, and a four-story warehouse. The original foundry at the South Works, which still operates today, remained the same size until a substantial addition in 1966. The machine shop and assembly areas continued to grow, with new additions every few years.

Since 1912, the Case company has diversified into construction equipment, producing road-building machines. It acquired several companies in the process, starting with the American Tractor Corporation in 1957. In 1985, through its parent company Tenneco, Inc., the company acquired some of the assets of International Harvester. By the mid-1990s, the company was the world's leading manufacturer of light- and medium-sized

Catalog page showing Case tractor available in 1918

Getting Started on Research

Reynold Wik's article "J. I. Case: Some Experiences of an Early Wisconsin Industrialist" in the *Wisconsin Magazine of History* traces the history of Case's early innovations and business practices. John Thompson's "Rise and Decline of the Wheat Growing Industry in Wisconsin" in the *Economics and Political Science Series* bulletin examines the historical and geographical aspects of wheat production in the state.

For primary material, the J. I. Case papers are in the Wisconsin Historical Society. You can also look through local newspapers from the period to find stories about late nineteenth- and early twentieth-century agricultural developments in your state and community.

construction equipment. It merged with New Holland to become CNH Global in 1999. J. I. Case's dream of helping farmers had grown way beyond even his own enormous imagination.

Think about the current state of agriculture. What are the major issues surrounding agriculture in Wisconsin? What processes and challenges are different from the ones in Case's lifetime? How are they similar? How has productivity and efficiency changed? What equipment or process has made the greatest impact? What do you think the future of Wisconsin's agriculture businesses will be like?

From Wheat to Dairy
How a Little Bug Made America's Dairyland

A crew of farm laborers take a break from harvesting wheat in Dane County, undated.

In the 1860s, southern and western Wisconsin were major wheat-producing areas. In fact, the state itself ranked third in the nation. Raising wheat was relatively easy for farmers, because crops required little attention between sowing and harvesting. Mechanized harvesting and threshing equipment increased yields, and Wisconsin's wheat crop helped make Milwaukee a major shipper of grain.

Then, disaster struck. In the late 1860s, tiny insects known as chinch bugs began devouring Wisconsin wheat crops. Farmers faced not only declining yields but falling prices. Large new lands for wheat farming opened on the prairies, particularly in Minnesota and the Dakotas, and Wisconsin farmers who did not follow the wheat west realized they needed to find a new source of income quickly. Dairying was an alternative, and it became a profitable, though labor intensive, answer to heading off economic woes.

Today, everyone knows that Wisconsin is a leading producer of milk and other dairy products. Our license plates proclaim Wisconsin as "America's Dairyland." Cheeseheads are familiar sights at Green Bay Packer games. However, fewer people know that during the mid-1800s, Wisconsin was a wheat-producing state. As the United States expanded westward, newly settled areas like Ohio, Indiana, Illinois, and Wisconsin became the nation's breadbasket. They fed America's growing population, as farms in New England were gradually wearing down.

Several reasons account for the rapid rise of the dairy industry in Wisconsin. First, many migrants from New York settled in the southern part of the state. At that time, New York was famous for its high-quality butter and cheese and was the leading dairy producer in the United States. These

New Yorkers brought with them their knowledge of commercial dairying. They convinced local farmers to invest in cattle that were better for milking. Also, they built cheese factories in many small towns. In fact, a New York native named Chester Hazen built Wisconsin's first neighborhood cheese factory at Fond du Lac.

Second, the University of Wisconsin actively promoted dairying through scientific research. William A. Henry, who became the university's first professor of agriculture in 1880, used the university's farm to experiment with new dairying methods. Dairying could not have been successful here if farmers had not found a way to store silage, or cattle feed, through the winter without having it spoil. The university promoted the use of cylindrical silos, which were innovations from the 1880s and 1890s. UW professor Stephen Babcock developed the first test for butterfat content in milk. The College of Agricul- ture pioneered testing for bacteria in milk and developed practical ways to pasteurize it.

To educate farmers about the benefits of dairying, in 1887, the University of Wisconsin began offering agricultural "short courses" and "winter courses" on the Madison campus. The university also hosted "farmers' institutes" around the state, which brought farmers and scientists together to share their knowledge.

Photograph by Steven Krauth, University of Wisconsin Department of Entomology

Photo of a chinch bug specimen

Getting Started on Research

Wisconsin's dairy industry is described very well in the PhD dissertation "The Rise of the Dairy Industry in Wisconsin" by Eric Lampard. For more on the role of the University of Wisconsin, find *Farm and College: The College of Agriculture of the University of Wisconsin* by Wilbur H. Glover. An online search of Wisconsin's dairy industry will provide several firsthand accounts and primary documents from inside Wisconsin's creameries, dairies, and cheese factories. Also, visit the Wisconsin Historical Society Archives (ArCat) Web site at http://arcat.library.wisc.edu/.

Finally, many Germans and Scandinavian immigrant families were quick to adopt dairying as a profitable way to run a farm. They took up the hard work of milking cows and delivering the milk to cheese factories. These immigrants also specialized in making European-style cheeses that appealed to consumers. Soon, Wisconsin became known for its Swiss cheese, but its Limburger cheese was popular as well. Today, Monroe cheese makers are the sole producers of Limburger cheese in the United States!

Wisconsin's dairy farms continue to be important elements of the state's economy (despite the fact that California recently surpassed the state in overall production). Much of modern Wisconsin dairying, however, would never have been possible unless a little bug had forced farmers to give up wheat production.

In what other ways have universities in Wisconsin encouraged the state's hardworking farmers to produce milk for creameries and cheese factories? What impact has been made by people from other states and countries on Wisconsin's dairy industry?

The University of Wisconsin Extension

Education for the People

The University of Wisconsin is known for its sprawling campus in Madison and several smaller campuses located throughout the state. The Badgers play Saturday afternoon football at Camp Randall Stadium, where several hall-of-famers played during their college days. But one of the most influential, yet least known, divisions of the university is the University Extension.

Founded in 1849, the University of Wisconsin began as a public institution. People believed that a democratic state required educated citizens and that the state had an obligation to provide a publicly funded college education to anyone who wanted it. Gradually, some at the university decided it could do even more for the people of the state, whether or not they attended classes in Madison. The University Extension essentially "extended" the university to all residents. It provided educational and cultural opportunities to everyone in every region of the state.

The University Extension was formally created in 1891, but its origins date back to

Poster advertising a Farmer's Institute in Arcadia, Wisconsin, which was administered by the Extension Service, 1922–1924.

efforts by the UW School of Agriculture to provide practical instruction to farmers. In 1885, the school initiated the first "Short Course," a program that brought farmers to the campus to learn new scientific farming methods for improving the state's agricultural production. That same year, the state legislature approved funding for Farmer Institutes, which were university-run, two-day workshops for farmers at various locations throughout the state. These institutes quickly became popular. In the winter of 1887 and 1888, the Extension ran 81 institutes that were attended by some 50,000 farmers! Such university support of state agriculture contributed mightily to Wisconsin's becoming a major dairy producing state.

But much more was to come. The president

Farmers attending a meeting with instruction on agricultural practices, early twentieth century.

of the university, Thomas Chamberlin, had even bigger ideas. If the university could provide practical education for farmers, perhaps it could do so for other occupations. The Extension began to introduce college courses in cultural education, such as history, literature, and science. These courses could be brought to everyone throughout the state, rather than being the activity of only those full-time students who could afford to attend the university in Madison.

In 1891, Chamberlin inaugurated the first extension programs. University officials developed a curriculum of 10 subjects. These included American history, English literature, Scandinavian literature, Greek literature, economics, antiquities of India and Iran, bacteriology, plant physiology, electricity, and geology. The courses were taught by popular university professors. Within months, 43 extension classes were underway all over the state. These university courses met with overwhelming popular response. History professor Frederick Jackson Turner gave seven classes in seven different towns, each attended by some 200 people. During its first year of operation, cities and towns requested 107 courses, but the university only had the resources to offer 50.

Farmers being instructed in how to do the Babcock test, early twentieth century.

WHS Archives

In the early years of the twentieth century, the University Extension was reinvigorated under the leadership of University President Charles Van Hise. Van Hise firmly believed that a public university should offer benefits not only to its students but to the people of the state. He promoted extension courses tirelessly. "I shall never be content," he said in 1905, "until the beneficent influence of the University reaches every family in the state."

The university had much to offer. It provided two-week courses for farmers and housewives, literature on contemporary issues for school children and adults alike, and traveling professors who brought university courses into towns and villages across the state. Under Van Hise's leadership, the university led the nation in democratizing education by making the best scholarship available to everyone.

What kinds of courses do you think would have appealed to people living in your community in 1900? What accounts exist of extension courses being given in or near your community? Local libraries, newspapers, and historical societies in your area can provide access to archives about the early years of the Extension.

Getting Started on Research

An excellent source of information about the creation of the University Extension is *The University of Wisconsin: A History* by Merle Curti and Vernon Carstensen. The University of Wisconsin Extension still offers a variety of continuing education and public services to the people of Wisconsin. You can visit its Web site at http://www1.uwex.edu/.

Primary documents can be found in the Wisconsin Historical Society's archives in Madison or through its online catalog (ArCat) at http://arcat.library.wisc.edu/. Use the keywords "University of Wisconsin Extension."

A New Cash Crop
The Hops Craze of Southern Wisconsin

People inside and outside the state know that Wisconsin produces a vast array of agricultural products. Milk and cheese are perhaps the most famous, followed closely by cherries and cranberries. But in the 1860s, most farmers depended upon wheat crops to sustain them, and Wisconsin was a leading national producer of wheat. About that time, a disease called wheat rust destroyed many crops, and chinch bugs infested Wisconsin by the billions. This disastrous event pushed many Wisconsin farmers west, especially to Minnesota and the Dakotas where they could grow more wheat, more cheaply. Those farmers who remained in Wisconsin had to find alternatives. In order to remain profitable, farmers were forced to find new, different, and more manageable crops.

Laffan hop yard near Wisconsin Dells, Wisconsin

WHI 215-1 (X3) 8323

Sauk County Historical Society

Needle and thimble used to sew bales of hops for shipping.

For some, hops seemed to be the answer. Hops' vines produce cone-like, green flowers. These contain bitter, aromatic oils, which are used in the making of beer. Dried hops give beer its "bite." Since the 1840s, people in the state had grown hops in small quantities, but the demand for the crop increased dramatically in the 1860s and 70s. As large numbers of Germans settled in Wisconsin, they brought with them an enjoyment of beer and traditional brewing methods. Almost every little community in the state had its own brewery. People found locally produced hops cheaper to purchase than commercially grown hops from the Atlantic states. The Civil War, too, increased the demand for hops as soldiers traveling away from home learned to like the taste of beer.

The big hops craze occurred in 1867. In New York and other eastern states, an infestation of the hop louse ruined crops, which drove up already-high prices. In 1861, one pound of hops sold for 25 cents. By 1867, however, the price for one pound

Getting Started on Research

To learn more about Wisconsin agriculture in the 1860s and 1870s, read chapter 13 of *The History of Wisconsin, Volume II: The Civil War Era, 1848–1873* by Richard Current. An outstanding source on Wisconsin's brief time as the "Hop King" is "Hop Culture in Early Sauk County," by Belle C. Bohn in the *Wisconsin Magazine of History.* You can contact the Sauk County Historical Society to see its collection of documents and artifacts from the hops craze.

was nearly 70 cents. As more and more farmers saw an opportunity, the state's total production increased from 135,587 pounds in 1861 to almost 7 million pounds in 1867!

Sauk County became the center of hops production in Wisconsin. In the 1860s, wheat dominated the county's agricultural production, but the lure of better profits from hops proved irresistible. In 1867, Sauk County alone grew one-fifth of the total crop of hops in the nation and brought in $1.5 million to county farmers! The boom was a benefit to laborers as well. When the hops were ready to be harvested, workers—including many women and children—came from far away to pick the crop. They could earn upwards of $2 per day, which was a remarkable wage for the time.

But all good things must end, and the hops craze was short-lived. In 1868, Wisconsin farmers set a record for harvesting 11 million pounds of hops. Unfortunately, that same year the eastern hops crop recovered, and the markets were flooded with a greater supply of hops

than the market demanded. The price dropped from 70 cents per pound to 10 cents per pound, which did not even cover the cost of production! Many disappointed farmers abandoned hops after that. A few farmers again tried raising the crop the following year, but they encountered the same market conditions. It only increased their losses.

After the hops craze of the 1860s, farmers kept looking for a new crop that would bring them steady profits. Sugar beets were popular for a time, as were flax (used to make linen cloth) and hemp. But not until dairying in the 1880s did Wisconsin farmers find a sure way to make consistent profits from the land. In the 1890s, dairy surpassed wheat as Wisconsin's most profitable form of agricultural enterprise.

What crops did farmers in your county raise in the 1870s? Are those crops still produced on a large scale? What, if anything, replaced them? What crops did Wisconsin farmers grow in the 1900s? How have things changed today? Your teacher or librarian can help you find histories that describe the evolution of agricultural progress in the nineteenth and twentieth centuries.

Sauk County Historical Society

Advertising card for a hops broker

Native Fruits

Wisconsin's Cranberry Industry

The American cranberry is one of the fruits native to the continent. Cranberries can be found along the northern United States from Maine to Wisconsin, and along the Appalachians to North Carolina. Cranberries are harvested for fresh fruit or are processed into products such as juice, craisens, or sauce. Until the 1940s, most people used hand-held scoops or mechanical harvesters to gather cranberries. Cranberry beds at that time were not artificially flooded, but more efficient water harvesting started in Wisconsin in the 1920s with a shallow flood method. A deeper flood method was developed in the early 1960s. Controlled artificial flooding works well because the air pockets in cranberries make them buoyant and therefore more easily harvested. Soon, all growers began water harvesting most of their acreage.

The story of cranberries in Wisconsin begins with the Native people living in the area. Wisconsin Indians used the cranberries they found for nutritional, medicinal, and decorative purposes. They gathered the berries for pemmican, a mixture of dried meat or fish and berries that was reduced to a pulp, shaped into a cake, and dried in the sun. They ate berries raw or cooked them into a sauce sweetened with maple sugar. Native people also combined cranberries with cornmeal to cure blood poisoning and processed them to treat sores and wounds. The juice from cranberries was also used as a textile dye.

On the northeast Atlantic coast, European colonists, too, recognized cranberries as a significant food source. They called the fruit "craneberry" probably because the flower, before it expands, resembles a crane. The name may also be rooted in the cranes' preference for the small, vibrant berries. Over the years, the name transformed into "cranberry." Settlers also found cranberries to be an excellent source of vitamin C. During long voyages, sailors consumed them to ward off scurvy, a disease caused by a lack of vitamin C in the body. Other sailors used limes for the same purpose, particularly the British.

Henry Hall, a farmer from Massachusetts, first cultivated cranberries in the United States. He noted that his vines flourished when exposed to dune sand. (Hall's observation is still used today. Modern cranberry beds receive a layer of sand every three to four years to promote new root and upright growth.) In 1816, he transplanted the stronger vines into a fenced area. The vines flourished,

Cranberry processing, date unknown

WHi (X3) 46033

Wisconsin Cranberry Company handbill from the late nineteenth century

and by 1820, he was sending cranberries to markets in Boston and New York City. To facilitate shipping, cranberries were packed in water in barrels holding 100 pounds of fruit. The barrel weighing 100 pounds became the standard measure of cranberry production, and this unique measurement is still employed today.

In the late 1800s, several factors influenced expansion in the cranberry industry. In the 1860s, Reverend Benjamin Eastwood's book on cranberry cultivation generated greater interest and expertise in the field. The railroad system, which could move cargo from one place to another more quickly and affordably, also contributed to the industry's growth.

In 1860, Edward Sacket arrived in Berlin, Wisconsin, and began cultivating cranberries on his land. Others in the area followed Sacket's lead, spawning an economic boom for the next two decades. Cranberry growing spread to Jackson, Juneau, Monroe, and Wood counties.

In 1874, cranberry production reached a peak of 30,000 barrels. But, the rain and floods of 1881 and frost of September 1882 greatly damaged Berlin's cranberry industry. By 1883, production had plummeted to only 3,000 barrels. In addition, acreage in other parts of the country continued to increase. The Berlin industry harvested a mere 27,640 acres as the years of the Great Depression were coming. Harvesting decreased even further from the 1920s to the 1940s because of the economic downturn and a disease in the eastern acreage.

However, cranberry growing rebounded in the late 1960s. Today, Wisconsin produces more cranberries than any other state in the nation. About 250 growers cultivate cranberries in 20 Wisconsin counties, making cranberries the state's number one fruit crop. More than 300 million pounds of fruit are produced annually. This is more than half of the 575 million or so pounds Americans consume yearly. According to the Wisconsin State Cranberry Growers Association, cranberry growing contributes more than $300 million to the state's economy and provides employment for some 7,000 people.

What impact has the cranberry industry made on your community? Do businesses in your area use cranberries? If so, what products containing cranberries are produced there?

Getting Started on Research

Paul Eck's *The American Cranberry* is a good place to start gleaning information about the cranberry industry in the United States. For more specific Wisconsin references, consult the United States Department of Agriculture or the Wisconsin State Cranberry Growers Association for statistics. The archives of the Wisconsin Historical Society contain photographs and documents from the past and present cranberry industry. You can find them by searching under the keywords "cranberry industry and Wisconsin" at the Wisconsin Historical Society Archives Web site at http://arcat.library.wisc.edu/.

The Milk Strikes
Dairy Farmers Respond to Low Prices

WHS Archives, Milwaukee Journal photo

Deputies waving nightsticks while guarding milk trucks, near Walworth-Waukesha county line, March 15, 1933.

In the 1930s, the United States endured a major economic crisis known as the Great Depression. For 10 years, the country struggled with high unemployment, loss of industrial production, and agricultural problems. Many people could barely afford to buy food, clothing, and other necessities. They stopped buying some things altogether.

This decline in purchasing caused a ripple effect in almost every area of America's industries. Unemployment grew as stores and factories had to lay off workers. Farmers were hit particularly hard. Even though people in towns and cities were desperate for food, they could not afford to buy farm produce at the prices that farmers required to stay in business! In Wisconsin, dairy farmers had a very tough time. Running their farms cost a lot of money, but milk prices were so low that many couldn't afford to keep going and went bankrupt.

Dairy farmers began suffering from falling prices in 1930. A year earlier,

Wisconsin farmers received about two dollars per hundred pounds of milk. By 1933, however, they could only get 85 cents for the same amount! Further decline in prices came as increasing numbers of people simply could not afford to buy much milk. Adding to the problem was the fact that the dairies were paying farmers lower and lower prices for the milk they sold. As more milk got produced than could be consumed, farmers were forced to sell their product at rock bottom prices.

As a result, some desperate farmers began to organize themselves in an attempt to assert more control over this situation. In 1932, Walter M. Singler formed the Wisconsin Cooperative Milk Pool. Singler encouraged farmers to demand a price that truly reflected their cost. At the time, this price was estimated at $1.40 per hundred pounds of milk. And, if markets would not pay the prices, the farmers withheld the milk. By February 1933, 67,000 farmers had joined the milk pool. By keeping milk from the market, farmers in the Fox Valley were able to shut down area dairies and factories producing cheese and butter. To expand the strike, the pool farmers blockaded roads and highways. Anyone who tried to get past them had

WHi (X3) 27919

Protestors dumping milk taken from stopped train, near Burlington, January 10, 1934.

their milk dumped onto the road! In several counties, sheriff's deputies used tear gas and clubs to break up these roadblocks. After Governor Albert Schmedeman agreed to study the problems dairy farmers faced, the strike was called off.

By May, however, when nothing had been done, pool farmers called a second strike. This time, the governor was prepared and ordered that milk not be sold in the 21 counties where the milk pool was strongest. The adjutant general put 2,500 national guardsmen on the roads to keep them open for milk producers. But the strikers adopted guerrilla tactics. Sometimes, they would spring upon a milk truck, dump out its contents, and scatter before the guardsmen appeared with their tear gas and guns. In Waukesha County, guardsmen with bayonets scattered blockading farmers in a violent encounter known as the "Battle of Durham Hill." Farmers were stunned by this response. City folks were angry with the farmers for striking and cutting off their milk supply. And when a third strike occurred in November, it was even more violent when seven cheese factories were bombed!

In the end, the strikes proved ineffective. They failed to solve the farmers' basic problem. They simply were not making enough money to pay for the production of their milk. The strikes also discouraged farm leaders from turning to the state and federal government for help. Franklin D. Roosevelt's

Getting Started on Research

Your librarian can help you find newspapers from the 1930s that describe the milk strikes. Even a brief search in libraries, historical societies, and the Web will bring results, because so much has been written about the strikes.

An excellent secondary source is *The History of Wisconsin, Volume V: War, a New Era, and Depression, 1914–1940* by Paul W. Glad. Read pages 409 to 419. You might also want to read "The Wisconsin Milk Strikes" in the *Wisconsin Magazine of History.* You can find a map of the Milk Strikes on page 72 of *Wisconsin's Past and Present: An Historical Atlas.* The visual archives at the Wisconsin Historical Society has several wonderful photographs from the tense encounter at Durham Hill.

New Deal programs helped many farmers. But it was not until WWII, when demand for milk greatly increased, that dairy farmers finally began to see real prosperity.

How was your community affected by the Great Depression? How did the events and federal programs of the 1930s affect farmers in your county? Was your county one of the 21 counties on which the governor ordered the embargo? What evidence remains in your community, city, or state that there ever was a series of milk strikes? Are milk and dairy cooperatives still around? What purpose do these cooperatives serve and what needs do they meet in your community today?

WHI (X3) 45437

Guardsmen charging with bayonets at Durham Hill during the milk strike, May 18, 1933.

Milk and Cheese Paradise
Wisconsin's Dairy Industry

Although dairy production, and in particular cheese, seems to many people to be the signature industry of Wisconsin, it wasn't always so. The cattle industry appeared in Detroit as early as 1707. Some cattle were distributed to various French outposts, and others were brought to Wisconsin by the British and American fur trade. Other importers of cattle included the Galena district lead miners and the U.S. Army. But these cattle were beef animals. Not until 1838, did Morgan Martin introduced milking stock to the state.

In the 1850s and 1860s, wheat trumped dairy by a large margin. At that time, the dairy industry was small and unassuming. Producing dairy products for a mass market was not common at all. Instead, farmers utilized their milk, butter, and cheese in their own households and exchanged a small percentage of these products with local stores for groceries. The market for dairy was virtually non-existent.

But by the late 1860s, wheat was on the decline because of overuse of the land, crop diseases, chinch bug infestation, and reduced prices. It was then that dairy businesses started to grow. In 1867, Wisconsin had 245,000 dairy cows. By 1912, that number had risen to 1,460,000! Two years later, the state was producing three million pounds of cheese. Ten years later, that number had quadrupled.

Several factors contributed to dairy's rise. The land that was deemed unsuitable for wheat cultivation proved ideal for livestock pastures. And the populations entering Wisconsin at that time—New Englanders, New Yorkers, and northern European immigrants—were experienced dairy farmers. The College of Agriculture at the University of Wisconsin fostered science and organization, and farmers established professional associations in which they exchanged practical dairy knowledge with one another.

Unfortunately, the rapid rise of dairy production caused a surplus in the western market, the main buyer of Wisconsin's dairy products. In 1871, cheese prices fell

WHI Image ID 2039

Highway billboard advertising Wisconsin cheese, September 28, 1942.

WHI D487 13014

Cheesecurds, cheesemaking, 1936

154

WHi Image ID 2211, photo by Milwaukee Journal-Sentinel

Cheesemaker storing cheese, 1952.

butterfat in milk. The test permitted rapid and accurate grading of milk at markets, discouraged adulteration and thinning practices, and made the testing of an individual cow's milk practical. These measures promoted the development of advanced breeding techniques in dairies, so superior strains of cattle could be produced.

Today, dairy ranks as one of Wisconsin's best performing industries. Although California now has the nation's largest dairy industry, in 2001, Wisconsin took first place in cheese dry whey production and second in milk and butter production. In that same year, Wisconsin possessed 14% of the nation's milk cows, surpassed only by California.

How has the dairy industry affected your part of the state? What related industries have grown up around it?

to eight cents per pound, and butter prices were equally dismal. To prevent this situation from getting worse, dairy producers formed the Wisconsin Dairymen's Association in February 1872. The organization served as a forum for discussion of innovations and successes. It also became a way for dairy farmers to introduce and promote their products to the significant eastern and British markets. This proved to be a very successful move, mainly because it provided secure dairy prices.

In 1887, the University of Wisconsin's College of Agriculture opened its Dairy School, the first of its kind in the nation. The school trained butter- and cheese-makers, while faculty and researchers spurred innovations. From 1887 to 1913, for example, Stephen Moulton Babcock was a professor of agricultural chemistry and chief chemist of the Wisconsin Agricultural Experiment Station. In 1890, he created the Babcock test, which measured the percentage of

Getting Started on Research

For a history of the state's dairy industry, consult *Wisconsin History: An Annotated Bibliography*, compiled by Barbara Dotts Paul and Justus F. Paul. The text has a series of entries for dairy in its subject index. Robert C. Nesbit's *Wisconsin: A History* also gives detailed background on dairy in Wisconsin. The *State of Wisconsin Blue Book*, compiled by the Legislative Reference Bureau, is also a useful source. The Wisconsin Agriculture Statistics Service Web site can be accessed at http://www.nass.usda.gov/wi/. The Wisconsin Department of Commerce Web site is at http://www.commerce.state.wi.us/. This site provides current data on dairy profits and production. The online archives of the Wisconsin Historical Society (ArCat) can be accessed at http://arcat.library.wisc.edu/. The archives contain numerous photographs, records, and other documents related to the dairy industry. Use the guided search online and type in keywords "dairy industry in Wisconsin."

German POWs
Easing Wisconsin's Agricultural Labor Shortages

Did you know that Wisconsin held German prisoners of war during World War II? Why were these POWs brought to Wisconsin and other parts of the United States in the first place? The Japanese attack on Pearl Harbor on December 7, 1941, brought America into the war. But by then, the war was well into its third year. The United Kingdom had been saddled not only with the task of fighting Adolf Hitler's German forces, but also with catering to the needs of the growing number of German POWs. Rumors began to circulate that Hitler planned to air-drop weapons to the several hundred thousand German POWs held in the UK. This would provide the German soldiers with weapons and avoid an actual military invasion by Germany itself. Soon, the United States reluctantly consented to take custody of all POWs who had been captured in the UK after November 1942.

Practically and militarily, the agreement posed problems. Transporting, imprisoning, guarding, and providing food for the POWs stateside (and overseas, too, for that matter) diverted troops and supply ships that could otherwise be used more directly in the Allied war effort. To keep some of the costs down, POWs coming to the United States

POWs stationed at Wisconsin Rapids during WWII are seen here working at the Bennett Cranberry Farm.

WHi (X3) 44179

traveled on returning empty ships and stayed at military bases that already had housing. These measures kept states from diverting resources into the construction of special centers to house the prisoners.

Once the POWs were in this country, they became useful in helping solve war-related labor shortages. The 1929 Geneva Convention and subsequent Red Cross Accords dictated that POWs could be used for labor as long as (1) officers were not forced to work, (2) the work was not directly related to the war effort, (3) the work did not endanger prisoners' safety and well-being, and (4) the work was not demeaning. Also, the workers were to be paid for their labor.

As people moved into urban centers for better-paying industrial jobs, it created severe

Wisconsin Rapids Daily Tribune

Prisoners of War To Work as Field Hands in This Area

Branch Camp Is Established at Tri-City Airport

A branch prisoner of war camp was opened here Sunday at the Tri-City Airport to provide agricultural and food processing labor and to meet the extreme shortage in seasonal field workers in this immediate area. The announcement was authorized by Colonel George H. Cushman, post commander of Fort Sheridan, Ill. The prisoners started on their jobs today with the first work details going to a number of cranberry marshes in the Central Wisconsin area. There are about 160 in the contingent according to Lt. Col. E. R. Schuelke, commander of the base prisoner of war camp at Fort Sheridan.

Captain Thomas R. Ryan of Detroit, Mich., is the commanding officer of the local camp.

Revamp Airport As Camp

The Wisconsin State Cranberry Growers association, of which Wm. F. Thiele is president and Vernon C. Goldsworthy is secretary, is acting as the contracting agent in the assignment of the prisoner of war...

Avoid Fraternization

BEST FOR PUBLIC TO IGNORE POW'S, SHERIFF STATES

"According to army advices, the best thing for the civilian population of Wisconsin Rapids and Wood county to do during the stay of prisoners of war here is to ignore them," Sheriff Henry J. Becker said today in commenting on the establishment of a branch German P. O. W. camp at the Tri-City airport and warning against trespassing on the grounds or violating other regulations.

The army does not presume to govern the conduct of local residents, Sheriff Becker pointed out, but there are certain restrictions which must be observed, any breach of which will bring prompt investigation. "Nobody is to enter the area which will be designated as a military compound and the boundaries will be patrolled regularly to discourage the curiosity seekers," the sheriff stated.

Front page headlines, *Wisconsin Rapids Daily Tribune,* May 7, 1945

labor shortages in rural agricultural areas. So, POWs filled the void. These POWs performed the same tasks as migrant agricultural workers, moving from crop to crop during harvest time. They picked corn, cherries, potatoes, beans, and other fruits and vegetables. They cut pulp wood in state forests and worked in dairies that produced canned or powdered milk and ice cream. In many of these locations, they worked alongside civilians.

At its peak, Camp McCoy in Wisconsin housed 9,000 POWs captured in the European and Pacific war zones. In addition, Fort Sheridan kept nearly 13,000 more POWs at the 38 branch camps stationed across the state. By the end of the war, Wisconsin was hosting more than three times as many POWs as Minnesota. For the economy in Wisconsin, POWs earned an estimated $3.3 million.

Patriotism brought on by the war effort and other factors discouraged cooperation with many POWs, and the media offered minimal coverage. The rural settings where the prisoners lived and worked

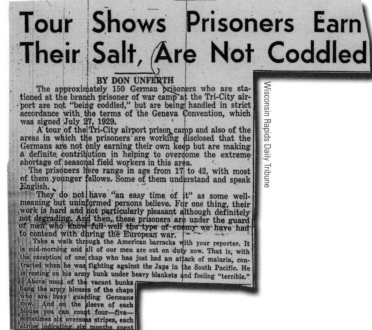

Front page headlines, *Wisconsin Rapids Daily Tribune,* May 7, 1945

kept contact with civilians at a minimum. So much so, that most Americans were unaware of their presence.

After the war, some prisoners wanted to stay in the United States. But, post-war policy dictated that all prisoners were to be returned to their home countries. The Secretary of Agriculture and some members of Congress lobbied the War Department to retain the prisoners for crop harvesting. President Truman announced a compromise: POWs would not be sent back for 60 days to allow them to help with the current harvest. All POWs, however, were to be sent back home by June 1946, and this is when the last POW left Wisconsin.

Were there POW camps in your county or POWs working there during World War II? Your local library or local historical society can help you investigate.

Getting Started on Research

Betty Cowley's *Stalag Wisconsin: Inside WWII Prisoner of War Camps* provides significant secondary information about daily life in the camps. It also includes the historical background that brought the prisoners to the camps and the social and economic effects of the prisoners' presence in Wisconsin.

Primary sources can be found in the Wisconsin Historical Society Archives, which contains photographs of prisoners held at Waupun and documents collected by Paul Mueckler regarding the POW facilities at Camp (now Fort) McCoy. Some of these are listed in the resource section and can be used as keywords for searches through the Wisconsin Historical Society's online archive catalog.

The Ho-Chunk Bison Ranch
Restoration of Native Community

In the 1800s, vast herds of bison roamed the Great Plains. These bison (usually called buffalo by non-Indian settlers) were critical to the survival of Native American tribes west of the Mississippi River. Bison provided not only food but also clothing and shelter—bison hides made warm robes and durable tepees. In 1800, an estimated 40 million bison existed in North America. But, by the 1880s, they had been hunted to near-extinction by American settlers and sportsmen, and only a few remained in captivity. Their destruction doomed American Indian communities, like the Lakota, who lost their principal source of food. The extinction of the bison was one of the great environmental disasters of American history. But today a few Native communities are working to restore the bison population.

As early as 1889, some recognized the growing tragedy of the bison's demise. In that year, William T. Hornady, superintendent of the National Zoological Park, reported on

Bison called "grandfather" from the Muscoda Bison Ranch.

the fate of the bison. He recommended saving a few specimens in order to keep the species alive. His advice was heeded, and today all bison in the United States are descended from those few hundred that were saved.

Today, the Ho-Chunk Nation of Wisconsin is working to preserve and restore the population of American bison. Historically, the Ho-Chunk lived in southern Wisconsin and northern Illinois and spoke a language similar to that of the Lakota people farther west. Both peoples used the bison for food and clothing. Into the 1820s, bison could be found in western Wisconsin (including Buffalo County, which is named for them). Non-Indian settlement, however, was the beginning of the end.

The federal government attempted to relocate the Ho-Chunk to Minnesota, South Dakota, and Nebraska, but the tribe was determined to keep its home. Many members of the Ho-Chunk Nation returned to

Herd of bison at the Muscoda Bison Ranch

Getting Started on Research

You can learn more about the American bison from the Wind Cave National Park's Web site at http://www.nps.gov/wica/bison.htm. The Ho-Chunk Nation's Muscoda ranch Web site can be accessed at http://www.muscodabison.com/. Tours are available (try to arrange an interview with someone working there). To learn more about the Ho-Chunk Nation, a good place to start is *Indian Nations of Wisconsin* by Patty Loew. A recent article about the bison ranch is "The Bison Will Return to Sauk Prairie" in the *Wisconsin Academy Review.*

Wisconsin, where they eventually purchased many parcels of land.

In 1993, the Ho-Chunk Nation joined the Inter-Tribal Bison Cooperative, a nonprofit group that assists American Indian nations in establishing their own bison herds. The Nation had just purchased a 639-acre farm near Muscoda along the Wisconsin River, and the site proved ideal for the bison. But the goal was not simply to own bison. The Ho-Chunk people wanted to restore the animals' natural habitat, allowing the bison to live in prairie conditions as they had in earlier centuries. The Nation joined the Bureau of Indian Affair's Circle of Flight program, which allowed tribal members to operate resource management programs. The herd started with only four bison, but within a few years, the herd had grown to more than 100.

Because bison meat is lower in fat than beef, one of the principal purposes of the herd was to provide a healthier source of food for the Nation. Older Ho-Chunk people tend to suffer from high rates of diabetes and heart disease, which led researchers to investigate the benefits of a more traditional diet. This diet included bison meat, which was much more common in the years before non-Indian settlement.

The Muscoda bison ranch provided meat for traditional feasts and meal sites for elders in Nekoosa, Wisconsin Dells, and other cities in central Wisconsin. The demand quickly outstripped the ability of the Muscoda herd to provide sufficient meat, and the Ho-Chunk Nation looked to expand the herd and perhaps sell the meat commercially. In addition to being more nutritious than commercial beef, bison meat is also more environmentally friendly. Organic farming became the way the Ho-Chunk Nation could ensure the health of the bison and the balance of nature. The bison now graze on restored prairie land without pesticides or fertilizers, and each bison receives about four acres of roaming space.

The Ho-Chunk bison ranch is fast becoming a model for organic, environmentally friendly agriculture. As more and more non-Indians become aware of the dangers of over-grazing and of the overuse of pesticides, the natural methods practiced by the Ho-Chunk Nation will likely become more common. The bison have returned, and they can lead us toward better methods of agriculture.

Herd of bison at the Muscoda Bison Ranch

Oginiiquay Fay Stone

AGRIGULTURE

Topic	Secondary Source Material	Primary Source Material
J.I. Case: Industry for Agriculture	Wik, Reynold. "J.I. Case: Some Experiences of an Early Wisconsin Industrialist." In *Wisconsin Magazine of History* 35, no. 1 (1951): 3–6. Thompson, John. "Rise and Decline of the Wheat Growing Industry in Wisconsin." In the *Economics and Political Science Series,* vol. 5, no. 3. Bulletin of the University of Wisconsin, No. 292. Madison: University of Wisconsin, 1909. (Reprint. New York: Arno Press, 1972. Based upon unpublished 1907 PhD dissertation).	The Wisconsin Historical Society Archives Web site at http://arcat.library.wisc.edu/ keywords: J. I. Case company papers
From Wheat to Dairy: How a Little Bug Made America's Dairyland	Lampard, Eric. "The Rise of the Dairy Industry in Wisconsin: A Study of Agricultural Change in the Midwest, 1820–1920." PhD diss., University of Wisconsin, 1955. Glover, Wilbur H. *Farm and College: The College of Agriculture of the University of Wisconsin, a History.* Madison, WI: University of Wisconsin Press, 1952.	The Wisconsin Historical Society Archives Web site at http://arcat.library.wisc.edu/ keywords: dairy industry in Wisconsin
The University of Wisconsin Extension: Education for the People	Curti, Merle and Vernon Carstensen. *The University of Wisconsin: A History.* Madison, WI: University of Wisconsin Press, 1949. The University Extension Web site at http://www1.uwex.edu/	The Wisconsin Historical Society Archives Web site at http://arcat.library.wisc.edu/ keywords: University of Wisconsin Extension

Topic	Secondary Source Material	Primary Source Material
A New Cash Crop: The Hops Craze of Southern Wisconsin	Current, Richard. *The History of Wisconsin, Volume II: The Civil War Era, 1848–1873*. Madison: State Historical Society of Wisconsin, 1976. Bohn, Belle C. "Hop Culture in Early Sauk County." In *Wisconsin Magazine of History* 18, no. 4 (1935): 389–394.	The Sauk County Historical Society Web site at http://www.saukcounty.com/schs.htm
Native Fruits: Wisconsin's Cranberry Industry	Eck, Paul. *The American Cranberry*. New Brunswick, NJ: Rutgers University Press, 1990. The United States Department of Agriculture Web site at http://www.usda.gov/ The Wisconsin State Cranberry Growers Association Web site at http://www.wiscran.org/	The Wisconsin Historical Society Archives Web site at http://arcat.library.wisc.edu/ keywords: cranberry industry in Wisconsin
The Milk Strikes: Dairy Farmers Respond to Low Prices	Glad, Paul W. *The History of Wisconsin, Volume V: War, a New Era, and Depression, 1914–1940*. Madison, WI: State Historical Society of Wisconsin, 1990. Jacobs, Herbert. "The Wisconsin Milk Strikes." In *Wisconsin Magazine of History* 35, no. 1 (1951): 30–35. The Wisconsin Cartographers' Guild. *Wisconsin's Past and Present: An Historical Atlas*. Madison, WI: University of Wisconsin Press, 1998. The Wisconsin Historical Society Web site at http://www.wisconsinhistory.org/	The Wisconsin Historical Society Archives Web site at http://arcat.library.wisc.edu/ keywords: milk strikes, milk pool

Topic	Secondary Source Material	Primary Source Material
Milk and Cheese Paradise: Wisconsin's Dairy Industry	*Wisconsin History: An Annotated Bibliography.* Compiled by Paul, Barbara Dotts and Justus F. Paul. Westport, CT: Greenwood Press, 1999. Nesbit, Robert C. *Wisconsin: A History.* 2nd ed revised and updated by William F. Thompson. Madison, WI: University of Wisconsin Press, 1989. The Wisconsin Agriculture Statistics Service Web site at http://www.nass.usda.gov/wi/ The Wisconsin Department of Commerce Web site at http://www.commerce.state.wi.us/	The Wisconsin Historical Society Archives Web site at http://arcat.library.wisc.edu/ keywords: dairy industry in Wisconsin

Topic	Secondary Source Material	Primary Source Material
German POWs: Easing Wisconsin's Agricultural Labor Shortages	Cowley, Betty. *Stalag Wisconsin: Inside WWII Prisoner of War Camps.* Oregon, WI: Badger Books, 2002.	The Wisconsin Historical Society Archives online catalog Web site at http://arcat.library.wisc.edu/ keywords: POWs, Mueckler, Waupun
The Ho-Chunk Bison Ranch: Restoration of Native Community	The Wind Cave National Park's Web site at http://www.nps.gov/wica/bison.htm Loew, Patty. *Indian Nations of Wisconsin: Histories of Endurance and Renewal.* Madison, WI: Wisconsin Historical Society Press, 2001. Members of the Ho-Chunk Nation. "The Bison Will Return to Sauk Prairie." In *Wisconsin Academy Review* 46 (Fall 2000): 38–39.	The Ho-Chunk Nation's Muscoda ranch Web site can be accessed at http://www.muscodabison.com/

Chapter Seven

Social Issues

DANGER !

Woman's Suffrage Would Double
the Irresponsible Vote

It is a MENACE to the Home, Men's
Employment and to All Business

- **The Bombing of Sterling Hall: Homegrown Terrorism on the UW Campus**

- **In the English Language: The Bennett Law Controversy**

- **School Vouchers: The Milwaukee Experiment**

- **Vitamin Research and the Wisconsin Alumni Research Foundation**

Pursuing Freedom
Wisconsin Defies the Fugitive Slave Law

Joshua Glover was a fugitive slave involved in Wisconsin's first trial under the Fugitive Slave Law.

In the years prior to the Civil War, tensions ran high between free Northern states and the Southern, slaveholding states. One of the biggest controversies was the Fugitive Slave Law. This law allowed slaveholders to pursue their runaway slaves into the free states, and it required northern law enforcement to help them do it! Citizens in free states were forbidden from assisting or protecting fugitive slaves. Slaves accused of running away could be taken back to the South without a trial. Northerners resented being forced to help Southern slave owners. In 1854, Wisconsin residents faced a controversial and violent encounter with the Fugitive Slave Law. In this case, the state refused to submit to a law it thought unwise and unjust.

On a March night in 1854, a deputy federal marshal and his associates stormed a shack four miles north of Racine. In the shack was Joshua Glover, a fugitive slave from Missouri, who was playing cards with two other men. After a struggle in which Glover was beaten and bloodied, the marshal took him to a jail in Milwaukee. The next morning, the mayor of Racine contacted antislavery newspaper editor Sherman Booth and asked him to find out if a proper warrant had been issued for Glover's arrest. Booth soon discovered that Glover's owner, Bennami Garland, had indeed obtained a warrant under the Fugitive Slave Law. Booth demanded a fair trial for Glover in a federal court, but the Fugitive Slave Law did not officially allow this option, and the federal judge denied his request. Infuriated, Booth rode through Milwaukee, calling interested citizens to a meeting to demand Glover's release.

The crowd grew outside the Milwaukee jail where Glover was being held. Those who gathered included not only sympathetic Milwaukeeans, but also a group of about 100 men from Racine who had come to the city with the Racine County sheriff. The sheriff wanted to arrest the federal marshal for the assault and battery of Glover. When the federal judge and marshal refused to listen to demands to free Glover, the mob decided to take matters into its own hands and rushed toward the jail door with a large timber, breaking open the door and allowing Glover to escape. A waiting wagon quickly took him to Waukesha. Supporters eventually placed him on a boat to Canada, where he was able to live in freedom.

Broadside from Milwaukee, 1854, announcing a meeting for those opposed to the Fugitive Slave Law.

166

Newspaper article about the first trial under the Fugitive Slave Law in Wisconsin, 1854

Getting Started on Research

A good place to learn more about Sherman Booth is "The Public and Private Affairs of Sherman M. Booth" by Diane S. Butler in the *Wisconsin Magazine of History* 82 (Spring 1999). You can also find more about abolitionism in 1850s Wisconsin in *The History of Wisconsin, Volume II: The Civil War Era, 1848–1873* by Richard Current. Wisconsin Public Television produced *Stand the Storm,* a program about Joshua Glover that may be available through your local library or be purchased from Wisconsin Public Television. The Sherman Booth case created a major sensation throughout the country, and your public librarian can help you find contemporary newspaper accounts of the incident.

Booth, meanwhile, bore the brunt of the blame for Glover's escape and rescue. He was quickly arrested and charged with violating the Fugitive Slave Law by helping a slave escape. With Booth in federal custody, his lawyer Byron Paine applied to the Wisconsin Supreme Court for a writ of habeas corpus. "Habeas corpus" means that the government cannot imprison anyone without just cause, and Associate Justice Abram D. Smith granted the writ on the grounds that the Fugitive Slave Law was unconstitutional. On July 19, 1854, the court affirmed Smith's decision, setting off a national furor over the controversial law.

Disregarding the court's action, a federal marshal again arrested Booth, who was tried in a federal court and convicted in January 1855.

But Booth did not give up. He appealed to the Wisconsin Supreme Court a second

Sherman Booth, abolitionist editor and antislavery leader

time for help. On February 3, 1855, the court once again ordered Booth's release on the grounds that the Fugitive Slave Law was unconstitutional. The case dragged on for another four years until the U.S. Supreme Court overturned the state court's action, decreed that it had no right to interfere, and ordered Wisconsin to return Booth to federal custody. The Wisconsin Supreme Court refused, but Booth was arrested once again.

By this time, the question was quickly being decided by other events. Within a year, 11 southern states seceded from the Union, and the nation was embroiled in a Civil War that would eventually abolish slavery altogether. Booth's courageous stand had encouraged many to oppose the Fugitive Slave Law and had increased antislavery feeling in Wisconsin and the North.

Some parts of the state, like Waukesha County, were decidedly antislavery. How did your community respond to abolitionism in the 1850s? What did your local newspaper report about the Booth incident?

Breaking the Color Line
Milwaukee Housing Segregation

In 1903, African American intellectual W.E.B. Du Bois wrote that the twentieth century's single greatest social issue would be the "color line." Race remains a prominent subject in this country, as Milwaukee housing segregation indicates.

By definition, *segregation* is the legal or social practice of separating people based upon race or ethnicity. But, segregation can take many different forms. *De jure,* or legal, segregation occurs when laws require or explicitly permit segregation. By contrast, *de facto* segregation, or segregation in fact, occurs when social practice, political acts, economic circumstances, and/or public policy separate people by race or ethnicity. It happens even when there's no law requiring that separation.

In the 1940s, the state's highest concentration of African Americans inhabited Milwaukee's "Inner Core," a near north neighborhood consisting of a 72-block area north of the Menomonee River and west of the Milwaukee River, bounded by Juneau Street and Brown Street. According to some accounts, the city was as segregated as Birmingham and Atlanta. By the 1960s, frustration with limited job opportunities, poverty, and segregation made the Inner Core a volatile area. On July 30, 1967, police broke up fights at a downtown entertainment spot. That night, riots erupted. Mayor Maier declared a citywide state of emergency, imposed an around-the-clock curfew, and asked the governor to call out the National Guard. Eight days later, four people were dead and more than 1,500 had been arrested, although most arrests were for curfew violations. The Milwaukee riot ranks third behind Detroit and Newark among that year's civil "disorders."

On August 28, 200 members of the Milwaukee NAACP Youth Council marched to Kosciuszko Park to protest the Common Council's refusal to pass an open housing ordinance. Three to five thousand white residents shouted obscenities and threw objects at the marchers, particularly concentrating their wrath on the march's leader, Father James Groppi. Groppi, a white Catholic priest, was an important and controversial civil rights figure. As one historian wrote: "To his followers and supporters, he was a selfless and charismatic figure; to his opponents he was abrasive, inflexible, and unrelenting."

In April 1968, the federal open housing law passed, preventing racial discrimination in 80% of the nation's housing units. On April 30,

WHi (X3) 52320

CORE picketing board of realtors at Coach House Motor Inn, in Milwaukee, January 1, 1964.

Father Groppi getting ready for a fair housing march in Milwaukee.

the Milwaukee Common Council approved a stronger law that exempted only owner-occupied dwellings with no more than two units.

Yet, weaknesses in the law, federal housing policies, and other factors permitted segregation to continue. As in other cities, Milwaukee had real estate agents, banks, and city zoning decisions, which shaped housing patterns. Real estate agents refused to show African Americans homes in white neighborhoods. Banks refused to loan money to African Americans moving into white neighborhoods, and city planners segregated neighborhoods through strategic decisions affecting the city's infrastructure and transportation network.

Suburbanization also contributed to increasing racial polarity. Whites increasingly fled urban centers for the suburbs, leaving the inner cities to poorer inhabitants, including African Americans. In 1968,

only two major American cities, Washington and Charleston, had black majorities. By 1990, more than 15 cities were predominantly African American.

Subject to limited educational opportunities and job discrimination, African Americans found it difficult to afford better housing. Also, as with other groups, African Americans chose to live near friends and family. Additionally, whenever blacks attempted to move into predominantly

Dilapidated houses in Milwaukee, April, 1936

white neighborhoods, they were often confronted with intimidation and violence.

The 1980 census indicated that only 2.5% of African Americans lived outside Milwaukee, ranking the city as the most segregated municipality among 16 urban centers of comparable size. Analysis of 2000 U.S. Census data demonstrates that residential segregation continues to persist between white Americans and African Americans in urban centers, despite the growth of the African American middle class.

Getting Started on Research

Several secondary sources provide relevant background information on Milwaukee's housing policies, including William Thompson's *The History of Wisconsin, Volume VI*, Ruth Zubrensky's "A Report on Past Discrimination Against African-Americans in Milwaukee, 1835–1999" (July 1999), Joe William Trotter Jr.'s *Black Milwaukee: The Making of an Industrial Proletariat, 1915–45*, and Kristin Bayer's thesis "Residential Segregation and the Section 8 Housing Allowances Program: An Exploratory Study of Milwaukee, Wisconsin."

An online search of the WHS Archives will yield many primary documents, including official records from Mayor Henry Maier's administration.

Dr. Kate Pelham Newcomb

Rural Healthcare on Snowshoes

In the early twentieth century, people in northern Wisconsin lacked easy access to medical care. Few decent roads linked this part of the state, and in winter, those roads became impassable. In addition, trained physicians were in short supply. This was before the arrival of Dr. Kate Pelham Newcomb.

Newcomb was born in Kansas in 1886. Three years later, her mother died during childbirth, and this early tragedy may have inspired her later interest in obstetrics. In September 1913, Kate began her medical studies at the University of Buffalo.

Newcomb earned her medical degree and specialized in obstetrics. For a short time, she practiced medicine on Manhattan's Lower East Side, where she delivered the first of the estimated 4,000 babies of her career. Soon after, she obtained an internship in Detroit, Michigan, where she met and married Bill Newcomb. When Bill became ill, a doctor prescribed a northern climate for his health. So in the winter of 1922, the couple

WHS Name File

Dr. Kate Newcomb

relocated to Boulder Junction in northern Wisconsin. Shortly after their arrival, the Newcombs lost their first child due to an incompetent physician. This tragic experience, coupled with caring for her ailing husband, prompted Newcomb to stop practicing medicine.

In 1931, she met Dr. Thomas Torpy. When he learned of Newcomb's medical training, he chided her for no longer practicing. Later that year, Torpy requested Newcomb's help with a patient he couldn't reach because of a blizzard. Newcomb protested that she hadn't practiced medicine in a decade and was not licensed in Wisconsin. But Torpy insisted. The woman lived eight miles from Newcomb's home and had severe pneumonia, so Newcomb grabbed her medical bag and left to treat the patient.

Shortly afterwards, Newcomb received her state license in Madison and began practicing in northern Wisconsin. Often, she drove 100 miles a day and logged many more miles on snowshoes or in

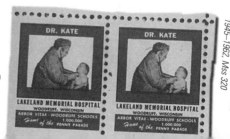

Stamps of Dr. Kate Newcomb
used to benefit hospital

a canoe, to serve the 7,000 people in the area. Because of her reliability in caring for patients, Newcomb earned the nickname "angel on snowshoes."

By the 1950s, area residents began thinking about building a hospital in Woodruff to decrease Dr. Newcomb's extensive and sometimes dangerous travels to various communities. In 1952, the structure's foundation was laid but could not be completed because of a lack of funds. Later that year, high school students came upon the concept of raising one million pennies to finish the construction. They reasoned that pennies, as the lowest valued coin, would be easier for donors to part with than dollars.

Called the Million Penny Parade, the drive to earn money for the hospital spread throughout the entire school. English classes competed to compose the best letter explaining the drive to potential donors. Thousands of letters were then sent to Newcomb's patients, local businesses, community organizations, and relatives. The community chipped in to defray postage costs, and donations started to pour in.

In 1953, the community celebrated the success of the Million Penny Parade with a real parade. Yet, the hospital fund was still $30,000 short of its goal. Newcomb's appearance on Ralph Edwards' popular *This Is Your Life* television program in March 1954 prompted a flood of money and supplies with totals eventually reaching $100,000.

The Lakeland Memorial Hospital in Woodruff was dedicated on July 21, 1954, and immediately diminished the workload of the over-extended physician. The hospital's mortgage

WHS Name File

Lakeland Memorial Hospital was also known as "Aunt Kate's" hospital.

was paid, the facility was fully supplied, and a surplus of $30,000 covered additional operating expenses.

Two years later, Newcomb fell, broke her hip, and died from complications in surgery. She was 69 years old, but the legacy of her service lives on in the Northwoods.

Cordelia Harvey

Northern Hospitals Close to Home

During the Civil War, Union and Confederate forces fought many bloody battles. Wisconsin regiments suffered their heaviest losses at the Battle of Shiloh in April 1862, in which more than 20,000 soldiers on both sides were either killed or wounded. In Madison, Governor Louis P. Harvey learned of the lack of hospital facilities and supplies, and he determined that volunteers from his state would not suffer in such conditions. He traveled to western Tennessee to take medical supplies to the wounded troops and inspect the conditions. On April 19, Harvey slipped while climbing aboard a ship and plunged into the Tennessee River. Despite frantic efforts to save the governor, he drowned. Wisconsin had not only lost many soldiers, but its governor as well.

Cordelia Harvey, the governor's widow, shared her husband's dedication to caring for Wisconsin's troops. After a few months of mourning her husband, she volunteered her services. In the autumn of 1862, the new governor Edward Salomon sent her to St. Louis as a sanitary agent to inspect hospital conditions and help care for wounded troops.

Mrs. Harvey was appalled at what she found. Incompetent doctors worked in badly supplied and poorly organized army hospitals. In the warm, balmy southern air, wounded soldiers lay in stuffy, unclean rooms where infection and diseases like pneumonia spread quickly. To ease the soldiers' discomfort, Mrs. Harvey brought in flowers and fruit, read letters to the soldiers, wrote letters for them, and helped arrange for several soldiers to go home to recover. She herself fell ill after visiting several southern hospitals during the spring of 1863, and she returned to Wisconsin and New York to regain her strength.

WHS Library

Letter from Mrs. Harvey—Our Sick at Memphis.

MEMPHIS, Tenn., March 20, 1862.

Governor Edward Salomon, Madison, Wis.:—DEAR SIR:—It is and has been next to impossible to send you anything like a correct report of what I am, and have been doing. For the last few weeks I have been laboring constantly in hospitals, seeking out soldiers broken in health to such a degree that they could in no possible way be of any further service to their country, and bringing such cases before the medical authorities, who, upon examination, discharge them. In this way I trust many a human life has been prolonged, at least until they reach their homes. This I believe to be just and merciful—just to the Government, and merciful to the man.

Letter from Harvey to Wisconsin governor Edward Salomon discussing sick soldiers in hospitals in Memphis, March 30, 1863.

Once back in the north, she thought of a new idea to help wounded soldiers recover. If the army would not allow them to

WHi image ID 10805

Engraving of Cordelia Harvey

return home to recuperate, then it should provide hospitals in the north where soldiers would be closer to their friends and family. The cooler climate would make them more comfortable and would lessen the spread of diseases that flourished in warm, damp weather. Northern governors embraced the idea, and Mrs. Harvey made it her mission to convince President Lincoln to set up army hospitals in the north.

Despite his generally sympathetic nature, Lincoln was unimpressed with the concept. In the fall of 1863, Mrs. Harvey visited the president and presented him with a petition signed by 8,000 people who wanted to establish northern hospitals. The president told her that soldiers kept in northern hospitals too close to home would desert. Harvey argued that many soldiers were simply dying in the hospitals down south. The meeting ended unsatisfactorily. When Mrs. Harvey returned the next day, Lincoln began to be annoyed at her persistence. "I believe this idea of Northern hospitals is a great humbug, and I am tired of hearing about it," he told her. But she refused to be dismissed so easily. "The people cannot understand why their friends are left to die, when with proper care they might live and do a good service for their country," she told the president. She went on to describe the conditions she had seen in the hospitals she had visited.

Cordelia Harvey's dedication worked. That afternoon, Lincoln gave the order to establish army hospitals in the north. When he told her the next day, Mrs. Harvey wept at the good news, and when he announced that he would name one of the Wisconsin hospitals after her, she insisted it be named after her late husband. Soon, three Wisconsin hospitals were established in Milwaukee, Madison, and Prairie du Chien. In Madison, the hospital occupied a familiar building, the three-story octagonal limestone mansion of former governor Leonard Farwell, renamed the Harvey United States General Hospital in 1863. More than 600 soldiers received treatment there during the war. After the war, the building was converted once again into a home for soldiers' orphans.

WHi Image ID 2690

The Soldier's Orphans Home, formerly the Harvey General Hospital, circa 1870

Getting Started on Research

To learn more about Wisconsin during the Civil War, an excellent place to start is *The History of Wisconsin, Volume II: The Civil War Era, 1848–1873* by Richard Current. Another excellent account is *Wisconsin in the Civil War: The Home Front and the Battle Front, 1861–1865* by Frank L. Klement. You can read about Cordelia Harvey in *Badger Saints and Sinners* by Fred L. Holmes. Reports of the Sanitary Commission can be found in the archives of the Wisconsin Historical Society. Search under Cordelia Harvey at http://arcat.library.wisc.edu/.

Temperance in Wisconsin
Frances E. Willard, Carrie A. Nation, and the WCTU

Carrie A. Nation and labor leader Michael Goldsmith

Wisconsin has had few visitors as colorful as Carrie A. Nation. As a member of the Women's Christian Temperance Union (WCTU), she traveled around the country in the early 1900s warning crowds about the evils of alcohol and saloons. This small, fiery speaker often surprised her audiences. On July 18, 1902, Nation spoke in Fond du Lac in front of a tavern, denouncing drinkers as they entered. When one angry customer dramatically presented her a bottle of whiskey, Nation pulled a small hatchet from beneath her dress and smashed the bottle! By closing the saloons, temperance reformers believed, hard-working men would be discouraged from

spending their money on alcohol and would be encouraged to spend more time with their families.

The hatchet-wielding Nation captured the public's imagination. But, by the time she visited Wisconsin, many people in the state had learned about temperance from Frances E. Willard, who grew up in Rock County in the late nineteenth century. She helped shape the WCTU into the first large, national women's organization in the United States. As the organization's president from 1879 to her death in 1898, Willard was one of the most influential women of her time. She was the only woman in the nineteenth century to be honored with a marble statue in the Capitol building in Washington, DC. Willard's leadership of the WCTU, however, went far beyond temperance. She enthusiastically supported equality for women and worked strategically to champion the cause of suffrage on the public arena. In fact, many suffragists learned their skills in the WCTU!

Frances Willard was born in 1839 in a small village outside Rochester, New York. At the age of seven, she came with her family by covered wagon to Wisconsin Territory to farm along the Rock River near Janesville.

Frances Willard

As a child, she hated housework and loved the outdoors, but she was also a serious reader in a devotedly Methodist household. In her autobiography, she recalls that, at 14, she clipped a temperance pledge from a juvenile magazine and pasted it into her family's Bible:

A pledge we make no wine to take,
Nor brandy red that turns the head,
Nor fiery rum that ruins home,
Nor brewers' beer, for that we fear,
And cider, too, will never do.
To quench our thirst, we'll always bring
Cold water from the well or spring;
So here we pledge perpetual hate
To all that can intoxicate.

Then, she insisted that all family members sign it! That persuasiveness became a hallmark of her personality, demonstrating the passionate dedication that marked her career.

The temperance movement won a significant victory that affected the late nineteenth and early twentieth centuries. The Eighteenth Amendment to the Constitution was passed, which prohibited the sale of alcoholic beverages. But, Prohibition, as it was called, could not completely put an end to the powerful tradition of brewing and beer-drinking in the country. This tradition was particularly strong among Germans in Wisconsin. Milwaukee was one of the leading beer-producing cities in the country. Convincing Wisconsinites to give up their beer was a tough challenge!

Despite the state's beer-drinking reputation, many in Wisconsin agreed with the concept of temperance. Wisconsin was home to a chapter of the WCTU, which eventually grew to nearly 10,000 members. Under Prohibition in the 1920s, fewer Americans drank, but the problems of enforcement proved too great. In 1933, Prohibition was repealed, and Americans,

Getting Started on Research

To learn more about Willard, Nation, the temperance movement, and Prohibition, read *The Alcoholic Republic* by W.J. Rorabaugh. For an excellent online resource, access the Wisconsin Bar Association's series of articles on the history of the women's suffrage movement in Wisconsin at http://www.wisbar.org/wislawmag/archive/history/pt14.html.

The Wisconsin Historical Society has many books in its library and documents in its archives about Frances Willard. Two books to help you get started are Ruth Bordin's *Frances Willard: A Biography* and Richard W. Leeman's *"Do Everything" Reform: The Oratory of Frances E. Willard.* Frances Willard's own *Glimpses of Fifty Years: The Autobiography of an American Woman* is a superb primary source.

despite the memory of Willard's famous speeches and Nation's hatchet, were glad they could drink legally again.

What were the effects of temperance in your community? Did Willard or Nation ever visit your hometown? What can you learn about these two women and how they influenced the social and political environment in the United States and in Wisconsin?

WHS Archives, Classified File 9415

National Platform of the Prohibition Party

We Won't Fight

German Immigrants Protest the Civil War Draft

You've probably heard about men who resisted the military draft during Vietnam, but did you know that men resisted the draft 100 years earlier, during the Civil War? In Wisconsin, many German immigrants resented the idea of being compelled to fight in a war they did not agree with, and they actively resisted attempts to conscript them into the army.

In 1862, the U.S. Congress passed a militia act that called for the governors of all states to produce a certain quota of men for military service. If they could not produce sufficient volunteers, then a forced draft would go into effect in their state. Governor Edward Salomon of Wisconsin established a quota for each county, hoping that large numbers of volunteers would make the draft unnecessary. In many counties, men filled or even exceeded the quota. But in areas near Lake Michigan dominated by German Catholics, the numbers lagged.

Many German immigrants felt unwelcome in the army, where they believed there would be few, if any, Catholic priests to serve them. Moreover, many did not support the abolitionist aims of the war and disagreed with Lincoln's administration on other matters as well. Most importantly, many Germans had fled Europe to escape compulsory military service and did not want to be forced to serve in their adopted country. German-speaking Catholics from Luxembourg, for instance, were vehemently opposed to such service, since their fathers and grandfathers had been forced to leave their farms to serve the foreign rulers of

their homeland. For all these reasons, resistance to the draft was sparked in predominantly German-Catholic communities.

After waiting months for enough volunteers, Governor Salomon finally ordered a draft in the counties that had not met the state's quotas. It was scheduled to begin on November 10, 1862. That day, riots broke out up and down the coast of Lake Michigan. In Brown County, hundreds of Belgian farmers armed with farm implements and guns marched on the home of U.S. Senator Timothy Howe. Twenty Germans attacked the draft commissioner in West Bend and drove him out of town.

The most serious attack occurred in Port Washington. The draft commissioner William Pors, a German Democrat, was a Protestant Mason accused of exempting his fellow Masons from the draft. As Pors began

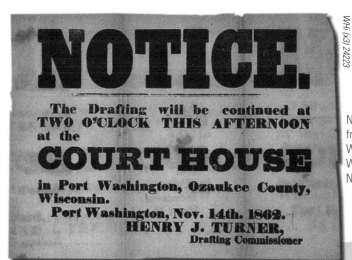

WHI (x3) 24223

Notice of draft from Port Washington, Wisconsin, November, 1862

Notice of draft from Dodgeville, Wisconsin, 1862

WHS Archives, Civil War Draft Artifacts, Wis Mss 6S

List of names subject to draft in Sheboygan County, Wisconsin

quota of militiamen. The state had already supplied enough troops so it had not even needed to draft any more! As for the arrested rioters, their fate was unclear. After lengthy court proceedings to determine whether they could be held as federal prisoners under martial law, they were quietly paroled. Wisconsin experienced no more trouble with the draft, and by the time the war was over, the state had achieved a noble record of assistance to the war effort.

Was your county ever under the Civil War draft? What would life have been like in your area in 1862? How did the Civil War, in general, affect the people and places in your community? Your public librarian can help you find local histories that might summarize your community's role in the war.

Getting Started on Research

The History of Wisconsin, Volume II: The Civil War Era, 1848–1873 by Richard Current is one of the best places to learn more about Wisconsin in the Civil War. The draft riots are also discussed in *Wisconsin in the Civil War: The Home Front and the Battle Front, 1861–1865* by Frank L. Klement. A good guide to use when researching people and places in the Civil War is *Exploring Civil War Wisconsin: A Survival Guide for Researchers* by Brett Barker. The Wisconsin Historical Society posts numerous primary documents and engaging activities about the 1862 Civil War militia draft, including a list of Wisconsin draft dodgers on its Web site at http://www.wisconsinhistory.org/teachers/lessons/civilwar/draft/.

to draw the names out of the draft box, a group of drunken Luxemburgers attacked him, dragging him out the door of the courthouse, throwing him on the steps, and finally, pelting him with rocks. The mob stormed through town, destroying the draft box, looting a warehouse, damaging the Masonic Hall, and smashing windows and furniture in the houses of several wealthy citizens. The governor immediately sent military reinforcements to surround and occupy the town. Nearly 150 protesters were arrested.

In the end, the draft proved unnecessary in Wisconsin. The War Department had neglected to inform Governor Salomon that when a state exceeded its quota of three-year volunteers, as Wisconsin had, it could apply those extra volunteers toward its

Don't Pick on Us!
Hispanic Farmworkers March to Madison

On August 18, 1966, fifteen tired migrant workers arrived in Madison. Led by 22-year-old Jesus Salas, they had walked all the way from Wautoma carrying images of the Virgin of Guadalupe and emblems of the United Farm Workers. The group marched five days to draw attention to the plight of migrant farmworkers, mostly Texas Mexicans, who labored in the fields during the summer months for many of Wisconsin's agricultural companies. Along the way, supporters waved and honked at

PH 3640

The migrant farmworkers on their way to Madison, August 1966

them on the roads. Some offered food or small cash donations.

Texas Mexicans first traveled to Wisconsin to harvest crops during World War II. In 1947, they numbered about 5,000,

and by 1961, more than 17,000 migrants worked in the state seasonally. Most workers harvested cucumbers in Waushara and Oconto Counties or picked cherries in Door County. These migrants arrived in the late spring and stayed for one to five months, most living and working under harsh conditions. In 1965, the Governor's Commission on Human Rights noted that migrant workers often made less than 85 cents an hour working from sunup to sundown with no overtime pay. Planting, weeding, and harvesting vegetables was back-breaking work, too. Can you imagine spending 14 hours a day hunched over, picking miles of cucumbers? The migrants lived in company camps that often lacked running water and toilet facilities. Laws already on the books set standards for migrant housing, but company officials often denied State Board of Health inspectors access to their camps.

So, Salas led the group to Madison to protest the conditions and to demand that state laws be enforced. The workers had five major demands (1) construction of a public restroom for migrants in Wautoma, (2) the addition of migrants to the Governor's Committee on Migratory Labor, (3) a $1.25

Wisconsin State Journal, August 19, 1966

Foot-Sore Migrants Arrive Here

By ROGER GRIBBLE
(State Journal Staff Writer)

"I never thought we'd make it today. It's been a long, long walk."

With those words, Jesus (pronounced hay-soos) Salas and 14 weary, foot-sore migrant workers from Wautoma completed their 4-mile "march for respectability" late Thursday afternoon.

The marchers passed Truax Field on Highway 51 shortly after 5 p.m. in their march to dramatize prevailing working conditions for migrant workers.

They were to be joined by others today to complete their march

to the State Capitol, where they will meet with state officials and a representative of the governor. The march today will begin at the Yahara bridge on E. Washington ave. at 10:30 a.m.

Salas, a student at Stevens Point University, kept tight control over his marchers. Thursday, as he warned them to keep off the highway and march in single file. Obviously fighting exhaustion, the group maintained a brisk pace along the final four miles of the march, despite the fact some limped.

A state patrolman told Salas about an hour before the march

ended that he had received complaints marchers were on the highway. Salas told him the marchers had stayed on the shoulder, and the patrolman agreed this was so.

Later, at a rest stop about a mile from Truax Field, a Dane county traffic patrolman addressed Salas by name and provided band-aids and other treatment for foot-sore marchers. Salas said he has nothing but praise for contacts he and his

*More Photos Page 4;
Story, Photo Sec. 2, P. 1*

group had with police during the march. "They have been very cooperative," he said. "One even told us the best way to get through a construction area."

The marchers wore casual clothes and some wore straw hats. The group carried an American flag and placards depicting Guadalupe, patron saint of the migrant mission at Wautoma.

Another marcher carried a red flag with a black eagle in its center, the symbol of the National Farm Workers Assn. Salas translated other placards in Spanish as follows:

"Unite to be recognized. Speak

Newspaper article discussing the arrival of the migrant farm workers after their march from Wautoma to Madison, August 19, 1966.

minimum wage for all migrants, (4) a state program to inform workers of their rights under the state's Workers Compensation program, and (5) enforcement of the state's migrant housing code. According to Salas, the workers also demanded "respect and dignity for their labor"—work that "had made Wisconsin a national leader in the harvesting, processing, and canning of vegetables."

The march had little immediate impact. At a series of public meetings afterward, migrant workers, growers, and processors discussed conditions. Still, the meetings mainly made the companies more hostile to the demands of migrant laborers. But the march had inspired migrant workers to organize.

In September 1966, workers at the Burns & Son potato plant in Almond asked Salas to help organize a union, even though he had very little experience with formal union organizing. With two of his brothers, he easily convinced the Mexican workers of the plant to organize *Obreros Unidos*—Workers United. But, Burns & Son refused to recognize the union and began a campaign to destroy it. Later in the fall, however, the Wisconsin Employment Relations Commission decided in the union's favor.

But by this late in the season, most of the workers had returned to Texas. Throughout, Salas remained determined to continue organizing.

In the early months of 1967, Salas and other organizers visited registered union members and other migrants in Texas before returning to Wisconsin the next summer. The Wisconsin AFL-CIO supported the efforts of the union. *Obreros Unidos* was able to create cooperative consumer groups, a newspaper *(La Voz Mexicana)*, and a free legal aid clinic. Although *Obreros Unidas* met with little success organizing transient farm workers, the union was more successful in Milwaukee and other urban areas.

What is the history of organized agricultural and migrant labor activity in your county? Your local librarian can help you find source materials.

Getting Started on Research

A lot of good information about Jesus Salas and the march to Madison can be found in local newspapers. Your public librarian can help you find copies from August 1966. The Governor's Commission on Human Rights published a pamphlet in 1965 on "Migrant Labor in Wisconsin." A good book on the subject is *Struggle for Justice: The Migrant Farm Labor Movement in Wisconsin* by Jesus Salas and David Giffey. The Wisconsin Historical Society and museum have archival and photographic material about the migrant labor movement.

Lloyd Barbee

Fighting Segregation in Milwaukee Schools

School desegregation pickets, 1964

In 1954, the Supreme Court case *Brown v. Board of Education of Topeka* established that racial segregation was unconstitutional. In a unanimous decision, the court ruled that racial segregation violated the constitutional requirement of equal protection under the law because segregated schools for African American children were inherently inferior. The next year, the court published guidelines requiring schools to desegregate "with all deliberate speed."

Despite this momentous decision, school segregation remained widespread. In many schools, segregation endured because the surrounding neighborhoods were segregated. Milwaukee is a significant example. In the 1950s, the city was one of the most segregated cities in the United States. In 1960, Milwaukee had an African American population of approximately 62,000, and 69% lived in the run-down area north of the Menomonee River and west of the Milwaukee River. Virtually all African American children in Milwaukee went to all-black schools.

In 1965, however, a major court case challenged Milwaukee's segregation. The principal mover behind this case was Lloyd Barbee. Barbee was born in Memphis, Tennessee in 1925 and attended the University of Wisconsin law school in 1949 after serving four years in the U.S. Navy. Discouraged by the racism he encountered from students and faculty on what was supposedly one of the most progressive campuses in the nation, he dropped out after one year. Barbee later returned and earned a law degree, but then had difficulty finding a Madison law firm that would take him as an intern. Eventually, he was admitted to the bar and opened a private practice in Milwaukee. Barbee campaigned hard for a fair-housing law that would ban racial discrimination, and he led a 13-day sit-in at the Capitol. He was also instrumental in getting a fair housing law passed in the state in 1965.

WHi image ID 5763

Lloyd Barbee, NAACP state president, walks out of a school board meeting, January 21, 1964.

In 1963, Barbee requested that the State Superintendent of Public Instruction order the desegregation of Milwaukee schools. The superintendent, Angus B. Rothwell, responded that Milwaukee schools were segregated only because of residential patterns and that there was nothing his department could do. Not satisfied with the state's or city's responses, on March 1, 1964, Barbee became chair of the Milwaukee United School Integration Committee (MUSIC) and led a boycott of public schools.

In October 1965, Barbee filed suit on behalf of the parents of 32 African American and nine white students demanding that Milwaukee end the de facto (illegal, but real) segregation of its schools. This was the first lawsuit of its kind in the nation. Barbee argued that the Milwaukee School Board had fostered segregation by drawing district boundary lines based upon segregated housing patterns and other discriminatory policies. As evidence, the plaintiffs cited the fact that 14 of 21 elementary schools in the Inner Core area had African American enrollment above 90%; most of the schools outside the core had less than 10% African American populations.

On January 19, 1976, Federal Judge John Reynolds ruled that Milwaukee Schools were illegally segregated and ordered the school board to take immediate steps to integrate the schools. But the board appealed the decision before the U.S. Supreme Court, which ordered a new trial. At the second trial, Barbee and his colleagues used testimony from a former school board member to demonstrate that the segregation was intentional. On March 1, 1979, the school board settled the case and agreed to implement a five-year desegregation plan. The plan was not perfect and minority schools remain a significant social, racial, and financial problem for the city, but without Barbee and others, the issue might never have been addressed.

Getting Started on Research

To learn more about segregation in Milwaukee schools, you can read *The History of Wisconsin, Volume VI: Continuity and Change, 1940–1965* by William F. Thompson. Lloyd Barbee's papers are stored at the Wisconsin Historical Society and are available to students who visit the headquarters building in Madison. The court case was well-chronicled in newspapers, especially the *Milwaukee Journal*. Your public librarian can help you find copies from the 1960s and 70s.

PH 4283

Lloyd Barbee

America's Longest Strike
The Kohler Company Strike of 1934–1941

In the history of the United States, workers have struggled for their share of social and economic justice. Labor controversies have often revolved around the issues of organized unions and collective bargaining. In the 1930s, the state's labor debate came to a head at a plumbing fixture plant near Sheboygan.

Annual Kohler Strike Memorial March, 1939

PH 6002

John Michael Kohler, the son of an Austrian immigrant, founded the Kohler Company in 1873. At 29, he bought the Sheboygan Union Iron and Steel Foundry and started producing cast iron and steel implements. Ten years later, he launched Kohler into the plumbing fixture business, and by the Depression era, the Kohler Company was producing an impressive array of bathroom fixtures.

As part of the New Deal, President Franklin Roosevelt signed the National Industrial Recovery Act on June 16, 1933. The most controversial portion, Section 7(a) of Title I, gave employees the right to organize and bargain collectively without employer restraint or coercion. Employers had to comply with approved hours and wage standards and were forbidden to require that workers join company-sponsored unions. However, labor leaders and company representatives offered very different interpretations of the law's language.

Encouraged by the legislation, the American Federation of Labor (AFL) Union 18545 presented 14 demands to the Kohler Company. The three most significant were (1) a minimum wage of 65 cents per hour,

(2) a 30-hour work week, and (3) the right to bargain collectively. Walter J. Kohler, the son of the company's founder and now president, rejected the union's demands on July 11, 1934. Five days later, the union mounted a strike against the company.

The strikers stopped coal deliveries to the Kohler power plant, which provided the entire village with water, sewer services, and fire protection. Reverend J.W. Maguire, a Catholic priest mediating the strike, convinced the strikers to allow one coal car to pass every other day, enough to keep the plant operating. Village authorities hid firearms at strategic points, acquired armored cars, and deputized volunteers. The strikers also prepared by collecting clubs, blackjacks, slingshots, and other weapons. On July 27, 1934, after the strikers refused a coal car, 100 Kohler deputies escorted the car to the power plant. That night, strikers and strike sympathizers damaged the plant with bricks and stones. The Kohler deputies responded with tear gas and bullets, killing two strikers and wounding approximately 40.

The next day, the National Guard restored order, but the strike continued.

After the regional labor relations office did not settle the strike, the case moved to the National Labor Relations Board (NLRB). The board heard testimony from Federal Labor Union 18545, the Kohler Company, and the management-sanctioned Kohler Workers' Association. An attorney for the AFL lodged three complaints against Kohler: that the company had fired employees for union activity, that it had refused to bargain collectively with union representatives, and that the company had interfered with union organizing efforts.

Although the NLRB found evidence substantiating the complaints, it decided that workers could choose between the AFL and the company-sponsored union. On September 27, workers elected the Kohler Workers' Association as their new bargaining agent, despite the insistence of the AFL that irregularities had existed in the polling process.

In 1941, the prolonged strike came to an unceremonious end. In hindsight, the strikers gained very little. Eventually, nearly all union members either relocated to areas more responsive to organized labor or accepted the Kohler company union. Also, the company met none of the workers' demands.

Have there been strikes in your community? What were the circumstances? What were the results?

Getting Started on Research

Paul Glad's *The History of Wisconsin, Volume V: War, a New Era, and Depression, 1914–1940* contextualizes the Kohler strike. Walter Uphoff's *The Kohler Strike: Its Causes and Effects* and Walter Uphoff's *Kohler on Strike: Thirty Years of Conflict* also bring the strike into focus within the overarching socioeconomic and political issues. For primary documents, search under Kohler and strike in the Wisconsin Historical Society Archives or read the essay "Salvos against the New Deal" about the strike by Garet Garrett published in the *Saturday Evening Post* from 1933–1940.

PH 6002

Kohler Strike Memorial, 1937

Sheboygan Press headline from July 28, 1934

Olympia Brown and the Women's Suffrage Movement

In colonial America, civil law perpetuated inequality between men and women. It viewed women as less reasonable in thought and behavior than men, a view that provided an ideological foundation for denying suffrage to women. *Suffrage* means the right to vote and to take advantage of the political privileges afforded by representative government. The women's suffrage movement in America was responsible for women gaining the equal right to vote in elections and referendums and to hold public office. But, the journey was long and hard.

WHi Image ID 1932

DANGER!

Woman's Suffrage Would Double the Irresponsible Vote

It is a MENACE to the Home, Men's Employment and to All Business

An anti-women's suffrage poster from Watertown, Wisconsin, 1912

Prior to the American Revolution (1776–1783), most voting rights laws in the colonies were based upon land ownership. Although women possessed property rights, their rights were limited. Only women from landed families could vote, and then only sometimes. In this period, American Quakers and other individuals, notably the political philosopher Thomas Paine, advocated for women's suffrage.

After the American Revolution, the framers of the Constitution allowed individual states to establish voting qualifications. By the early nineteenth century, most states had eliminated property qualifications and extended voting rights to all adult males. Ironically, enfranchising more men stripped women of their rights! Laws granting men the right to vote excluded women based solely upon gender. By eliminating property ownership as a voting requirement, these laws removed women's best legal claim to the right to vote.

The women's rights movement in the United States began during this time. In July 1848, the Seneca Falls Convention established suffrage as the primary goal of the women's movement. Although not present at that convention, Olympia Brown was instrumental in advancing women's rights. At a time when few women graduated from college, Brown received her Bachelor of Arts degree from Antioch College in Yellow Springs, Ohio, in 1860. Three years later, she became the first female to graduate from a regularly established theological school at St. Lawrence University. She was ordained

Olympia Brown

as a minister in the Universalist church—a religious faith incorporating many Christian tenets and whose adherents believe in universal salvation. As a result, she became the first female minister acknowledged by a denomination.

In 1864, Brown obtained her first full-time parish ministry in Weymouth Landing, Massachusetts, and became active in the women's rights movement. By 1870, she was working for a parish in Bridgeport, Connecticut, but she resigned her ministry there in 1874 and moved to Racine, Wisconsin, to rejuvenate a floundering Universalist parish. Nine years later, after having reenergized the parish and established it as a community educational and cultural center, Brown left full-time ministry to devote her time to women's rights. She led the Wisconsin Suffrage Association for a number of years and served as Vice President of the National American Women's Suffrage Association, promoting a broad range of reforms, such as education and suffrage for women.

In 1913, Alice Paul and Lucy Barnes started the National Woman's Party, an organization that encouraged a more confrontational approach than the conservative National American Women's Suffrage Association. Brown was a charter member of the party, and despite the political dangers, she participated in many protests. In fact, she publicly burned President Wilson's speeches in front of the White House to protest his lack of support for women's rights.

In 1919, the passage of the 19th Amendment to the U.S. Constitution, guaranteed suffrage to women. Brown was one of the few original suffragists still alive to witness the victory. In 1920, at age 85, she voted in her first presidential election. For the rest of her life, Brown dedicated herself to promoting world peace and remained active as one of the original members of the Women's International League for Peace and Freedom. In 1926, she died in Baltimore at age 91 and was buried beside her husband in Racine's Mound Cemetery. The Racine church where Brown had preached was later renamed the Olympia Brown Unitarian Universalist Church, and in 1975, an elementary school in Racine was named in her honor.

Getting Started on Research

Charlotte Cote's full-length biography *Olympia Brown: The Battle for Equality* is an excellent place to start your research. Olympia Brown's papers and assorted documents relating to her career are held at the Schlesinger Library of the Radcliffe Institute at Harvard University in Cambridge, Massachusetts; the Wisconsin Historical Society; and in the archives of the National Woman's Party at the Library of Congress. Brown herself published *Olympia Brown: An Autobiography*, an excellent primary source.

THE NATURE OF THE RIGHT.

The right of suffrage has by some one been called "the right preservative of all other rights." It is the weapon of defense in a free, peaceful and civilized country; it is at once a stimulus to honorable ambition, a means of education, and a protection against injustice.

It stands for fair play in the working world. It is the consent which the individual gives to the government by which he is controlled.

An extract from "Woman's Suffrage" that Brown wrote in 1907, which advocated for the right of women to vote

Helping Hands
Wisconsin's Schools for the Deaf and Blind

Every day when you go to school, you listen to your teacher and you read your books. Most students in class can solve math problems, read and discuss literature, and take notes on lectures without much difficulty. Many enjoy working on art projects and participating in school athletics. But all these things are difficult, even impossible, for students who do not see or hear. From its earliest years as a state, Wisconsin has made a commitment to providing education to all of its children. Parents in the state continue to be able to send their visually or hearing impaired children to special schools to be educated.

Even before Wisconsin became a state, some citizens recognized the need to provide educational facilities that addressed the needs of visually and hearing impaired children. In 1843, Increase A. Lapham urged the Territorial Council to petition Congress for funds to establish such schools, but no action was taken. Education in a frontier state was uncommon for any child, let alone those needing special assistance.

The first state charitable institution began in Janesville when private citizens organized the first state school for impaired students. One Janesville resident, J.T. Axtell, a graduate of the Ohio Institution for the Blind, arranged a village meeting that took place on August 27, 1849. After Axtell explained several methods for instructing children with defective vision, 30 residents promised $430 to start a school and purchase the required equipment. That October, eight visually impaired children attended the first school for the visually impaired in the state, operated out of a private home.

In 1850, the students exhibited some of their work to the legislature. Members of the legislature were so impressed that they immediately incorporated the Wisconsin Institution for the Education of the Blind and made the school tax-supported, appropriating $2,500 dollars to keep it running. In establishing the school, the state made a firm commitment to the principle of universal education. According to state statute, the institute would ensure visually impaired children "the enjoyment of the blessings of a free government, obtaining the means of subsistence and discharging those duties, social and political, devolving upon American citizens." In other words, the

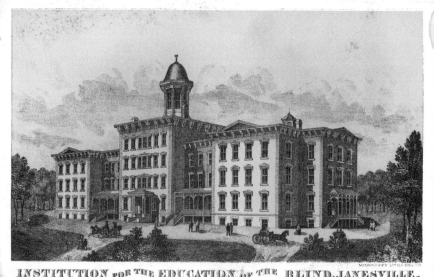

INSTITUTION FOR THE EDUCATION OF THE BLIND, JANESVILLE.

Institute for the Education of the Blind, Janesville, Ohio

Getting Started on Research

You can learn more about the state schools for visually and hearing impaired children on the Internet at the Wisconsin Center for the Blind and Visually Impaired Web site at http://www.wcbvi.k12.wi.us/ and the Wisconsin School for the Deaf Web site at http://www.wsd.k12.wi.us/.

A good history of both institutions is *A History of the State Board of Control of Wisconsin and the State Institutions: 1849–1939* by Bernett O. Odegard and George M. Keith. The archives of the Wisconsin Historical Society contain a variety of records and documents from both schools, which can be accessed through a guided search at http://arcat.library.wisc.edu/.

school's goals were to provide an education, to teach its students how to make a living, and to ensure that its students could become self-sufficient citizens.

In a similar story, a young teacher from New York named Wealthy Hawes came to the farm of Ebenezer Cheeseboro near Delavan in 1850 to teach his hearing impaired daughter Ariadna. One year later, there were eight hearing impaired children in this private school. Few people could afford such a school, however, and in 1851, the school closed from lack of funds. The Cheeseboro family, however, circulated a petition requesting that the legislature establish a school specifically to educate hearing impaired children. In 1852, the representative from Delavan introduced the bill, and on April 15, Governor Leonard Farwell signed the measure. The bill established the Wisconsin Institute for the Education of the Deaf and Dumb at Delavan on land donated by a local resident. At the institute, vocational training was a priority, and students learned income-producing skills, such as shoemaking and cabinetmaking, so that they could become independent citizens.

Both schools continue to operate, although the educational focus has moved beyond vocational training. The schools originally were administered under the state Board of Control and later under state welfare agencies. In 1947, however, they were transferred to the Department of Public Instruction, which continues to ensure that visually and hearing impaired children receive a productive education.

Are there any specialized educational or training institutions in your community? What populations are their focus, what are their goals, and what subjects are taught? How have the school(s) changed over time?

WHS Archives, Lithographs of State of Wisconsin Buildings, M99-119

Institute for the Deaf and Dumb, Delavan, Wisconsin

Senator Joseph McCarthy
The Rise and Fall of an Anti-Communist

WHS Archives, Joseph McCarthy Files, 1946–1957, M75–079

After World War II, the Cold War gripped the world. During this period, the United States and its allies competed with the United Soviet Socialist Republics (USSR) and its allies for global political dominance. This tense rivalry continued until the fall of the Soviet republic in the early 1990s. In the years between, the Cold War shaped almost every aspect of international politics. The United States and its allies worked to foster democracy and capitalism around the world, while the Soviets and their allies pushed equally hard to make communism a worldwide movement.

Such efforts fueled Americans' suspicions that communism was gaining strength. In 1948, the communists, backed by the Soviets, took control of Czechoslovakia, and the Soviets blockaded West Berlin. In 1949, the communists rose to power in China, and the Soviets tested an atomic bomb. The following year, former State Department official Alger Hiss was convicted on two counts of perjury, stemming from accusations that he was a communist and had provided information to the Soviets. Adding fuel to the anti-communist zeal, Senator Joseph McCarthy in the 1950s used people's fears of encroaching communism to launch his infamous anti-communist campaign. Some admired McCarthy's patriotic fervor, while others despised his aggressive tactics.

Part of a speech given by Joseph McCarthy on the Senate floor, June 2, 1950, about his desire to root out communism.

Born in 1908 in Grand Chute, Wisconsin, Joseph McCarthy defeated Robert M. La Follette Jr. in 1946 to become Wisconsin's junior Republican senator. His early career was unimpressive, but he soon distinguished himself in a 1950 speech in Wheeling, West Virginia, during which he announced that he knew of 205 communists currently working in the U.S. State Department. Later, he changed the figures and altered his testimony, but McCarthy never changed the part of his story about communists infiltrating the government and influencing foreign policy. His contentious announcement vaulted him into public prominence and supplied a strong political platform for his re-election.

McCarthy was easily re-elected in 1952. As chairman of the Senate Permanent Investigations Subcommittee, he attempted to expose communists and their sympathizers. During his first year as chairman, the subcommittee privately interrogated 395 witnesses and publicly interrogated 214 others. McCarthy's

Joseph McCarthy

PETITION FOR RECALL

I, the undersigned, a qualified elector of the County of ...., State of Wisconsin, hereby petition for the recall of United States Senator Joseph R. McCarthy of the City of Appleton, Outagamie County, from the United States Senate.

Signature of Petitioner	Town, City or Village of Residence	Street and No. or Rural Route of Post Office	Date

Signatures Here

(The following information to appear following signatures at the bottom of each petition).

AFFIDAVIT OF CIRCULATOR

State of Wisconsin
County of ....

.................., being duly sworn, deposes and swears that he is a qualified elector of the County of ...., and resides at No................ on .... Street or Avenue in the city, town or village of ....; that he is personally acquainted with all the persons who have signed the foregoing petition; that he knows them to be electors of the COUNTY named therein; that they signed the same with full knowledge of the contents thereof; that their respective residences are stated therein; that each signer signed the same on the date stated opposite his name, and that he, the affiant, resides within the district which the candidate named therein presently represents.

.... Signature of Circulator

.... Post Office Address or Rural Route Number

Signed and sworn to before me this .... day of ....

.... Seal of Notary, Justice, Judge or Town, Village, City or County Clerk

This petition was originally printed in the *Sun Prairie Star*, March 18, 1954. Citizens opposed to McCarthy were urged to sign this petition to try to get McCarthy out of office.

accusations were often unsubstantiated, but they garnered him power in a political climate filled with fear and paranoia. In January 1954, in the nation's first televised congressional hearings, McCarthy indirectly attacked President Eisenhower and directly attacked Secretary of the Army Robert Stevens.

When McCarthy investigated Army dentist Major Irving Peress, the Army decided McCarthy had finally gone too far. In 1954, the Army charged that McCarthy was seeking preferential treatment for his assistant David Schine, who had been drafted in 1953. His own subcommittee addressed the charges in the Army-McCarthy hearings. These televised hearings—the very format that McCarthy had utilized to advance his anti-communist cause—were his downfall. Despite the fact that he presented no real evidence for his claims, McCarthy belligerently continued to insist that his allegations were true.

In December 1954, the Senate officially rebuked McCarthy for "conduct unbecoming a senator" by a vote of 65 to 22. This public disgrace forever marred his career. Although McCarthy continued to serve in political office, his power, influence, and credibility quickly eroded. He descended into obscurity and alcoholism, dying of a liver ailment in Bethesda, Maryland on May 2, 1957.

In power for only a short time, McCarthy attained global recognition, epitomizing for his detractors the negative aspects of American foreign policy. Fear and intimidation were his trademarks, and he was a genius at creating publicity for himself. At the peak of his power, even Presidents Harry Truman and Dwight Eisenhower proceeded cautiously in their policy making, hoping not to incur McCarthy's wrath. McCarthyism, coined by *Washington Post* cartoonist Herbert Block, is still used today to describe fanatical patriotism and the notion of blind loyalty to a charismatic leader.

Getting Started on Research

For an excellent overview of the life and times of Joseph McCarthy, start with the comprehensive Web site developed by the Outagamie County Historical Society and the University of Wisconsin's Oshkosh Area Research Center at http://www .foxvalleyhistory.org/mccarthy.

For more detailed background information, find Thomas Reeves' *The Life and Times of Joe McCarthy.* For insightful political analysis of McCarthy, see Stanley Kutler's *The American Inquisition: Justice and Injustice in the Cold War.* Robert Griffith's *The Politics of Fear: Joseph R. McCarthy and the Senate* offers an astute overview of McCarthy's rise and fall. In May 2003, the U.S. Senate released 9,000 pages of previously sealed transcripts of McCarthy's closed-door interrogations (1953–1954), which can be accessed online at http://www.gpoaccess .gov/index.html. (Just type the keywords Joseph McCarthy into the Search window at the top of the screen to access these and other primary sources.) The full text of McCarthy's official censure by the Senate can be read online at http://usinfo.state .gov/usa/infousa/facts/democrac/60.htm

You'll find many documents relating to McCarthy's career by doing a guided search in the Wisconsin Historical Society Archives at http://arcat.library.wisc.edu/

Emil deAntonio's film *Point of Order,* about the Army-McCarthy hearings, is available through the WHS Center for Film and Theater Research at http://www.wisconsinhistory.org/wcftr/.

The Posse Comitatus
Rural Terrorism at Tigerton Dells

The early 1980s brought hard times to American farmers. In the previous decades, high crop prices had encouraged many to take out high-interest loans to purchase more land and more equipment. But in 1981, a world-wide recession caused crop prices to plummet. Suddenly, many farmers lost much of their income, incurred massive debt, and faced the prospect of losing their farms and homes. In turn, the farmers searched for ways to ease the mounting pressures. Some sought answers by blaming others.

In Wisconsin, one person who claimed to have the answers was James Wickstrom, who lived in a 570-acre compound in Shawano County near Tigerton. Wickstrom claimed to be a minister for the Life Science Church and the National Counter-Insurgency Director for the Posse Comitatus. The Posse Comitatus was an anti-government, anti-Semitic organization that denied the legitimacy of state and federal government. Its leaders asserted that the only legitimate government existed at the county level; the term "posse comitatus" literally means "the power of the county." Members of the posse refused to pay taxes and to abide by court decisions. The Life Science Church was, on one hand, a fundamentalist religious organization, but on the other, it served as a way to dodge taxes. Members would sign over real estate to the church so they could be exempted from paying property and income taxes.

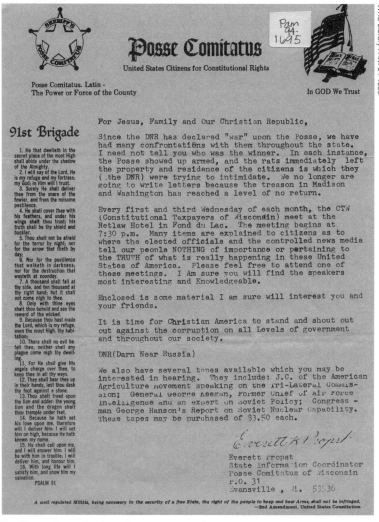

The Tigerton Posse Comitatus's newsletter for their members

The Posse Comitatus first came to Wisconsin in 1974, in response to farmers who felt they were losing control of their property to the state's Department of Natural Resources. But by 1980, the organization had evolved into an anti-government organization that encouraged people to stop paying taxes, defy local zoning ordinances, and prepare for an economic (even nuclear) crisis that would drive urban-dwellers into the countryside.

The largest membership was in northern Wisconsin. No one knew how many people in Shawano County—or elsewhere in central and northern Wisconsin—belonged to the organization, but its members armed themselves and sent out vigilante groups to intimidate game wardens, judges, and anyone else who refused to acknowledge the authority of the posse's "Constitutional Township of Tigerton Dells." Many poor and frustrated rural citizens sympathized with and even supported Wickstrom, and he received 16,000 votes in a 1980 senate race and 7,700 votes in a 1982 run for the governorship. Dozens of reporters attended his press conferences, and he spoke to audiences throughout the country, even appearing on the nationally popular Phil Donahue television program.

At Tigerton, posse members hoarded food and collected guns and ammunition. They were convinced that a crisis was coming that would force them to defend themselves against state and federal authorities. Signs posted near their property warned, "No Trespassing—Survivors Will Be Prosecuted." Whenever they felt threatened by agents from the Internal Revenue Service or the state's Department of Natural Resources, posse members retaliated by trying to intimidate the agents and by filing million-dollar liens in court to tie up the personal finances of judges or other public officials. One Wisconsin member named Donald Minniecheske was convicted under the so-called "Posse-Comitatus Law" of illegally filing fraudulent claims. Wickstrom himself was convicted of impersonating a public official—he claimed to be the "mayor" of Tigerton Dells—and served several months in prison.

Newspaper and national television coverage did much to reveal the hatred that inspired Posse Comitatus leaders, and the posse's terrorist tactics alienated many

Getting Started on Research

A good book on the Posse Comitatus movement is *Bitter Harvest* by James Corcoran. Wisconsin newspapers covered the posse on an almost daily basis. At the Wisconsin Historical Society's Web site, you can find many primary sources by doing a guided search using the keywords "posse comitatus." Your school librarian can help you find newspaper accounts, particularly from the summer of 1980. You can also ask older residents of Wisconsin what they remember about these events.

would-be members. Although it gradually faded from the spotlight, the organization has never disbanded and still has some adherents in rural areas. Its reputation for viciousness reminds us that the solutions to economic problems lie in cooperative, legal action and not in vigilante action.

Article from the *Milwaukee Journal,* July 27, 1980

The Bombing of Sterling Hall

Homegrown Terrorism on the UW Campus

During the 1960s, the University of Wisconsin–Madison gained the reputation of being a radical campus. Students marched to protest the Vietnam War, burned draft cards, and confronted army recruiters. In 1967, police used mace and clubs to break up a student protest at the Dow Chemical Company, a company that was producing the deadly chemical napalm for the U.S. military. But nothing was more horrifying than the early-morning events of August 24, 1970. A group of men detonated a bomb outside Sterling Hall, killing a university researcher and injuring four others. The bomb also destroyed vast amounts of scientific and scholarly research.

An August 24, 1970, *Capital Times* headline about the bombing of Sterling Hall

The men behind the bombing were Karl Armstrong, Dwight Armstrong, Leo Burt, and David Fine. On January 1, 1970, the two Armstrong Brothers flew a light plane over the Badger Army Ammunition Plant in Baraboo and dropped a small bomb, but it failed to go off. After this attack, they called themselves "The New Years Gang." They were responsible for bombing the ROTC offices and U.S. draft board that spring.

The New Years Gang believed that university research associated with the Army Mathematics Research Center aided the war effort and resulted in the deaths of thousands of innocent men, women, and children in southeast Asia. Many on campus and in Madison agreed, but few sympathized with using violence to make a point. While visiting their uncle in Minneapolis, the Armstrong brothers learned of the Kent State shootings, in which National Guard members fired into a crowd of students, killing four. That incident convinced Karl to tell Dwight, "They're killing us now. We're in the endgame. Army Math is next." So the New Years Gang prepared for their biggest attack.

Sterling Hall after the bombing, August 1970

In the early morning hours of August 24, the gang drove a stolen van packed with 2,000 pounds of ammonium nitrate soaked in jet fuel and parked it in front of Sterling Hall where the Army Math Research Center was located. At 3:42 a.m. on the 24th they detonated the bomb. The blast injured four researchers and killed Robert Fassnacht, a physicist. Fassnacht had been working late that night to finish a project and was planning to leave for San Diego later in the day with his wife and three children. People living 30 miles away heard the explosion, which shattered windows for blocks. The damage was estimated at 6 million dollars.

The New Years Gang had planned for the bomb to go off at a time when they thought no one would be in the building. At first, they were jubilant that the explosion had worked, but when they heard news reports that they had killed someone, they were horrified. All four fled to Canada. Karl Armstrong was captured in 1972 and served seven years in prison. In 1976, police arrested and captured David Fine in California, and he received a three-year

prison sentence. That year Dwight Armstrong was also arrested and served four years. Leo Burt has never been apprehended.

The Sterling Hall bombing was the New Years Gang's last attack. Many feared that the bombing would only escalate tensions on campus and encourage others to adopt such violent means of protest. But the bombing instead completely discredited the peace movement and quieted the protestors. Some activists continued protesting, but instead of 10,000 students showing up at a rally, usually just a few hundred actually came. For several years, student activism almost completely stopped. Today, Sterling Hall still stands, scarred by the attack, and university students continue to remember the bombing that brought an abrupt end to the '60s peace movement on campus.

Getting Started on Research

An excellent book on the Sterling Hall bombing is *Rads: The 1970 Bombing of the Army Math Research Center at the University of Wisconsin and Its Aftermath* by Tom Bates. There is also an excellent video documentary of UW campus activism and the bombing called *The War at Home.* Both are commonly available at local libraries. The bombing was headline news across the country. Your librarian can help you find microfilmed newspaper accounts from local and national papers, and the archives at the Wisconsin Historical Society contains numerous photographs and accounts of the bombing.

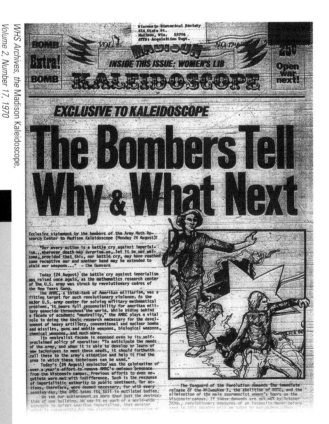

WHS Archives, the Madison Kaleidoscope, Volume 2, Number 17, 1970

The *Madison Kaleidoscope* was a radical newspaper devoted to protesting the war in Vietnam.

In the English Language
The Bennett Law Controversy

WITH INTENT TO CONTINUE SUCH attendance, then the penalty provided by this act shall not be incurred.

SECTION 5. No school shall be regarded as a school, under this act, unless there shall be taught therein, as part of the elementary education of children, reading, writing, arithmetic and United States history, in the English language.

SECTION 6. Prosecutions under this act shall

The Bennett Law, passed in 1889, required the instruction of students to be in English.

Sometimes the government enacts well-intentioned laws that have unforeseen consequences. In 1890, a measure to promote public education became a major controversy because it required children to be taught "in English." Many Wisconsin communities were made up of German and Scandinavian immigrants who continued to speak their native language at home and in school. As a result, the Bennett Law became one of the most controversial laws ever passed in the state.

Education reform was not new—for years people had recommended that children attend school at least a few months every year. A young assemblyman from Iowa County named Michael J. Bennett introduced the bill, which sailed through both houses of the legislature without debate. Governor Hoard signed the bill into law on April 17, 1889. The new law required each child to attend either a public or private school to learn "reading, writing, arithmetic and United States history in the English language."

No one questioned the concept of compulsory education, but the language requirement of the

Bennett Law ignited a storm of criticism. Beginning that summer and continuing into the spring of the next year, the English-language provision of the law was hotly contested across the state.

Defenders of the legislation, including the editor of the *Milwaukee Sentinel*, Horace Rublee, complained about immigrants who became citizens without learning English. But many others opposed the law. He praised the requirement as a way to assimilate immigrants into American culture more quickly. Both Lutheran and Catholic Wisconsin Germans, operated parochial schools and resented any attempt to force teachers to teach exclusively in English. They worried that their children would arrive at school and not understand anything the teacher said!

Other ethnic groups also opposed the law. Wisconsin's Irish already spoke English, but they were wary of any potential interference involving their Catholic schools. Even some Scandinavians who favored the language provision of the Bennett Law were skeptical of the state's requirement that children attend school in their district. They wanted the right to send their children to any school that they wanted.

Governor Hoard was shocked by the response and insisted on the need for public education. He reiterated that children of immigrants needed to learn English in order to be useful citizens. During the election of 1890, the Republican party came out

Governor WIlliam Dempster Hoard

Getting Started on Research

To learn more about the Bennett Law, a good place to start is "Wisconsin Ethnic Groups and the Election of 1890" by Roger E. Wyman in the *Wisconsin Magazine of History* 51 (Summer 1968), 269–293. During the late nineteenth century, numerous ethnic groups lived in Wisconsin. You can read about them in *Old World Wisconsin* by Fred L. Holmes. For papers by several prominent people who commented on the law, access the WHS online archives and type "Bennett Law" into the guided search feature. Also in these archives, you can find Robert Ulrich's dissertation "The Bennett Law of 1889: Education and Politics in Wisconsin," which will point you to a variety of other primary documents.

I have, I believe, as friendly a feeling towards our German-American population as any man in this country; and if I did not believe that the Bennett Law would assist in the advancement of their youth I would certainly oppose its continuance upon our statute books. I want the little German boy and girl, the little Norwegian, the little Bohemian and the little Pole, the children of all foreign born parents, to have the same chance in life as my children. Without a knowledge of the English language they can not have this chance. This is a very plain proposition, with which I know you will agree. I plead for these children of foreign born parents for the reason that I personally know many who were born in this country who are handicapped by ignorance of the language of the country. Should not something be done to give these bright young people an opportunity to rise according to the ability God has given them? Advancement in life for them is out of the question without a knowledge of the language of the country.

Governor Hoard wrote this in support of the Bennett Law, circa 1890–1891.

in favor of the law, but Democrats demanded its repeal. Joining the Democrats were Lutheran and Catholic organizations that wanted to protect their parochial school systems. Germans—Wisconsin's largest ethnic group—called the law an attack on their mother tongue and their heritage, and most German communities voted solidly

Democratic. Scandinavians, normally dependable Republican voters, either voted Democratic or simply did not vote.

The conflict resulted in a major Democratic political victory led by George W. Peck of Milwaukee. The Democrats won every state office, captured a majority of the legislature, and won all but one of Wisconsin's seven congressional seats. In 1891, the legislature promptly repealed the Bennett Law, but remnants of the issue remain today as the state continues to struggle to find the best ways to educate its children. Many of today's students in Wisconsin are immigrants from Mexico, Laos, and Puerto Rico, and their first language is not English. A century after it became law, the phrase "in the English language" remains a sensitive and controversial topic.

How did people in your community respond to the Bennett Law and what was its local impact? Your librarian can help you find local histories and newspaper accounts that describe your community's school system in 1890 and the ethnic groups that lived there.

An illustration from the pamphlet "The Bennett Law Analyzed"

School Vouchers
The Milwaukee Experiment

When our nation began, the founders sought to avoid the religious divisiveness that had plagued European countries. In framing the U.S. Constitution, they purposefully sought to separate government and religion. In 1789, James Madison wrote the First Amendment to the U.S. Constitution, which was ratified in 1791. Later, the first ten amendments became known as the Bill of Rights.

The First Amendment guarantees the right of free speech, the right to practice the religion of one's own choosing, the right to petition and to peaceably assemble, and the right of the press to communicate freely and openly. The Constitution provides a framework for these principles, and the judicial system is given the authority to interpret them. The First Amendment outlines the rights, yet the debate concerning the separation of church and state continues today. The role of religion in the United States is at the center of many contested social issues, including abortion, freedom of speech, sexual preference, cloning, and others.

The nation's public schools, for example, have become a hotbed of controversy regarding the separation of church and state. Appropriate funding, curriculum content, and assessment have always been part of the education debate, but in the last few years, criticism has mounted against public schools for not meeting students' needs. The criticism has spurred reforms that include charter schools, different academic standards, and private school voucher programs.

In 1990, Wisconsin became the first state to implement a large-scale voucher program. The Milwaukee Parental Choice Program (MPCP), which provides state-paid tuition vouchers for eligible low-income students to enroll in private schools in the city of Milwaukee, started with about 340 students (.4% of Milwaukee Public School enrollment).

In 1995, legislation included religious schools in the voucher program and expanded enrollment. By the 1998–1999 school year, religious schools constituted roughly 75% of the participating schools. Sectarian schools across the nation account for about 85% of the private school enrollment in the United States, meaning that Wisconsin is in keeping with this national trend.

By the 2000–2001 school year, enrollment had grown to 9,638 students

Letter to the editor, May 18, 2001, expressing opposition to the private school voucher program in Milwaukee.

Milwaukee Journal, May 18, 2001

SCHOOL CHOICE

Voucher program not improving MPS

I must rebut the letter from Annie Oliver ("Kids being lost in political shuffle," May 14).

The decline in Milwaukee Public Schools enrollment due to vouchers has meant $25 million lost in school aid. Voucher money has followed 10% of MPS students to mainly Catholic schools. What about the 90% of MPS students whose parents either believe in MPS or do not want their children in Catholic schools? Why not fix the problems Oliver laments, as we all do, instead of gutting the system?

It is disgraceful that MPS has been allowed to sink this low. Perhaps former MPS Superintendent Howard Fuller could have addressed these very problems rather than championing private schools.

Vouchers cannot be accepted as a valid method of improving MPS "through competition." They are unfair to non-voucher students; they fly in the face of the separation of church and state; they are a misleading panacea to fixing what's wrong with our public schools. Get rid of vouchers!

Eve Sylvester
Retired MPS teacher
Fox Point

(9.2% of MPS enrollment) participating in the voucher program, with approximately 6,000 enrolled in parochial schools. The 1999 Wisconsin Act 9 dictated that program costs would derive from state funds earmarked for both Milwaukee and the rest of the state's school districts, rather than just money for Milwaukee. The following school year, approximately $49 million of state funding was applied to MPCP. Opponents criticized this funding structure, saying that it diverted much-needed resources from public schools.

School voucher advocates argue that vouchers give poor families the same opportunities afforded the affluent, such as the ability to "choose" a private school. Opponents counter that parents are not legally guaranteed the "choice" of parochial schools and to give public money for religious instruction brings church and state together when the two should maintain their separation.

In 1992, the voucher program was tested in court, and the Wisconsin Supreme Court upheld Milwaukee's program as constitutional by a 4–3 vote. In 1998, the U.S. Supreme Court declined to hear the appeal of the Wisconsin Supreme Court decision, which allowed the decision to stand. In 2002, the U.S. Supreme Court ruled that the existence of publicly funded school vouchers does not violate church-state separation.

Supporters and detractors from all sides of the political, economic, and social spectrum continue to speak out about the topic. They range from people who want to shape educational policy to parents concerned about the quality of their children's education to activists and others committed to maintaining the separation of church and state. Numerous factors, including educational funding, what and how our children

should learn, and the role of religion in our society continue to keep the issue at the forefront of the social agenda.

Milwaukee Journal, March 4, 1992

In 1992, the Wisconsin State Supreme Court upheld Milwaukee's voucher program.

Getting Started on Research

Several secondary sources can aid your research. Try *Education: Opposing Viewpoints*, edited by Mary Williams, and *False Choices: Why School Vouchers Threaten Our Children's Future*, edited by Robert Lowe and Barbara Miner. Also, *Public School Choice vs. Private School Vouchers*, edited by Richard D. Kahlenberg, provides an excellent analysis.

For more information about the voucher system in Wisconsin, access the Wisconsin Education Association Council Web site at http://www .weac.org/. The National Education Association is also an excellent resource. Its Web site is at http://www.nea.org/. You can access the August 2001 report by the U.S. General Accounting Office Government titled "School Vouchers: Publicly Funded Programs in Cleveland and Milwaukee" on the Internet at http://www.gao .gov/new.items/d01914.pdf. The report provides valuable information regarding program funding and results. The Legislative Reference Bureau also provides updated information about the program through its search feature at http://www.legis.state .wi.us/lrb/index.htm.

Also, local newspapers and magazines provide examples of primary source material on both sides of the issue. Many can be found at your local library and on the Web.

Vitamin Research and the Wisconsin Alumni Research Foundation

Vitamins are tiny organic molecules that are critical to human life. Research has shown that vitamin C strengthens the body's immune system and that vitamin K is required for normal blood clotting. But until the early years of the twentieth century, these substances were unknown. Scientists did realize that people could eat plenty of food but still become sick when they did not eat the right *kinds* of food. Without vitamin D, for example, otherwise healthy people would suffer from deformed and weakened bones, a condition known as scurvy.

In the first two decades of the 1900s, the University of Wisconsin played a major role in making vitamins well-known and understood by the general public. In 1914, E.V. McCollum of the UW College of Agriculture discovered a fat-soluble substance that he named "vitamin." This was vitamin A, and the first announcement of its discovery was printed in *Hoard's Dairyman*, Wisconsin's foremost agricultural newspaper. Soon thereafter, McCollum discovered water-soluble vitamin B. In 1917, McCollum left the University of Wisconsin for Johns Hopkins University, where he discovered vitamin D.

But, exciting discoveries continued in Madison. Henry Steenbock learned that yellow corn contained vitamin A but white corn did not, which meant that all varieties of a particular food were not equally healthful. Edwin B. Hard discovered that chickens suffering from leg weakness lacked sufficient vitamin D in their diets.

Harry Steenbock working on his research.

Steenbock and his colleagues also discovered that sunlight helped cure rickets, a research finding that established a link between the sun and vitamin D.

The discovery of a connection between vitamin D and sunlight raised important questions about the role of research at a public university. Steenbock had discovered how to create vitamin D in foods by exposing them to ultraviolet light. This was a major breakthrough in nutrition and could help millions of people, and it meant that Steenbock could patent the process and become rich. This was a dilemma—should he deliberately not patent the process to make it available to the public or open the door to unscrupulous industrial firms abusing the process for their own profit?

To protect his research, Steenbock proposed that the university create a trust to take the patent. Harry Russell, the Dean of the College of Agriculture, and Charles Slichter, Dean of the Graduate School, met with a Madison attorney and drew up articles of incorporation for the Wisconsin Alumni Research Foundation (WARF). WARF was formally organized in 1925 as an alumni group to receive patents from university research and to fund additional research projects. Money received from the patent then was divided between the researcher (who received 15%) and a trust fund. WARF supervised the trust fund and provided grants, scholarships, and fellowships to fund research in the natural sciences.

Since its creation in 1925, WARF has become a driving force in university research. Its most significant contribution to science bears its name: Warfarin. The discovery came in the early 1930s when Professor Karl Paul Link began investigating a possible connection between spoiled sweet clover and a disease that killed cattle by causing their blood to stop clotting. Link isolated the cause of the disease, an anticoagulant called Dicumarol, which WARF patented under the name Warfarin. It has since become the most important drug in treating victims of heart attacks. And it all started with a pursuit of the mysterious substances called vitamins.

In what ways do vitamins affect our lives? What other research has the University of Wisconsin undertaken in the last century and how has this research improved medicine and agriculture?

Getting Started on Research

Learn more about the University of Wisconsin and its research in *The University of Wisconsin: A History* by Merle Curti and Vernon Carstensen. Footnotes and bibliography will lead you to primary resources. You can also read about the work of the College of Agriculture in newspapers from the 1920s and 1930s. Your public librarian can help you find issues of *Hoard's Dairyman* and other farm journals.

One useful idea to help get you started is getting the address from the Web site and writing or calling the foundation to ask about their papers, or to interview a researcher who may be working on a current project, or to find someone who can describe the foundation's history. For primary resources, consult the WARF Web site at http://www.warf.ws/aboutus/.

Milwaukee Journal

Our Debt to Steenbock

The name of Harry Steenbock may be little known or unknown today to millions of the world's people who remain deeply in his debt. But the vitamin D research of the University of Wisconsin biochemist four decades ago did much to eliminate rickets, a childhood disease now rare in the western world.

The retired professor died Monday in Madison in his 81st year. Behind him lay the researcher's good life of inspiration, perspiration, discovery and notable service to humanity.

It was Prof. Steenbock who, in 1924, demonstrated that irradiation by ultraviolet light increased the vitamin D potency of foods. The discovery resulted in the healthful irradiation of certain foods, especially milk.

Rickets once was a common disease of infancy and childhood, caused by a deficiency of vitamin D and resulting in bone deformity. Thanks to the Steenbock discovery, it now can be prevented by the regular prescription of supplemental vitamin D.

Some men might have enriched themselves by the discovery. Prof. Steenbock signed his vitamin D process over to the then new Wisconsin Alumni Research Foundation which he and an associate had helped plan. The royalties made a major contribution to the foundation which has contributed so much to the university, providing generous seed money for investment, growth and future research.

The names of yesterday's men of genius, vision and idealism may be forgotten by many. But the good that they brought to their world remains and grows.

Article from the *Milwaukee Journal*, December 27, 1967, recounting Steenbock's accomplishments.

S O C I A L   I S S U E S

Topic	Secondary Source Material	Primary Source Material
Pursuing Freedom: Wisconsin Defies the Fugitive Slave Law	Butler, Diane S. "The Public and Private Affairs of Sherman M. Booth." *Wisconsin Magazine of History* 82, no. 3 (1999). Current, Richard N. *The History of Wisconsin, Volume II: The Civil War Era, 1848–1873*, Madison, WI: State Historical Society of Wisconsin, 1976. *Stand the Storm.* VHS. Madison, WI: Wisconsin Public Television in cooperation with the Wisconsin Supreme Court, 1998.	The Wisconsin Historical Society Archives: http://arcat.library.wisc.edu/ keywords: Sherman Booth, Joshua Glover
Breaking the Color Line: Milwaukee Housing Segregation	Thompson, William. *The History of Wisconsin, Volume VI: Continuity and Change, 1940–1965*. Madison, WI: State Historical Society of Wisconsin, 1988. Zubrensky, Ruth. "A Report on Past Discrimination Against African-Americans in Milwaukee, 1835–1999." July 1999. Trotter, Joe William Jr. *Black Milwaukee: The Making of an Industrial Proletariat, 1915–45.* Urbana: University of Illinois Press, 1985. Bayer, Kristin. "Residential Segregation and the Section 8 Housing Allowances Program: An Exploratory Study of Milwaukee, Wisconsin." Thesis. Madison, WI: University of Wisconsin, 1991.	The Wisconsin Historical Society Archives: http://arcat.library.wisc.edu/ keyword: Henry Maier

Topic	Secondary Source Material	Primary Source Material
Dr. Kate Pelham Newcomb: Rural Healthcare on Snowshoes	Comandini, Adele. *Dr. Kate, Angel on Snowshoes: The Story of Kate Pelham Newcomb, M.D.* New York: Rinehart, 1956. The Dr. Kate Museum in Woodruff can be reached at 715-356-6896. The museum's Web site is available at http://north-wis.com/drkmuseum/	The Wisconsin Historical Society Archives: http://arcat.library.wisc.edu/ keyword: Dr. Kate Pelham Newcomb
Cordelia Harvey: Northern Hospitals Close to Home	Current, Richard N. *The History of Wisconsin, Volume II: The Civil War Era, 1848–1873.* Madison, WI: State Historical Society of Wisconsin, 1976. Klement, Frank L. *Wisconsin in the Civil War: The Home Front and the Battle Front, 1861–1865.* Madison, WI: State Historical Society of Wisconsin, 1997. Holmes, Fred L. *Badger Saints and Sinners.* Milwaukee, WI: E.M. Hale and Company, 1939.	The Wisconsin Historical Society Archives: http://arcat.library.wisc.edu/ keyword: Cordelia Harvey
Temperance in Wisconsin: Frances E. Willard, Carry A. Nation, and the WCTU	Rorabaugh, W. J. *The Alcoholic Republic: An American Tradition.* New York: Oxford University Press, 1981. Leeman, Richard W. *"Do Everything" Reform: The Oratory of Frances E. Willard.* Westport, CT: Greenwood Press, 1992. Bordin, Ruth. *Frances Willard: A Biography.* Chapel Hill, NC: University of North Carolina Press, 1986. The Wisconsin Bar Association Web site: http://www.wisbar.org/wislawmag/archive/history/pt14.html	Willard, Frances E. *Glimpses of Fifty Years: The Autobiography of an American Woman.* Chicago, IL: H.J. Smith and Company, 1889.

Topic	Secondary Source Material	Primary Source Material
We Won't Fight: German Immigrants Protest the Civil War Draft	Current, Richard N. *The History of Wisconsin, Volume II: The Civil War Era, 1848–1873.* Madison, WI: State Historical Society of Wisconsin, 1976. Klement, Frank L. *Wisconsin in the Civil War: The Home Front and the Battle Front, 1861–1865.* Madison, WI: State Historical Society of Wisconsin, 1997. Barker, Brett. *Exploring Civil War Wisconsin: A Survival Guide for Researchers.* Madison, WI: Wisconsin Historical Society, 2002.	The 1862 militia draft on the Wisconsin Historical Society's Web site: http://www.wisconsinhistory.org/teachers/lessons/civilwar/draft/
Don't Pick on Us!: Hispanic Farmworkers March to Madison	Salas, Jesus and David Giffey. *Struggle for Justice: The Migrant Farm Worker Labor Movement in Wisconsin.* WHS Pamphlet Collection, 1998: 98–187. *Migrant Labor in Wisconsin.* Governor's Commission on Human Rights, 1965. WHS Government Pubs., Call No.: GO RI.2:M 5/6.	The Wisconsin Historical Society Archives: http://arcat.library.wisc.edu/ keyword: migrant labor The Wisconsin Historical Society Museum: http://www.wisconsinhistory.org/museum/
Lloyd Barbee: Fighting Segregation in Milwaukee Schools	Thompson, William. *The History of Wisconsin, Volume VI: Continuity and Change, 1940–1965.* Madison, WI: State Historical Society of Wisconsin, 1988.	The Wisconsin Historical Society Archives: http://arcat.library.wisc.edu/ keyword: Lloyd Barbee
America's Longest Strike: The Kohler Strike of 1934–1941	Garrett, Garet. "Salvos against the New Deal: Selections from the Saturday Evening Post, 1933–1940." Caldwell, ID: Caxton Press, 2002. Glad, Paul. *History of Wisconsin, Volume V: War, a New Era, and Depression, 1914–1940.* Madison, WI: State Historical Society of Wisconsin, 1990.	The Wisconsin Historical Society Archives: http://arcat.library.wisc.edu/ keywords: Kohler strike

INSTITUTION

Topic	Secondary Source Material	Primary Source Material
Olympia Brown and the Women's Suffrage Movement	Cote, Charlotte. *Olympia Brown: The Battle for Equality.* Racine, WI: Mother Courage Press, 1988.	The Schlesinger Library of the Racliffe Institute at Harvard University: http://www.radcliffe.edu/schles/index.php The Wisconsin Historical Society Archives: http://arcat.library.wisc.edu/ keyword: Olympia Brown The Library of Congress Web site: http://www.loc.gov/ keywords: National Woman's Party Papers Brown, Olympia. *Olympia Brown: An Autobiography.* Ed. Gwendolen B. Willis. Racine, WI: G. Willis, 1960.
Helping Hands: Wisconsin's Schools for the Deaf and Blind	The Wisconsin Center for the Blind and Visually Impaired Web site: http://www.wcbvi.k12.wi.us/ The Wisconsin School for the Deaf Web site: http://www.wsd.k12.wi.us/ Odegard, Bernett O. and George M. Keith. *A History of the State Board of Control of Wisconsin and the State Institutions: 1849–1939.* Madison, WI: State Board of Control, 1939.	The Wisconsin Historical Society Archives: http://arcat.library.wisc.edu/ keywords: Wisconsin School for the Deaf, Wisconsin School for the Blind

TION OF THE BLIND, JANESVILLE.

Topic	Secondary Source Material	Primary Source Material
Senator Joseph McCarthy: The Rise and Fall of an Anti-Communist	The Outagamie County Historical Society and University of Wisconsin's Oshkosh Area Research Center Web site: http://www.foxvalleyhistory.org/mccarthy Reeves, Thomas. *The Life and Times of Joe McCarthy*. New York: Stein and Day, 1982. Griffith, Robert. *The Politics of Fear: Joseph R. McCarthy and the Senate*. Amherst, MA: University of Massachusetts Press, 1987. The Wisconsin Center for Film and Theater Research Web site: http://www.wisconsinhistory.org/wcftr/	Full text of McCarthy's official censure by the Senate available online at: http://usinfo.state.gov/usa/infousa/facts/democrac/60.htm The Wisconsin Historical Society Archives: http://arcat.library.wisc.edu/
The Posse Comitatus: Rural Terrorism at Tigerton Dells	Corcoran, James. *Bitter Harvest: Gordon Kahl and the Posse Comitatus—Murder in the Heartland*. New York: Penguin Books, 1991.	The *Milwaukee Journal*, July 27, 1980, p. 1. The Wisconsin Historical Society Archives: http://arcat.library.wisc.edu/ keywords: posse comitatus
The Bombing of Sterling Hall: Homegrown Terrorism on the UW Campus	Bates, Tom. *Rads: The 1970 Bombing of the Army Math Research Center at the University of Wisconsin and Its Aftermath*. New York: HarperCollins Publishers, 1992. *The War at Home*. VHS. A First Run Features Presentation. A Catalyst Films/Madison Film Production Company Production. Produced and directed by Glenn Silber and Barry Alexander Brown. Publisher: First Run Features Home Video, 1998.	The Wisconsin Historical Society Archives: http://arcat.library.wisc.edu/ keywords: Sterling Hall bombing

Topic	Secondary Source Material	Primary Source Material
In the English Language: The Bennett Law Controversy	Wyman, Roger E. "Wisconsin Ethnic Groups and the Election of 1890." *Wisconsin Magazine of History* 51, no. 4 (1968), 269–293. Holmes, Fred L. *Old World Wisconsin: Around Europe in the Badger State.* Madison, WI: University of Wisconsin Press, 2003. Ulrich, Robert. "The Bennett Law of 1889: Education and Politics in Wisconsin." PhD diss., University of Wisconsin at Madison, 1965.	The Wisconsin Historical Society Archives: http://arcat.library.wisc.edu/ keywords: Bennett Law
School Vouchers: The Milwaukee Experiment	*Education: Opposing Viewpoints.* Mary E. Williams, ed. San Diego, CA: Greenhaven Press, 2000. *False Choices: Why School Vouchers Threaten our Children's Future.* Robert Lowe and Barbara Miner, eds. Milwaukee, WI: Rethinking Schools, Ltd., 1992. *Public School Choice vs. Private School Vouchers.* Ed. Richard D. Kahlenberg. New York: Century Foundation Press, 2003.	The Wisconsin Education Association Council Web site: http://www.weac.org/ The National Education Association Web site: http://www.nea.org/ Download the "School Vouchers: Publicly Funded Programs in Cleveland and Milwaukee" report from the U.S. General Accounting Office Web site at http://www.gao.gov/new.items/d01914.pdf The Legislative Reference Bureau Web site: http://www.legis.state.wi.us/lrb/index.htm
Vitamin Research and the Wisconsin Alumni Research Foundation	Curti, Merle and Vernon Carstensen. *The University of Wisconsin: A History.* Madison, WI: University of Wisconsin Press, 1949.	*Hoard's Dairyman* The WARF Web site: http://www.warf.ws/aboutus/

Chapter Eight

Arts, Entertainment, and Sports

- Ed "Strangler" Lewis: Wisconsin's World Champion Wrestler

- Lunt and Fontanne: First Couple of the American Stage

- Of Woods and Prairies: Children's Author Laura Ingalls Wilder

- Packers as Packers: Meatpackers and Wisconsin's Favorite Team

- Three Ring Circus: How Wisconsin Became America's Circus Capital

- Vinnie Ream Hoxie: The Woman Who Carved Lincoln

- Frank Lloyd Wright: Legendary Architect

- Wheel Speed: Wisconsin's Link to Auto Racing

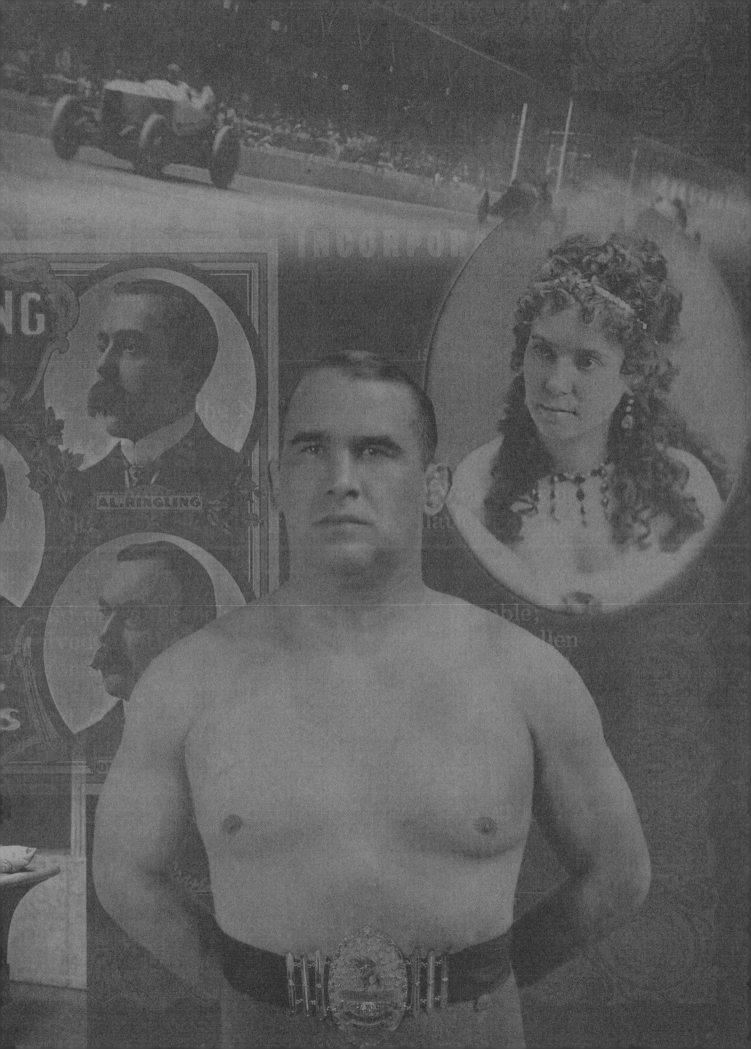

Ed "Strangler" Lewis
Wisconsin's World Champion Wrestler

Just about every Wisconsinite has heard of Curly Lambeau, the founder of the Green Bay Packers and one of the most famous Wisconsin sports figures. But have you ever heard of Ed Lewis? During the 1920s and 1930s, he was as famous as baseball legend Babe Ruth and boxer Jack Dempsey. Lewis was the world wrestling champion five times between 1920 and 1931, but more importantly, he popularized the sport nationwide.

Lewis was born Robert Friedrich in Sheboygan on June 30, 1891. When he was 13, his family moved to Wood County, and he began wrestling in high school. That year, his team played a match near Wisconsin Rapids, and he defeated the local champion after a tough bout before 300 spectators. Every small town had its hometown champ, and a champion was what young Lewis was determined to be. Lewis took on all

Ed "Strangler" Lewis

challengers and most often won. He briefly attended Ripon College, but he dropped out to pursue a professional wrestling career.

In the early twentieth century, wrestling was very different than it is today. There were many wrestling matches, or "shoots," and the emphasis was on athletic ability, rather than on brightly-colored costumes and over-the-top showmanship. Gaining the advantage over an opponent through sheer strength and leverage required skill and concentration. The goal was to pin the opponent to the mat–a victory required two out of three "falls." Some matches lasted hours. On July 4, 1916, Lewis was involved in what remains one of the longest wrestling matches in history. He wrestled Joe Stecher, a former champion himself, for five and a half hours!

The match ended in a draw. But in 1920, Lewis defeated Stecher to earn his first-ever World Champion title. Lewis was well-suited to be a star

Jack Pfefer Collection, University Libraries of Notre Dame

wrestler–he was powerfully built with a 56-inch chest and weight of around 250 pounds. Lewis got his nickname "Strangler" because he used a variation of a move known as "the sleeper hold." To spectators, the maneuver gave the impression that Lewis was strangling his opponents. An earlier wrestler named Evan Lewis had been nicknamed "The Strangler," so the young boy from Wisconsin adopted "Ed Lewis" as his professional name, in part to hide his career from his parents.

Lewis claimed that he wrestled in more than 6,200 matches during the 1920s and 1930s, losing only 33. In 1937, he quit after becoming disgusted that the sport had become both violent and showy. Lewis called it "slam-bang wrestling" and complained, "if you put on a good scientific match, they [the fans] walked out. They wanted to see slamming." But, Lewis could not resist the ring's allure and occasionally continued to get back in the ring.

Lewis's last match was in 1947 in Honolulu. After leaving professional wrestling, he opened a restaurant and tried acting. But, wrestling was in his blood. He returned to the sport

Getting Started on Research

Obituaries are one of the best ways to learn about people. Your public librarian can help you find newspaper accounts of Lewis's life and his death (August 7, 1966). Also, several Web sites provide biographical details and photographs, including the National Wrestling Hall of Fame and others, at http://www.wrestlinghalloffame.org and http://www.puroresu.com/wrestlers/lewis_ed/.

For secondary sources, consult Charles Morrow Wilson's *The Magnificent Scufflers: Revealing the Great Days When America Wrestled the World*, Don Nardo's *Wrestling*, Kristian Pope and Ray Whebbe Jr.'s *The Encyclopedia of Professional Wrestling: 100 Years of History, Headlines, & Hitmakers*.

to train and manage his protégé, the world champion Lou Thesz. Lewis's chief pastime in retirement was bridge. He became an expert at the game, but the loss of his sight in the early 1960s forced him to give it up. He had begun to suffer from trachoma, a degenerative eye disorder common to professional wrestlers and boxers. He spent a sizeable fortune to save his sight, and his vision did improve for a time, but by 1962, he was completely blind. When Lewis died on August 7, 1966, in Muskogee, Oklahoma, newspapers across the nation remembered him as the father of modern professional wrestling.

What sports are popular in your area, and what led to their popularity? Has an athlete from your community ever become famous? If so, in what sport?

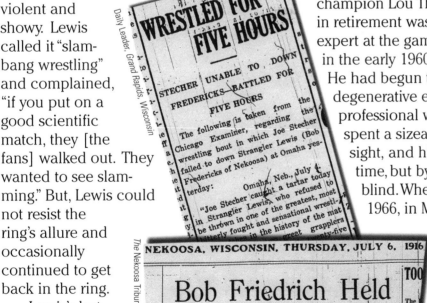

Article from Grand Rapids, Wisconsin, about Lewis' match on July 4, 1916

Daily Leader, Grand Rapids, Wisconsin

WRESTLED FOR FIVE HOURS

STECHER UNABLE TO DOWN FREDERICKS—BATTLED FOR FIVE HOURS

The following is taken from the Chicago Examiner, regarding the wrestling bout in which Joe Stecher failed to down Strangler Lewis (Bob Fredericks of Nekoosa) at Omaha yesterday:

Omaha, Neb., July 4.

"Joe Stecher caught a tartar today in Strangler Lewis, who refused to be thrown in one of the greatest, most bitterly fought and sensational wrestling matches in the history of the mat...

The Nekoosa Tribune

NEKOOSA, WISCONSIN, THURSDAY, JULY 6. 1916

Bob Friedrich Held the great Stetcher to a draw July 4th

The boys were at it for four hours and fifty-five minutes. Bob broke the scissors hold three times. The reports received vary so we are obliged to wait until we get word first hand.

Article from Lewis' hometown, Nekoosa, Wisconsin, about his famous July 4th match

Lunt and Fontanne
First Couple of the American Stage

Lunt and Fontanne in a scene from *Amphitryon*. Lunt's character relaxes while Fontanne's character darns his socks.

WHi Image ID 10507

Lynn Fontanne and Alfred Lunt were born on either side of the Atlantic Ocean. Fontanne was born in the English county of Essex on December 6, 1887, and Alfred Lunt was born in Milwaukee on August 12, 1892. Both aspired to acting careers at a very young age. During Washington, DC's summer stock in 1919, Fontanne met Lunt, and they performed in three plays together. Who would have guessed that they would become known as the aristocracy of the American stage?

In 1922, Lunt and Fontanne married, and after 1931, they often appeared together in productions. Their dedication to the craft of acting bordered on obsessive. Wanting to hone every element of a performance to perfection, they rehearsed constantly. Through their work, they developed a naturalistic style of speaking on stage, a synchronized "body language" that almost seemed choreographed, and a rapid-fire banter that became their trademark.

They were not known as the most handsome or most beautiful, but they exuded a sense of tremendous glamour and class, which helped them become popular and enduring icons of the art.

When the two grew tired of starring in light comedies, they joined the New York Theatre Guild in 1924. This guild was known for its serious literary and dramatic work, and in their five years as members, Lunt and Fontanne acted together in several plays, including George Bernard Shaw's greatest works: *Pygmalion* (1926), *Arms and the Man* (1925), and *The Doctor's Dilemma* (1927).

Although Lunt and Fontanne acted in many dramas, they were best-known for their work in comedies, many of which focused on marital infidelities. They pushed the boundaries of acceptability onstage with memorable performances in Noël Coward's *Design for Living* (1933) and in two Eugene O'Neill plays: he in *Marco*

Millions (1928) and she in *Strange Interlude* (1928).

Although Lunt once claimed to be a "slave of the playwright," the couple often altered the plays in which they appeared, sometimes without the playwright's consent! But, the result always led to magnificent performances. Often, playwrights commented that the Lunts brought out elements of the play that even they hadn't envisioned.

Despite their antics onstage, the Lunts maintained an interesting balance offstage between excess and modesty. When President Johnson awarded them with separate Presidential Medals of Freedom in 1964, both shied away from the cameras, believing it inappropriate for two mere actors to be photographed with a such a powerful figure as the president of the United States.

They retired from the stage in 1958, and the old Globe Theatre in New York City was renamed the Lunt-Fontanne Theatre in their honor. *The Sound of Music* and Disney's *Beauty and the Beast* became musical legends at this Broadway venue. The Lunts

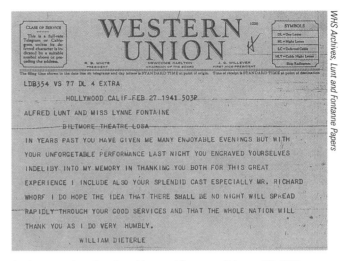

A telegram written by a fan of Lunt and Fontanne, February 27, 1951.

emerged from retirement in 1965 to act in *Magnificent Yankee* for the *Hallmark Hall of Fame* television series, garnering Emmy awards for their performances. Two years later Fontanne appeared alone in a television production of *Anastasia*, which was her first performance without Lunt since *Strange Interlude* in 1928.

In retirement, Lunt and Fontanne lived in the farmhouse they remodeled and named Ten Chimneys in Genesee Depot, Wisconsin. They filled the house with antiques from their travels and invested as much time and energy into decorating, cultivating friendships, and entertaining as they had put into their acting careers. Some of the best known names in film and theater graced the doorway of Ten Chimneys.

In 1971, both received special Tony awards for lifetime contributions to the theater. Alfred Lunt died on August 3, 1977, and Fontanne passed away on July 30, 1983. Without their income to sustain the estate, Ten Chimneys fell into disrepair for decades until May 2003, when it was restored and opened to the public.

Getting Started on Research

Several biographies of the Lunts provide interesting background information, including Maurice Zolotow's *Stagestruck: The Romance of Alfred Lunt and Lynn Fontanne,* Margot Peters' *Design for Living,* and Jared Brown's *The Fabulous Lunts.* The Wisconsin Historical Society Archives houses many primary and secondary documents regarding the couple. To experience a bit of their life, visit the Lunts' Wisconsin home, Ten Chimneys, at Genesee Depot. Open to visitors since 2003, the house maintains the furnishings just as they were when the Lunts lived there. Tours of Ten Chimneys are offered between March 30–October 30, Tuesday–Saturday. To make reservations, call 262-968-4110.

Of Woods and Prairies
Children's Author Laura Ingalls Wilder

The books of beloved children's author Laura Elizabeth Ingalls Wilder have been making frontier life real to young readers for more than 70 years. She was born to Charles and Caroline Ingalls on February 7, 1867, near Pepin, Wisconsin. In 1868, the Ingalls family moved to Missouri, but they didn't stay long. Motivated by the 1862 Homestead Act, Charles bought land near Independence, Kansas. The family built a house and a stable, but left in the fall of 1870. Rumors had circulated that the government was going to break its promise concerning the Homestead Act and forcibly remove the settlers. So, the Ingalls family returned to Wisconsin.

Little House in the Big Woods begins just after their return in 1871. Four-year-old Laura lived in a log cabin with her family and the family dog, Jack. The book depicts the hardships of pioneer life, such as securing food for the long, cold winter; curing bear meat; and sapping maple trees. But, the narrative also highlights the simple joys of living on the frontier, including celebrating Christmas with homemade toys and treats, planting in the spring, harvesting, making the first trip into town, and falling asleep to the sound of her father's fiddle. Laura relates several major adventures: a snowstorm, a panther attack, and a wild sled ride.

In 1874, the Ingalls bought a farm near Walnut Grove, Minnesota, where the family lived in a dugout until they could build a house. The wheat crop was bountiful that year, but a "cloud" of grasshoppers destroyed it. The family tried again the next year, but the grasshopper eggs from the previous harvest hatched and the insects once again destroyed the crop. After living in

Iowa, the Ingalls family soon returned to Walnut Grove in the summer of 1877. This time, they lived in town and Charles did carpentry and opened a butcher shop. In 1879, the family moved to De Smet in the Dakota Territory. One after another, blizzards besieged the area from October 1880 to May 1881, hindering travel and preventing trains from delivering supplies.

At age 15, Laura began teaching at Bouchie School, located 12 miles from her home. While boarding with the Bouchies, Laura grew increasingly frightened of Mrs. Bouchie's erratic behavior, which was apparently induced by the isolation she felt in the barren, lonely settlement. A farmer from De Smet named Almanzo James

Harper and Brothers, New York and London, 1932

CHAPTER I

Little House in the Big Woods

ONCE upon a time, sixty years ago, a little girl lived in the Big Woods of Wisconsin, in a little gray house made of logs.

The great, dark trees of the Big Woods stood all around the house, and beyond them were other trees and beyond them were more trees. As far as a man could go to the north in a day, or a week, or a whole month, there was nothing but woods. There were no houses. There were no roads. There were no people. There were only trees and the wild animals who had their homes among them.

Wolves lived in the Big Woods, and bears, and huge wild cats. Muskrats and mink and otter lived by the streams. Foxes had dens in the hills and deer roamed everywhere.

To the east of the little log house, and to the west, there were miles upon miles of trees, and only a few little log houses scattered far apart in the edge of the Big Woods.

First page of Laura Ingalls Wilder's *Little House in the Big Woods,* 1932

Getting Started on Research

Secondary materials include William Anderson's *Pioneer Girl: The Story of Laura Ingalls Wilder* and John Miller's *Becoming Laura Ingalls Wilder: The Woman behind the Legend*. For primary sources on Laura and Almanzo's life, read the *Little House* series. You can also visit her various home sites, including a replica of her home in Pepin, Wisconsin. For more information about her home and the Laura Ingalls Wilder Park and museum in Pepin, visit the Discover Pepin, Wisconsin Web site at http://www.pepinwisconsin.com/.

died on February 10, 1957, at Rocky Ridge Farm. She was 90 years old.

Laura Ingalls Wilder's novels are recognized as historical fiction, not autobiography, because she sometimes changed factual events to suit her dramatic purposes. However, her books provide a snapshot of the times from a child's perspective. The books have become immensely popular and even inspired the *Little House on the Prairie* television series that aired in the 1970s and 1980s.

Wilder took it upon himself to offer Laura a ride to her home every weekend. Over the next few years, Laura grew to love Almanzo. The two married on August 25, 1885, and their daughter Rose was born the in December of the following year.

Life remained complicated and dangerous. Droughts and hailstorms ruined their crops, which kept the Wilders in debt. Almanzo contracted diphtheria, leaving him crippled. Shortly afterward, their second child died, and their house burned down after a kitchen fire. Exhausted by the tragedies, Almanzo and Laura moved in with his parents in Spring Valley, Minnesota. Hoping a warmer climate would restore Almanzo's health, they moved to Westville, Florida, and in 1892, the three returned to De Smet.

In 1894, the Wilders purchased Rocky Ridge Farm in Mansfield, Missouri, where Laura and Almanzo would live out the rest of their lives. In the 1930s, Laura's daughter Rose inspired her to record her memories of growing up on the frontier. The first of the Little House books, *Little House in the Big Woods,* was published in 1932, and the last of the series, *These Happy Golden Years,* was published in 1943. Almanzo died on October 23, 1949, at the age of 92. Laura

Harper and Brothers, New York and London, 1932

Illustration from page 46 of the 1932 edition of *Little House in the Big Woods,* illustrated by Helen Sewell

Qackers as Packers

Meatpackers and Wisconsin's Favorite Team

Many people love to watch football on Sunday afternoons in the fall, especially when the Green Bay Packers are playing at Lambeau Field. But the Packers are unusual in several ways. For one thing, Green Bay is the smallest city in the country with a National Football League team. In the early years of the NFL, many smaller cities— Canton, Ohio, and Providence, Rhode Island, for example—had teams, but the teams relocated to larger cities that could provide big crowds to watch the games. Yet the Packers remain in little Green Bay. Why? And then, there's the name. Lions and Bears are fierce, but just what is a Packer?

The answer to both questions lies in the team's origins. In 1919, the team was founded by Ed "Curly" Lambeau and George Calhoun. Lambeau's employer, the Indian Packing Corporation, provided money for jerseys and the use of its athletic field. People called the team the "Packers," even though the Indian Packing Company

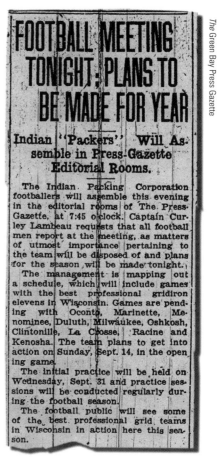

The Green Bay Press Gazette

FOOTBALL MEETING TONIGHT; PLANS TO BE MADE FOR YEAR

Indian "Packers" Will Assemble in Press-Gazette Editorial Rooms.

The Indian. Packing Corporation footballers will assemble this evening in the editorial rooms of The Press-Gazette, at 7:45 o'clock. Captain Curley Lambeau requests that all football men report at the meeting, as matters of utmost importance pertaining to the team will be disposed of and plans for the season will be made tonight.

The management is mapping out a schedule, which will include games with the best professional gridiron elevens in Wisconsin. Games are pending with Oconto, Marinette, Menominee, Duluth, Milwaukee, Oshkosh, Clintonville, La Crosse, Racine and Kenosha. The team plans to get into action on Sunday, Sept. 14, in the opening game.

The initial practice will be held on Wednesday, Sept. 31 and practice sessions will be conducted regularly during the football season.

The football public will see some of the best professional grid teams in Wisconsin in action here this season.

This article from August 29, 1919, uses the nickname "Indian Packers" for the team after the Indian Packing Company.

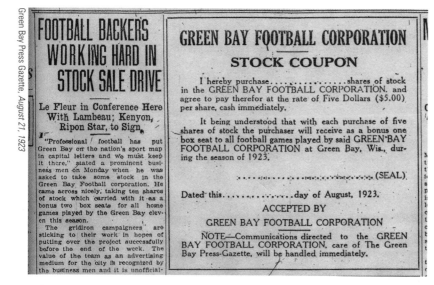

Green Bay Press Gazette, August 21, 1923

FOOTBALL BACKERS WORKING HARD IN STOCK SALE DRIVE

Le Fleur in Conference Here With Lambeau; Kenyon, Ripon Star, to Sign.

"Professional football has put Green Bay on the nation's sport map in capital letters and we must keep it there," stated a prominent business men on Monday when he was asked to take some stock in the Green Bay Football corporation. He came across nicely, taking ten shares of stock which carried with it as a bonus two box seats for all home games played by the Green Bay eleven this season.

The gridiron campaigners are sticking to their work in hopes of putting over the project successfully before the end of the week. The value of the team as an advertising medium for the city is recognized by the business men and it is unofficial

GREEN BAY FOOTBALL CORPORATION
STOCK COUPON

I hereby purchase................shares of stock in the GREEN BAY FOOTBALL CORPORATION. and agree to pay therefor at the rate of Five Dollars ($5.00) per share, cash immediately.

It being understood that with each purchase of five shares of stock the purchaser will receive as a bonus one box seat to all football games played by said GREEN BAY FOOTBALL CORPORATION at Green Bay, Wis., during the season of 1923.

.... (SEAL)

Dated this................day of August, 1923.

ACCEPTED BY

GREEN BAY FOOTBALL CORPORATION

NOTE—Communications directed to the GREEN BAY FOOTBALL CORPORATION, care of The Green Bay Press-Gazette, will be handled immediately.

Article and form for first team stock sale in 1923

had closed before the team completed its first season. The name stuck because it appealed to the city's working-class residents. Named for humble meatpackers, the team has been known as the Packers ever since.

Still, why did the Packers stay in Green Bay? The NFL was formed in 1921 when it consisted of 13 teams from industrial cities in the East and Midwest. Few people followed the sport, and many teams folded quickly. Through the 1920s, 49 different teams played in the NFL, but by 1934, there were just 11. Except for the Packers, all the surviving teams had homes in the big cities of Boston, Detroit, Pittsburgh, Cincinnati, St. Louis, Pittsburgh, Philadelphia, and two each in Chicago and New York. The population of a small town simply could not support an NFL team, and the Packers were in bleak financial shape almost every year during the 1920s.

By 1922, a sparsely attended game could lead to bankruptcy. Andrew B. Turnbull, the publisher of the *Green Bay Press-Gazette* and others, paid Lambeau's debt and rallied the people behind the team. In August 1923, the men reorganized the club as the Green Bay Football Corporation, a non-profit company. Local merchants raised $5,000 by selling stocks for five dollars per share. Tough times continued, however, and in 1935, the team actually did go bankrupt. Afterward, the corporation was reorganized into the Green Bay Packers, Inc., and a new public stock offering raised $15,000 to save it. Additional public offerings were held in 1950 and 1997, and both times the response was overwhelming. Because people from all over the state purchased stock in the team, Packers finally gained a firm financial footing.

Today, the Green Bay Packers are the only publicly owned team in the National Football League. An annual meeting of stockholders elects a board of directors, which, in turn, elects an Executive Committee of seven members. Only the president receives a salary. With this organization, the Packers are not beholden to a single owner or group of owners; the team management answers to the fans themselves.

Currently, more than 111,000 stockholders own approximately 4.7 million shares, and despite the fact that the team plays in the NFL's smallest television market, the Packers have stayed in their original home and remain one of the most successful sports franchises ever.

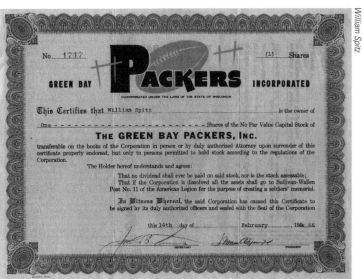

Share of Packer Stock belonging to William Spitz, February 14, 1966

Getting Started on Research

You can learn about the Packers' history at the team's official Web site at http://www.packers.com/. Newspapers didn't report on professional football very well in the NFL's early years, but your librarian can help you find accounts from the 1930s and 1940s, when the sport began to grow in popularity. By searching the archives at the Wisconsin Historical Society, you'll find the records of the Green Bay Area Chamber of Commerce and assorted documents describing the way the Packers' presence affected the greater community. Type the keywords "Green Bay Packers" into the search function at http://arcat.library.wisc.edu/. For secondary information, try David Maraniss' *When Pride Still Mattered: A Life of Vince Lombardi.*

Three Ring Circus
How Wisconsin Became America's Circus Capital

Did you know that one of the most famous and successful American circuses began right here in Wisconsin? The Ringling Brothers Circus, which later merged with Barnum & Bailey, was known as "The Greatest Show on Earth," and originally began in Baraboo. The Ringling brothers were Al, Otto, Alf, Charles, and John, the

Al learned to juggle and do acrobatics, and along with his other brothers, formed the Ringling Brothers' Classic and Comic Concern Company. They began to take their comic skits, songs, and juggling acts around Wisconsin, and they held their first performance in the little town of Mazomanie. After the success of this first tour, they expanded their operations and toured all over southern Wisconsin, and in the Iowa and Dakota territories. By 1884, the brothers had made enough money to expand and become a big-top circus troupe. They hired showman Yankee Robinson and formed the Yankee Robinson and Ringling Brothers Great Double Shows. By 1888, they were successful enough to add two elephants, a band, and several new acts.

Ringling Brothers poster, 1905

WHi Image ID 6050

sons of German immigrant parents who settled in Wisconsin in the 1870s. When the Ringlings lived in McGregor, Iowa, in the 1860s, the five boys became excited about circuses after seeing a troupe come to their town. The performance of the John Stowe and Company circus impressed them so much that they began to create their own circus act.

Each brother had his own role in the troupe. Al was the director, as well as the strongman, who impressed audiences with his ability to balance a plow on his chin. John planned the route for the show, Alf was the press agent, and Otto and Charles were performers and musicians. Al's wife took charge of the wardrobe and

Lou performed on horseback during the show. By 1890, their circus was a "railroad show" with 18 cars of attractions, including hippopotamuses, camels, hyenas, and elephants. In 1892, the Ringling Brothers actively competed with the other premier circus of the era, not the least of which was Barnum & Bailey. That summer, both shows performed in Milwaukee, and, after the Ringling Brothers drew the larger audience, they began to expand their tours to ever larger venues.

Much of the Ringling Brothers' success stemmed from their use of pageantry. They staged elaborate pageants as part of their circus performance, which included "The Fall of Rome," "Jerusalem and the Crusades," and "Cinderella." The lush costumes and music impressed young and old audiences and captured their imaginations. The rivalry between the two circuses continued until 1908, when the Ringling Brothers purchased Barnum & Bailey. In 1919, the show officially became the "Ringling Bros. and Barnum & Bailey Circus."

Baraboo remained home to the Ringlings, even after success took them on tours around the world. Al built an elaborate residence and opened the Al Ringling Opera House in 1915, just months before he

Getting Started on Research

To learn more about Al Ringling and his circus, you can read "Master of the Tinsel Ring" in *Badger Saints and Sinners* by Fred L. Holmes. Circuses were among the most popular entertainments before television and movies. You can learn more about the Ringling Bros. and Barnum & Bailey circus, and circuses in general, in *American culture in The Circus Age* by Janet M. Davis. If your community was a regular stop on the circus tour, your public librarian can help you find newspaper accounts of the tours. Of course, you can visit Circus World Museum in Baraboo or on the Web at http://www.circusworldmuseum.com/. Do an online guided search under "circus Wisconsin" to find many primary sources about Wisconsin circuses in the archives at the Wisconsin Historical Society at http://arcat.library.wisc.edu/. You can also find images and information by searching under "Ringling" at http://www.wisconsinhistory.org/whi/.

died. Otto had died four years earlier in 1911, and by 1936, all five brothers were deceased. Although Baraboo stopped functioning as the circus's winter quarters after the acquisition of Barnum & Bailey, the town continued to be proud of their native sons and honored the circus with a Golden Jubilee in 1933. Today, Circus World Museum remains a tribute to the Ringling Brothers' lifelong achievements.

The Ringling Brothers were just one of the many circus groups that originated in Wisconsin. Why did the circus hold so much appeal for midwestern audiences and those in other parts of the United States during so much of the twentieth century?

WHI (M4911)

WHI (X3) 39957

Al Ringling's residence, Baraboo, Wisconsin, 1918

Al Ringling Theatre, Baraboo, Wisconsin

Vinnie Ream Hoxie

The Woman Who Carved Lincoln

Vinnie Ream Hoxie

In the 1800s, few women were professional artists, and those who were, seldom received major commissions. Wisconsin's Vinnie Ream, however, proved that women could produce works of art rivaling the nation's best. In 1866, the federal government granted Ream a $10,000 commission to sculpt a life-sized marble statue of president Abraham Lincoln for the U.S. Capitol. The request made Ream the first woman to gain such a significant commission. Many people doubted her ability, yet Ream's statue was greatly praised and is still regarded as one of the best representations of the former president.

Ream's statue of Abraham Lincoln

Born in 1847, Ream lived in Madison for the first 10 years of her life until her parents moved to Missouri. During the Civil War, she and her family moved to Washington, DC. After a chance visit to the studios of famed sculptor Clark Mills in 1863, she began to sculpt. "I felt at once that I, too, could model and, taking the clay, in a few hours I produced a medallion of an Indian chief's head," she recalled. Mills immediately accepted her as his pupil. Word of Ream's abilities circulated, and she began sculpting busts of prominent men. Among them were General George Armstrong Custer, Congressman Thaddeus Stevens, and New York editor Horace Greeley.

In 1864, some friends arranged for her to sculpt a bust of Lincoln. At first, the president refused to pose for Ream. Then, after learning that she was a young woman struggling to support herself, he granted her daily half-hour sittings. For five months, she visited the president and worked on a clay model, carefully replicating the lines that had creased Lincoln's face over the past three years of strife and war. The bust she created captured Lincoln's likeness impressively, and in 1866, it led to the commission for the life-sized marble statue.

After winning the congressional commission for the Lincoln statue, Ream moved to Italy to copy her model into marble. She and her parents lived in Rome for three years. During that time, she continued to produce other works, including a bust of composer Franz Liszt. In 1871, when her statue was unveiled, it was received enthusiastically by Washington society. Other commissions followed. In 1875, she received a federal commission of $20,000 to sculpt a bronze statue of Admiral David Glasgow Farragut, the Civil War hero.

While working on her Farragut statue, Ream met and married Lieutenant Richard Hoxie. Their son Richard Ream Hoxie was born in 1883. Vinnie followed her husband's wishes and stopped accepting commissions, although she continued to sculpt for personal enjoyment.

Ream's studio in the U.S. Capitol

In 1906, Vinnie briefly returned to the professional world when the State of Iowa commissioned her to sculpt a statue of Civil War Governor Samuel Kirkwood for Statuary Hall in the U.S. Capitol. But by this time, she was in poor health. Her husband rigged a rope hoist and chair so she could finish the statue.

Her final work was yet another statue for Statuary Hall in the Capitol. It was a likeness of Sequoya, inventor of the Cherokee language in written form, commissioned by the State of Oklahoma. The state later named the town Vinita after her. She completed the clay model just before she died

of uremic poisoning in November 1914, leaving another artist to cast the statue in bronze. Ream was buried in Arlington National Cemetery, just across the Potomac River from the U.S. Capitol, the home still today of three of her statues.

What public sculpture or historical artwork exists in your community? Perhaps it's on the street, in a park, at the public library, in the courthouse or other government building, or in a museum or private home. What is the work, who created it, and when was it completed? Your public librarian or local historical society can help you research this topic.

WHi Image ID 3808

Getting Started on Research

You can learn more about Vinnie Ream Hoxie at the Arlington National Cemetery Web site at http://www.arlingtoncemetery.net/vrhoxie.htm/ and at http://www.vinnieream.com/. Primary documents about her may be found at http://www.firstgov.gov/fgsearch/index.jsp.

Her papers and many other related documents are in the archives of the Wisconsin Historical Society, which are available at http://arcat.library.wisc.edu/. Type keywords "Vinnie Ream Hoxie" in the search function of ArCat. You can also see a statue by Vinnie Ream Hoxie in the Wisconsin State Capitol—"The West" is located on the first floor.

Frank Lloyd Wright
Legendary Architect

A hundred years ago, many architects and designers fought against traditional European styles. Through the early part of the twentieth century, innovators from the United Kingdom, Austria, and Spain created exciting new ways to think about design. In the United States, the Prairie School applied many of these concepts to the design of private dwellings. From 1900 to 1920, the Prairie School forever changed how people in this country and abroad looked at home design. The architect chiefly responsible for the changes was Frank Lloyd Wright.

Born in 1867 in Richland Center, Wisconsin, Wright spent his teenage summers on his uncle's farm near Spring Green. In the rolling hills of the Driftless Area, he grew to love and respect natural beauty. He briefly attended the University of Wisconsin and studied engineering, but that was the extent of his formal education. On his uncle's farmland in 1886, he got his first up-close-and-personal experience with building design when Chicago architect Joseph Lyman Silsbee built a Unitarian chapel

there. The following year Wright moved to Chicago to work with Silsbee.

Once there, he spent six years at the Dankmar Adler and Louis Sullivan firm. Architect Louis Sullivan was famous for streamlined buildings with elaborate ornamental design based on naturalistic elements. He instilled in Wright the idea that all good design demonstrates its links with nature. Wright thrived at the firm, but his position as head draftsman was not enough for the gifted and ambitious young man. In 1893, Sullivan discovered that his protégé was "moonlighting," designing homes for clients outside the firm. When Sullivan confronted him, Wright quit to pursue his own projects.

Wright began to experiment with different styles, and in 1901, he presented a project for the *Ladies' Home Journal*, which would become the Prairie style prototype. Wright referred to the Prairie style as "organic" architecture that exemplified several key design features: an emphasis on open space; integration of the building with the

WHS Historic Preservation

The Jacobs I House by Wright in Madison, Wisconsin

Getting Started on Research

Good secondary sources of Wright's life and work include H. Allen Brooks' *Frank Lloyd Wright and the Prairie School,* which offers a general overview of how Wright fit into the emergence of the Prairie School. Also, Kristin Visser's *Frank Lloyd Wright and the Prairie School in Wisconsin: An Architectural Touring Guide* provides in-depth knowledge about Wright's personal and professional career. You can also consult the WHS Archives' John H. Howe Collection of Architectural Books and Periodicals for primary sources. Your library will have books showing many of Wright's designs originally published in women's magazines from the period, such as the *Ladies' Home Journal.* You can also read Wright's own account, entitled simply, *An Autobiography.*

On the Web, you can find photographs and information on many of Wright's designs, including http://www.wrightplus.org/robiehouse/. See examples of Wright's work in Wisconsin on the Wright in Wisconsin Web site at http://www.wrightinwisconsin.org/.

surrounding landscape; and use of new technologies and materials. Like Sullivan, Wright believed that design should adapt to practical use, rather than being dominant, and his credo became "form follows function." Such design principles strongly drew upon Japanese domestic architecture, which Wright first witnessed at Japan's Ho-o-den exhibit at the World's Columbian Exposition held in Chicago in 1893. Afterward, Wright pioneered an open floor plan and grid system that were based upon these ideas.

Initially, Wright worked out of his Oak Park, Illinois, home and studio. But after 1911, he worked at Taliesin, the home and studio he built on his family's property in Spring Green, Wisconsin.

Taliesin is Welsh for "shining brow," a reference to the building's location on the "brow," rather than on the crest, of a hill. This sensitive placement of his home demonstrated his desire to make his own home an organic part of its surroundings, not a dominating element for its own sake. Each time Taliesin burned down, Wright rebuilt it, and it became not only his studio but a training center for apprentices. In the mid-1930s, Wright built Taliesin West in Scottsdale, Arizona, and every winter thereafter, Wright and his apprentices worked there.

Among Wright's most prominent designs were the Frederick C. Robie house (1909) on Chicago's south side, the S.C. Johnson headquarters in Racine (1939), and the Guggenheim Museum in New York City (1959). And perhaps his most famous home is Fallingwater, which was built in 1936 for Pittsburgh department store magnate Edgar Kaufmann. Wright died two months prior to his 92nd birthday in 1959, leaving a legacy of more than 1,000 designs and nearly 500 structures.

WHS Historic Preservation

Hardy House by Wright in Racine, Wisconsin

Wheel Speed

Wisconsin's Link to Auto Racing

PH 6233

Car and driver from an auto race in Milwaukee, Wisconsin, 1912

When people think of auto racing, they probably think of Indianapolis or Daytona. But, did you know that Wisconsin has a historical link to these great racing institutions? Today, NASCAR racing is one of the most popular sports in the country. Wisconsinite Matt Kenseth from Cambridge won the 2003 NASCAR championship. But the connection goes much deeper. In the 1870s and 1880s, Wisconsin inventors were at the forefront of the creation of the "horseless carriage," or steam-powered automobile. The first automobile intended for highway and street use was a high-wheeled buggy designed by Dr. John W. Carhart in 1872 in Racine. The steam-powered contraption didn't catch on right away, but it stirred a lot of interest in self-propelled modes of transportation, especially after an epidemic incapacitated the horses most of the city's population depended upon for transportation.

Sensing the need for reliable man-made transportation, the Wisconsin state legislature in 1875 offered a $10,000 prize for the invention of "a self-propelled [vehicle] ... which shall be a cheap and practical

substitute for the horse and other animals on the highways and farms." This incentive was irresistible to mechanics and dabblers interested in self-powered mechanical transportation. In 1878, the makers of two machines stepped forward to claim the prize. Their cars were named after the cities in which they were built: the *Oshkosh* and the *Green Bay*. The challenge to determine the winner was a race. Both machines were to drive from Green Bay to Madison by way of Janesville and Beloit.

On July 16, the two steamers began their competition in front of spectators who lined the streets of Green Bay to watch the historic event. Once outside the city limits, however, the *Green Bay* broke down and had to go back to the shop for repairs! The

THE STEAM WAGONS.

Arrival of the Oshkosh Machine—Details of the Tour—The Unfortunate Green Bay Engine.

A year or two since the Legislature offered a prize of $10,000 for a perfect steam wagon for general agricultural and hauling purposes, to be able to stand such tests as a board of three Commissioners should propose; among other things, the contesting machines were to

An update about the steam wagon race printed July 24, 1878, in the *Wisconsin State Journal*.

Wisconsin State Journal

PH 6233

Scene from an auto race in Milwaukee, Wisconsin, 1912

Oshkosh continued south, impressing gaping onlookers along the way. People thought the car made excellent time, traveling the 90 miles between Green Bay and Appleton in about eight hours! The two vehicles competed in speed trials in Oshkosh, and although the *Green Bay* was faster, it kept breaking down. The *Oshkosh* completed two heats, running one mile in just over four minutes and thirty seconds.

On July 23, the *Oshkosh* triumphantly entered Madison to claim its prize while the *Green Bay* languished in a ditch in Jefferson. The *Oshkosh* had indeed established a good record. It had traveled the 201 miles in 33 hours and 27 seconds and had demonstrated its capacity to haul loads of more than 5,000 pounds. The *Oshkosh* was driven around the streets of Madison before being left at the Park Hotel, where hundreds of curious residents viewed it. The state commission charged with awarding the $10,000 prize, however, was not impressed. The group determined that the vehicle had not actually met the criteria of being "cheap and practical," so it gave the owners of the *Oshkosh* only half the money.

The same year that the legislature offered the $10,000 prize, Harry Miller was born in Menomonie. After traveling around the country, Miller returned to Menomonie and worked at the Globe Iron Works. In his spare time, he tinkered with motorcycles and developed a four-cylinder, four-stroke engine. This early experimentation led him into a career of designing automobile engines and parts, and his carburetors and spark plugs dominated the auto industry for many years. In 1911, Miller went to Indianapolis and began building racecar engines that were popular throughout the 1920s. At the 1928 Indianapolis 500, Miller had built the engines of nine of the top 10 finishers, including the winner!

Much has changed in the racing industry since the Oshkosh ambled into Madison and Harry Miller's cars dominated Indy, but the sport remains as exciting as ever. What other Wisconsin inventors brought innovations to the automobile industry?

Getting Started on Research

A good place to learn more about Harry Miller is Timothy Gerber's "Built for Speed: The Checkered Career of Race Car Designer Harry A. Miller" in the *Wisconsin Magazine of History* 85 (Spring 2002), 32–41. You can see a photograph of the *Oshkosh* and other early autos in *Portrait of the Past* by Howard Mead, Jill Dean, and Susan Smith. To learn more about the 1878 competition, check out the Wisconsin Stories Web site at http://www.wisconsinstories.org/2002season/car/index.cfm. For secondary resources, visit the Wisconsin Historical Society Archives at http://arcat.library.wisc.edu/.

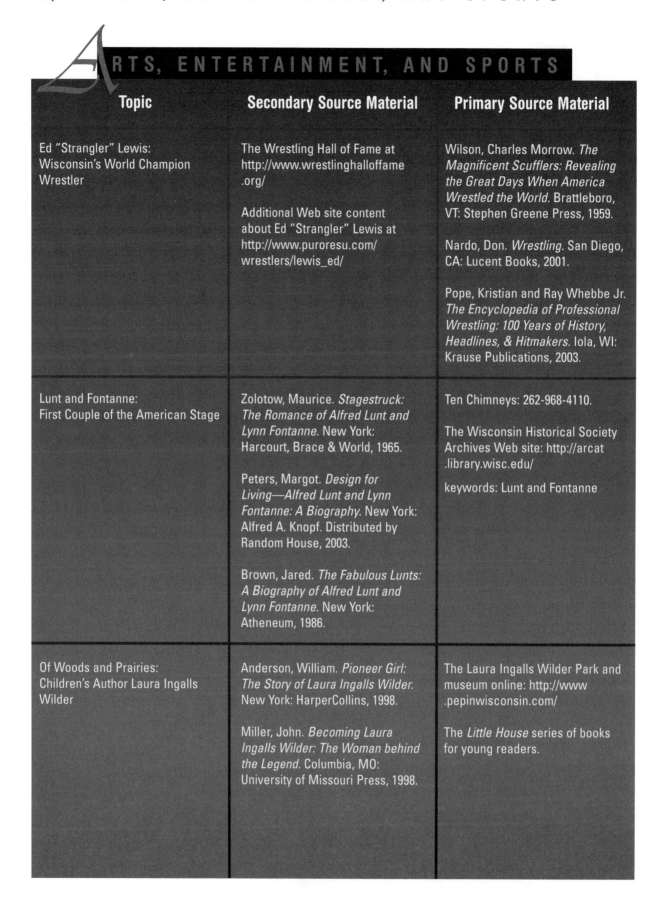

RTS, ENTERTAINMENT, AND SPORTS

Topic	Secondary Source Material	Primary Source Material
Ed "Strangler" Lewis: Wisconsin's World Champion Wrestler	The Wrestling Hall of Fame at http://www.wrestlinghalloffame.org/ Additional Web site content about Ed "Strangler" Lewis at http://www.puroresu.com/wrestlers/lewis_ed/	Wilson, Charles Morrow. *The Magnificent Scufflers: Revealing the Great Days When America Wrestled the World.* Brattleboro, VT: Stephen Greene Press, 1959. Nardo, Don. *Wrestling.* San Diego, CA: Lucent Books, 2001. Pope, Kristian and Ray Whebbe Jr. *The Encyclopedia of Professional Wrestling: 100 Years of History, Headlines, & Hitmakers.* Iola, WI: Krause Publications, 2003.
Lunt and Fontanne: First Couple of the American Stage	Zolotow, Maurice. *Stagestruck: The Romance of Alfred Lunt and Lynn Fontanne.* New York: Harcourt, Brace & World, 1965. Peters, Margot. *Design for Living—Alfred Lunt and Lynn Fontanne: A Biography.* New York: Alfred A. Knopf. Distributed by Random House, 2003. Brown, Jared. *The Fabulous Lunts: A Biography of Alfred Lunt and Lynn Fontanne.* New York: Atheneum, 1986.	Ten Chimneys: 262-968-4110. The Wisconsin Historical Society Archives Web site: http://arcat.library.wisc.edu/ keywords: Lunt and Fontanne
Of Woods and Prairies: Children's Author Laura Ingalls Wilder	Anderson, William. *Pioneer Girl: The Story of Laura Ingalls Wilder.* New York: HarperCollins, 1998. Miller, John. *Becoming Laura Ingalls Wilder: The Woman behind the Legend.* Columbia, MO: University of Missouri Press, 1998.	The Laura Ingalls Wilder Park and museum online: http://www.pepinwisconsin.com/ The *Little House* series of books for young readers.

Topic	Secondary Source Material	Primary Source Material
Packers as Packers: Meatpackers and Wisconsin's Favorite Team	The Green Bay Packers official Web site at http://www.packers.com/ Maraniss, David. *When Pride Still Mattered: A Life of Vince Lombardi.* New York: Simon & Schuster, 1999.	The Wisconsin Historical Society Archives Web site: http://arcat.library.wisc.edu/ keywords: Green Bay Packers
Three Ring Circus: How Wisconsin Became America's Circus Capital	Holmes, Fred L. "Master of the Tinsel Ring." In *Badger Saints and Sinners.* Milwaukee, WI: E.M. Hale and Company, 1939. Davis, Janet M. *The Circus Age: Culture and Society under the American Big Top.* Chapel Hill, NC: University of North Carolina Press, 2002. The Circus World Museum Web site at http://www.circusworldmuseum.com/	The Wisconsin Historical Society Archives Web site: http://arcat.library.wisc.edu/ keywords: Wisconsin circuses Find additional information online at http://www.wisconsinhistory.org/whi/
Vinnie Ream Hoxie: The Woman Who Carved Lincoln	The Arlington National Cemetery Web site at http://www.arlingtoncemetery.net/vrhoxie.htm	The Vinnie Ream Web site at http://www.vinnieream.com/ The FirstGov search site at http://www.firstgov.gov/fgsearch/index.jsp The Wisconsin Historical Society Archives Web site at http://arcat.library.wisc.edu/ keywords: Vinnie Ream Hoxie

Topic	Secondary Source Material	Primary Source Material
Frank Lloyd Wright: Legendary Architect	Brooks, H. Allen. *Frank Lloyd Wright and the Prairie School.* New York: Braziller. Published in Association with the Cooper-Hewitt Museum, the Smithsonian Institution's National Museum of Design, 1984. Visser, Kristin. *Frank Lloyd Wright and the Prairie School in Wisconsin: An Architectural Touring Guide.* Madison: Prairie Oak Press, 1998. The FLW Preservation Trust Web site at http://www.wrightplus.org/robiehouse/ The Wright in Wisconsin Web site at http://www.wrightinwisconsin.org/	The Wisconsin Historical Society Archives Web site at http://arcat.library.wisc.edu/ keywords: John H. Howe Collection of Architectural Books and Periodicals and Frank Lloyd Wright Wright, Frank Lloyd. *An Autobiography.* New York: Duell, Sloan and Pearce, 1943, 1958 printing.

Topic	Secondary Source Material	Primary Source Material
Wheel Speed: Wisconsin's Link to Auto Racing	Gerber, Timothy. "Built for Speed: The Checkered Career of Race Car Designer Harry A. Miller." *Wisconsin Magazine of History* 85, no. 3 (2002), 32–41. Mead, Howard, Jill Dean, and Susan Smith *Portrait of the Past: A Photographic Journey through Wisconsin.* Madison, WI: Wisconsin Tales and Trails, 1971–1973. The Wisconsin Stories Web site at http://www.wisconsinstories.org/2002season/car/index.cfm	The Wisconsin Historical Society Archives Web site at http://arcat.library.wisc.edu/ keywords: auto racing

Chapter Nine

Government

ursuing Reform
The Life and Work of Robert M. La Follette

November 4, 1890, was a sad day for Bob La Follette. He was running for re-election to the House of Representatives against Democrat Allen Bushnell. At 11 o'clock that evening, he came home and told his wife Belle, "Bushnell is elected to Congress from the Third District, and I am elected to practice law." For many politicians, such a defeat would have ended their careers. But for La Follette, the defeat marked the beginning of a lifelong fight with political corruption and political reform. It also signaled the beginning of the Progressive Movement.

La Follette's career as a reformer began a few months later when a leading Republican named Philetus Sawyer offered him a bribe to influence the judge in a lawsuit against several former Republican state officials. The judge was La Follette's brother-in-law, Robert Siebecker. La Follette was furious that Sawyer and others would try to use money to corrupt the legal system. He refused the bribe and began to actively oppose the influence of money in politics and the ways in which a few wealthy Republicans selected candidates in party meetings and shut out the voice of the people. For nearly 10 years, he traveled the state speaking out against the influence of crooked politicians and the power that railroad companies and other industries used for political gain. In 1900, he was elected governor of Wisconsin and began to institute his own brand of political reform.

Other reformers had suggested ways to make politics more democratic, and La

Follette quickly adopted many of their ideas. In his five years as governor, he convinced the legislature to pass measures instituting primary elections, giving the people the right to choose their own candidates. He got another measure passed that regulated the behavior of railroad companies and other important industries. And he

A 1911 political cartoon giving Bob La Follette credit for reforming the railroad laws in Wisconsin.

influenced taxation policies to make them more fair. La Follette worked closely with professors from the University of Wisconsin to help the state become "a laboratory of democracy." As a result of his efforts, La Follette became a famous political name throughout the country.

In 1906, the Wisconsin legislature elected La Follette to the U.S. Senate (until 1914, senators were elected by their state legislatures). La Follette worked hard in Washington to promote the same kind of reforms he had established in Wisconsin. He often spoke at length on the senate floor, denouncing government corruption and the abuses of industrial workers and consumers. His work ultimately led to the direct election of senators by the people and to the exposure of the Teapot Dome scandal. Often, La Follette worked so hard that he made himself sick and occasionally collapsed from fatigue and overwork. He supported economic reform efforts that included the Federal Reserve System and the national income tax.

Both Robert and his activist wife, Belle La Follette, believed that disputes should be resolved peacefully, and he opposed American entry into World War I. Although many people charged that he was unpatriotic and disloyal, he bravely stood his ground, believing that a war would end democratic reform at home. In 1922, the people of Wisconsin re-elected him senator despite the ridicule he endured, and in 1924 La Follette ran for president on the Progressive ticket. He received 4.8 million votes (about 16.5 % of the total) but lost to Republican Calvin Coolidge. The next year, La Follette died. National recognition for his efforts to reform American democracy came when his statue was placed in the Washington, DC Capitol in 1929. His legacy continues to inspire reformers today.

How does La Follette's example relate to politics today? How did your community vote when La Follette ran for president in 1924? Which candidate won your local district?

WHi Image ID 5455

Robert La Follette delivering a speech.

Getting Started on Research

La Follette wrote about his experiences in "La Follette's Autobiography: A Personal Narrative of Political Experiences." A good secondary source on his life and work is *The La Follettes of Wisconsin* by Bernard Weisberger. Weisberger's book is based on newspaper accounts from La Follette's time, which can be found at your library. Personal papers from the La Follette family that were used in the book are stored at the Wisconsin Historical Society in Madison and the Library of Congress in Washington, DC. The book's bibliography provides many other sources to look for. You can also track the highlights of his career through online resources and local Wisconsin newspapers.

Wisconsin's War Effort
Liberty Loans and the Four-Minute Men

In April 1917, after German submarines attacked American ships on the Atlantic Ocean, the United States entered World War I. The European conflict had been going on since August 1914, when Great Britain, France, and Russia went to war against the German and the Austrian-Hungarian empire. Americans had wanted to stay out of the war, but repeated German attacks against American ships forced the United States to take action. In mid-1917, American troops arrived in France to fight the German army.

Despite the fact that Wisconsin had a large German population and was home to Robert M. La Follette, a leading opponent of the war, the state enthusiastically supported the war effort. Just six days after Congress declared war, the Wisconsin legislature organized a State Council of Defense to administer federal war policies and teach citizens what they could do to help on the homefront. Under the council's guidance, families saved food by embracing "meatless Tuesdays" and "wheatless Wednesdays." They grew their own vegetables in backyard "Victory Gardens." People conserved energy by shutting off lights and using less coal to heat their homes. Everyone joined in to do their part to help American troops.

One significant way that Wisconsin citizens aided the war effort was by purchasing government bonds, called "Liberty Loans." Liberty loans were like modern savings bonds—people purchased them from the government. Essentially, people loaned money to the government to pay for the war, and the government later repaid them with interest.

Four Liberty Loan drives were carried

Parade in Hartford Wisconsin, July 1918

out during the war. At first, Wisconsin citizens were not interested in buying the bonds. Because interest rates were low, many people did not think bonds were a good investment. Other people, especially in the northern part of the state, simply could not afford them. The federal government had set Wisconsin's quota of war bonds at $44 million during the first drive in 1917, but Wisconsin fell $10 million short of its goal. During the fall of 1917, Wisconsin again fell short of its $91 million quota by almost $4 million.

The Council of Defense used "patriotism" as a way to motivate buyers. This massive, propagandistic approach made those who did not buy the bonds, for whatever reason, seem unpatriotic. This worsened the rising tension between those who openly supported the war and those who did not. Many who questioned the war effort, including Senator Bob La Follette, were bullied and assaulted. One group beat up a man for refusing to buy more liberty bonds and then painted a yellow stripe down his back!

To convince more people to buy bonds, the War Department (later the Department of Defense) also sent public speakers into states to urge crowds to support the Liberty Loan. For months, 900 men and women in every county appeared at community gatherings with a sales pitch. Because the speeches were supposed to last just four minutes, these speakers became known as "Four-Minute Men." The Four-Minute Men urged citizens to prove their patriotism and love of country by reaching into their pocketbooks to support the war effort. It worked. In the third and fourth Liberty Loan drives, Wisconsin exceeded its quotas by wide margins. By the end of the war, Wisconsin citizens had purchased more than $333 million in war bonds.

Getting Started on Research

To learn more about Wisconsin during World War I, a good place to begin is *The History of Wisconsin, Volume V: War, A New Era, and Depression, 1914–1940* by Paul W. Glad. The state summarized its efforts in the *1919 Blue Book*, available at most public libraries and on the Internet. The Wisconsin Historical Society archives has a wealth of materials and images on World War I at http://www.wisconsinhistory.org/teachers/classroom/ (Click on the World War I and World Power link). Also see http://www.wisconsinhistory.org/military/ww1/.

How did World War I affect your community? What individuals or groups in your area disapproved of the war? How did they show their disapproval? Your librarian can help you find newspaper accounts that describe the liberty loan and the Four-Minute Men efforts in your county and across the state. After the war, many counties constructed war memorials that were often dedicated to soldiers in this war that was fought "to make the world safe for democracy," according to President Woodrow Wilson. Where are the war memorials in your community? What people, groups, and events do they represent? What is the general feeling in your community about these memorials today?

A pennant encouraging people to buy Liberty Bonds.

WHI (X3) 48934

Protecting Workers
John Commons and Workmen's Compensation

WHi (X3) 12622

John Commons

In the 1800s, the United States became the world's leading industrial power. American factories were producing an ever-increasing variety of manufactured goods at an astonishing rate. In Wisconsin, Milwaukee became a major industrial city. Smaller cities like Sheboygan, Manitowoc, Appleton, and Superior were home to large factories that created jobs and brought prosperity. But these factories were often dangerous places in which to work. Vast, complex machines could quickly injure workers, and the rapid pace of labor often led to accidents. Every year, thousands of Wisconsin factory workers were killed or maimed on the job. At a time when medical care was difficult to come by, any serious workplace injury could mean disaster for an employee. Who would pay the medical bills? Who would support the family while the employee was unable to work? What if the worker could never work again?

Employees had the right to sue factory owners for damages, but the burden was on the worker to prove that the factory owners had somehow been negligent. Few unemployed workers could afford to do this. And even those who did were still left disabled. A more realistic goal was to make the workplace safer for all employees. By the time the twentieth century arrived, many reformers were working to reduce the number of workplace injuries and to provide some degree of support for workers who became disabled.

WORKMEN'S ACCIDENT INSURANCE
JOHN R. COMMONS
SECRETARY AMERICAN ASSOCIATION FOR LABOR LEGISLATION

The remarkable opportunity offered by workingmen's accident insurance legislation of bringing hostile employers and unions together when both are honestly guided, is strikingly shown in Minnesota. Just as remarkable is the effort of cheap machine politics to keep them separated, also shown in that state.

The Minnesota Employers' Association has for several years conducted a vigorous and largely successful attack on the unions. The State Federation of Labor has stoutly defended itself and has aggressively moved for protective legislation. Recently the executive committees of the two bodies met in the office of the newly appointed labor commissioner, Mr. McEwen, himself the former secretary of the State Federation of Labor. They were accompanied by a similar committee

stitutional systems, and equitable as between the employer, the employe, and the state.

2. An act requiring all employers, and employes, too (in so far as possible), and all policemen and firemen, and hospitals and doctors, rendering relief to the injured or deceased, to report the natures and the causes of the accidents with reasonable details, including wages, through proper channels to enable the statistics to be gotten by the Labor Department of this state, and the accidents classified according to the various industries to get a proper basis from which the commission may determine, and include, an equitable system in its report.

Our reasons for this petition are, briefly stated:

1. That there are a great many thousand accidents in this state, the exact number of which, and the classified reasons therefor, cannot from any data now made be obtained; there were in 1907, 92,178 either killed or injured throughout the United States in the course of their employment on 229,951 miles of single track railroads, or about one for

Workmen's Accident Insurance from *Charities and the Commons*, March 1909, written by Commons.

Release Wednesday afternoon, July 16, 1930.

Address by John R. Commons, at Annual Meeting of Wisconsin
State Federation of Labor, 11 o'clock a.m. at La Crosse,
Wisconsin on

UNEMPLOYMENT INSURANCE

On the subject of unemployment insurance nothing can
be done, without the cooperation of employers. For this reason
I advocate the principle embodied in the Huber Bill, as
revised in 1925. It is an Unemployment Compensation bill,
modeled after the Accident Compensation law of Wisconsin.
It recognizes that neither the state nor the trade unions
can prevent unemployment. They can only relieve it and cannot prevent it.

Commons's speech from the Annual Meeting of the Wisconsin
State Federation of Labor, La Crosse, Wisconsin, July 1930

Beginning in 1905, Frederick Brockhausen, a socialist labor leader from Milwaukee, introduced a workers' compensation bill at every session of the state assembly. He designed his program to provide benefits for injured workers. For six years, the legislature took no action, but by 1909, public opinion was turning in favor of Brockhausen's idea. University of Wisconsin economist and labor historian John R. Commons took the lead in advocating such a program. He promised employers that this kind of insurance system would create safer working environments and protect them from costly litigation. In 1909, the legislature appointed a special committee to investigate the matter and produce a report.

The task of drafting the bill fell to Commons. He had the difficult task of developing an insurance program that would be agreeable both to employers and to workers. Commons's bill required employers to set up self-insurance programs or join mutual insurance pools with other companies. Firms that had fewer than four employees were exempted, including farmers. Those that refused to join insurance programs had to bear the burden of proof in the case of litigation. On May 3,

1911, the nation's first workers' compensation law went into effect. After the state supreme court ruled the law constitutional, most Wisconsin firms adopted insurance programs and assumed responsibility for workplace accidents.

In the long term, the Wisconsin Workers' Compensation program benefited employers as well as employees. By making employers responsible for their injured employees, the law provided a strong incentive to make workplaces safer. Safe workplaces meant lower insurance premiums and more profitable companies. The legislature also created the Wisconsin Industrial Commission to set standards and oversee safety conditions in factories, with Commons as one of its first commissioners.

What factories were operating in your community in 1911? How do you think they were affected by the Workers' Compensation Law? What did your local newspapers report about the passage of the law and it effects?

Getting Started on Research

For a detailed description of the law, look at the "1911 Wisconsin Workmen's Compensation Law: A Study in Conservative Labor Reform" by Robert Asher in the Wisconsin Magazine of History 57 (Winter 1973–74). You can learn more about John R. Commons in John D. Buenker's *The History of Wisconsin, Volume IV*, which has excellent footnotes. Page 668 lists all relevant government documents in Wisconsin that relate to labor and industrial issues. For primary sources, search the WHS Archives using the keywords "workmen's compensation."

Edwin Witte and Social Security

A New Deal for American Workers

Today, when people lose their jobs or retire, they can receive unemployment wages or get monthly social security payments from the government. But this was not always the case. During the Great Depression (1929 to 1939), millions of Americans were without jobs and had no protection whatsoever against the financial burdens of unemployment. Capable young, but unemployed, people and retired citizens faced poverty under such circumstances. The Social Security Act of 1935 was designed to assist with these disasters. The architect of that plan was a man named Edwin Witte, who learned much of what he knew about government and economic programs while studying in Wisconsin.

Witte was a student of the well-known University of Wisconsin economics professor John Commons. After earning his PhD in the 1920s, Witte worked for the state government as head of the Legislative Reference Library (LRL). The LRL is a body of in-house experts who helped legislators research difficult issues and prepare bills. When the Great Depression began, Witte regularly sent memos to Governor Philip La Follette describing the economic conditions of the state and working with others to develop new programs. He was instrumental in developing Wisconsin's Unemployment Compensation program, the first in the nation to offer benefits to the unemployed.

But by the mid-1930s, it was clear that no single state could fully respond to the challenges of a national economic depression. When President Franklin D. Roosevelt took office in 1933, he promised a "New Deal" for the American people and began instituting a series of programs that provided emergency cash relief for the poor, work programs for the unemployed, and economic measures focused on reform. One of the most successful and long-lasting of these reforms was the Social Security program. In 1934, Roosevelt created the Committee on Economic Security to investigate the unemployment and pension programs of other nations and to make recommendations to develop similar approaches in the United States. Arthur Altmeyer, the assistant

WHi (X3) 21814

Edwin E. Witte

Getting Started on Research

Both Witte and Altmeyer wrote memoirs of their experience with the Social Security program. *The Development of the Social Security Act* by Edwin Witte and *The Formative Years of Social Security* by Arthur Altmeyer are insightful and valuable primary sources. To learn more about the men's Wisconsin background, see *The History of Wisconsin, Volume V: War, a New Era, and Depression, 1914–1940* by Paul W. Glad (Chapter 11). Your public librarian can also help you find microfilm copies of newspapers from 1934 and 1935 when Witte worked to develop the program. Edwin Witte's papers are housed at the Wisconsin Historical Society Archives. You can find them described online through the WHS ArCat search function.

Secretary of Labor who drafted the president's order creating the committee, knew exactly who should head it. Altmeyer had been the secretary of the Wisconsin Industrial Commission under Philip La Follette and remembered Witte's work. So, in the summer of 1934, Witte was summoned to Washington to create a new federal program.

After a great deal of investigation and debate, Witte devised a program that established a national retirement-age insurance system in which employees would participate. Employers and employees paid into the system through taxes. Then, at the age of 65, workers could retire and receive a monthly pension based upon their individual earnings during their working years. The Social Security program also established a federal-state system of unemployment insurance and provided aid to dependent mothers and their children, the visually impaired, and others who could not work.

The new law required that current workers fund the pensions for retired persons, with some domestic workers and agricultural workers excluded altogether. But these short-comings actually have kept the system working. Roosevelt himself once noted, "We put those payroll contributions there so as to give the contributors a legal, moral, and political right to collect their pensions and their unemployment benefits. With those taxes in there, no politician can ever scrap my social security program." For the first time, the federal government guaranteed help to society's neediest citizens: the unemployed, the aged, and the disabled.

Wisconsin has often been called a "laboratory of democracy" because it has a history of enacting creative solutions to complex economic and political problems. Nowhere does this legacy shine so clearly as it does with the Social Security program that Wisconsinite Edwin Witte helped create.

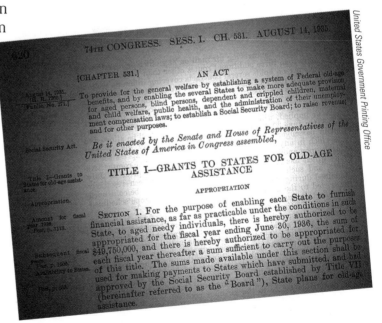

Part of the Social Security Act, August 14, 1935, which Witte helped to create

United States Government Printing Office

Mr. Berger Goes to Washington
Milwaukee Demands Representation

In November 1918, voters in Wisconsin's Fifth Congressional District (the northern half of Milwaukee County) elected Victor Berger to the House of Representatives. Even though Berger previously had served one term in Congress (1911–1913), he was a controversial choice to represent Milwaukee. First, he was a member of the Socialist Party. Although Berger was a loyal citizen and proud of the United States, many regarded him—and all Socialists, for that matter—with suspicion, especially after radical Socialists had overthrown the Russian government in the Bolshevik Revolution of 1917. Second, Berger opposed American involvement in World War I, and

the government had suspended the mailing privileges of his newspaper, the *Milwaukee Leader*. Finally, Berger had been convicted and sentenced to 20 years in prison for violating the federal Espionage Act and criticizing the war. While he waited for his appeal to be heard, he traveled to Washington to claim his congressional seat. No one was sure what would happen.

On May 19, 1919, Congress convened to swear in new members. The visitors' galleries were packed with those who came to watch the day's activity. But, when Berger walked to the speaker's desk to take his oath of office, the speaker refused to administer the oath! Instead, he appointed a committee to decide whether Berger had a right to his seat. Under the Constitution, each house of Congress had the right to judge its own elections and could refuse to seat whomever it wanted. The committee met in June 1919 and sifted through Berger's record as editor of the *Leader*, as well as the charges that he was disloyal. Despite Berger's impassioned defense that every citizen has a right to free speech, the committee recommended Berger not be seated because of his conviction for opposition to the war. On November 10, 1919, the House passed a resolution formally denying the seat to Berger. Only one congressman, Edward Voigt of Wisconsin, voted in Berger's favor.

In Wisconsin, Governor Emanuel Philipp called a special election for the Fifth District's seat. The Socialist Party nominated

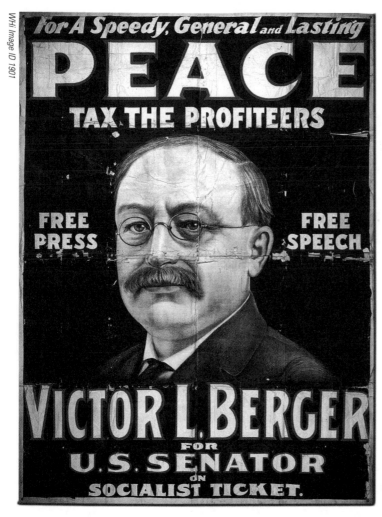

WHi Image ID 1901

For A Speedy, General and Lasting PEACE

TAX THE PROFITEERS

FREE PRESS   **FREE SPEECH**

VICTOR L. BERGER

FOR U.S. SENATOR

ON SOCIALIST TICKET.

Campaign poster for Victor Berger

Berger again. Only one other candidate, Henry Bodenstab, ran for the seat, but when the votes were counted, Berger had won by 4,806 votes! In 1918, he had received a scant plurality in a three-way race, but this time he had the majority of votes. The people of Milwaukee had chosen the man they wanted in Congress, and they were not going to let Washington tell them otherwise.

But on January 20, 1920, the House again refused to seat the duly-elected Berger when he arrived in Washington. Undaunted, Berger returned home and ran again in November 1920. This time, he was defeated by the Republican candidate William H. Stafford. Even though Berger lost the election, he experienced other victories in his life. The federal government restored the *Leader's* mailing privileges and allowed the newspaper to circulate freely once

Getting Started on Research

A good place to begin learning more about Victor Berger is *Victor Berger and the Promise of Constructive Socialism, 1910–1920* by Sally M. Miller. Berger's wife, Meta Berger, was an important figure in her own right, and in her autobiography *A Milwaukee Woman's Life on the Left,* you'll find her perspective of her husband's congressional career. Your public librarian can help you find newspaper articles on Berger's elections.

again, and a federal appeals court threw out his conviction. The sweetest victory came in the fall of 1922, when Berger again ran for Congress and won. This time, the House quietly acquiesced to the demands of the people of Milwaukee and allowed Berger to take his seat. He served three terms in Congress until 1929, when he returned to his editorial work in Milwaukee. He died there after an automobile accident in 1929.

In 1919, how did your local newspapers report about the Victor Berger story? Did the paper seem to support or oppose him? How does your local paper's coverage compare to that of the *Milwaukee Leader* or other Milwaukee newspapers? Does it surprise you that Milwaukee had a Socialist mayor for 50 years? In earlier years, why was the Socialist Party so popular in Wisconsin?

WHS Archives, Pamphlet Collection

Berger platform card

WHS Archives, Pamphlet Collection

This flier describes the platform of the Socialist Party, in German on this side and English on the reverse.

Ending Vietnam
The Legacy of Melvin Laird, Secretary of Defense

Although United States citizens did not realize it at the time, the Vietnam War actually began in 1954 after France left the country divided into two governing units. North Vietnam was on the side of the Soviet Union and China, and South Vietnam was allied with the United States. The two countries continually fought each other, and gradually the United States began to supply more and more aid and soldiers to South Vietnam. By 1969, more than 500,000 U.S. troops were stationed in Vietnam, and another 1.2 million were positioned elsewhere in Southeast Asia. Although Congress never officially declared war, the Vietnam "conflict" took the lives of many U.S. soldiers and changed America forever.

In 1969, President Richard Nixon assumed office and promised to reduce American involvement in the war. To oversee this initiative, he appointed Melvin Laird of Marshfield, Wisconsin, as Secretary of Defense. Laird was born in Omaha, Nebraska, in 1922. After graduating from Carleton College in 1942, Laird served four years with the U.S. Navy in the Pacific, finally leaving the service in 1946

Melvin Laird

with a Purple Heart and other decorations. His father, Melvin Laird Sr., was the Wisconsin senator representing Clark, Taylor, and Wood Counties. When Melvin Laird Sr. died in 1946, Melvin Laird Jr. won the seat and served in the senate until 1952, when he was elected to the U.S. House of Representatives from the 7th District, which included much of central Wisconsin.

While in the House, Laird was active in defense issues. He served on the Defense Subcommittee of the House Appropriations Committee, and in 1966 became an outspoken critic of President Lyndon Johnson's administration and its handling of the Vietnam War. He charged that the administration had invested too much of its defense budget in Vietnam and that it had misled the American people about how much the war would cost.

In 1969, Laird reluctantly left Congress when President Richard Nixon appointed him Secretary of Defense. When Laird took the position, he was given three goals: to get Americans out of Vietnam, to turn the war over to the South Vietnamese, and to end the draft. He accomplished the first two goals

Getting Started on Research

To learn more about the Vietnam War, find *A Bright Shining Lie* by Neil Sheehan. As part of a National History Day project, D.C. Everest High School students interviewed Laird. The interview is on the Internet at http://www.dce.k12.wi.us/srhigh/socialstudies/histday/vietnam.htm/.

Learn more about Laird's time as Secretary of Defense by reading newspaper articles from 1969 to 1973. School and public librarians can help you consult the *Reader's Guide to Periodical Literature* when you begin your search. See the Melvin Laird's Papers, 1904–1979, in the WHS Archives for microfilm, photographs, and tape recordings of his correspondence with national leaders.

battlefield. Because he had been in the armed service himself, he recognized the value of those who served. The Vietnam War ended during Laird's service at the Pentagon. Peace talks had just begun under President Johnson, and on January 27, 1973, representatives of North Vietnam and the United States signed a peace accord in Paris. The negotiators agreed to a cease-fire, the withdrawal of U.S. troops, and the release of prisoners of war (POWs). Laird's one regret was that the United States failed to follow through with its promise to the South Vietnamese army to supply replacement arms and equipment. Without U.S. support, the government fell to North Vietnam in 1975.

through a policy of "Vietnamization," which meant turning over more and more responsibility to the South Vietnamese army to ease the involvement of more American troops. The United States, however, would still supply arms and equipment. During Laird's four years as Secretary of Defense, the number of American troops serving in Southeast Asia declined from 500,000 to just 69,000. Laird also successfully met

Melvin Laird and then-Vice President Richard Nixon at a testimonial dinner for Laird in Wisconsin Rapids, November 12, 1959.

his third goal. He reduced the number of young men being called to duty through the draft from 300,000 in 1969 to slightly more than 50,000 by 1972. In 1973, Laird suspended the draft altogether.

One of the first things Laird did as Secretary of Defense was to visit South Vietnam and the troops. He was concerned about their morale and the difficult conditions on the

Despite the outcome, Laird left a significant legacy. He ended the draft that had been in place since 1939, and he greatly improved relations between the Pentagon and Congress, which enabled him to gain approval and funding for many of his initiatives. Since retiring from public life, Laird has written extensively about national and international affairs.

Help for the Unemployed
Wisconsin's Unemployment Compensation Law

Today, as in generations past, talk about jobs and the economy almost always includes discussions about unemployment. When the economy takes a downturn, many people lose their jobs and find themselves in the difficult position of looking for new work. When an economy is healthy, the unemployment rate is usually around 5%. During the Great Depression however, unemployment was a major problem in the United States. At times, 25% of American workers were without a job! The families of

compensation for years. But the bill he wrote was repeatedly introduced into the legislature during the 1920s without success. In that relatively prosperous decade, few people thought the state would ever need to worry about the jobless. But between 1929 and 1933, Wisconsinites lost more than 10,000 jobs, and people suddenly saw how much the state needed to implement such a program. Governor Philip La Follette, son of "Fighting Bob" La Follette, made passage of an unemployment compensation law a top priority.

In the fall of 1931, representative Harold Groves, a University of Wisconsin–Madison economics

Front of the first unemployment check issued in Wisconsin, August 17, 1936, for $15.00

WHi image ID 3491

WHi image ID 5485

Photo of Neils Ruud receiving the first unemployment compensation check issued in Wisconsin from Voyta Wrabetz, chairman of the state industrial commission. Also shown is Edwin Witte, university economist and author of the national Social Security Act; Professor John Commons, university economist; and Ruud's employer H.H. Brockhausen.

those who had lost their jobs faced disaster when they could not pay for food, clothing, and shelter for their families. Faced with this crisis, Wisconsin enacted the nation's first unemployment compensation law to provide some degree of support for unemployed workers.

University of Wisconsin economist John R. Commons had promoted unemployment

professor, introduced an unemployment compensation bill in the assembly. The program was to work like this: Every firm that employed 10 or more people had to contribute 2% of its payroll to a state-controlled account. Every employer had a separate account. When the money in the account reached $55 per employee, the employer's contribution dropped to 1%. When the account reached $75 per employee, the employer's contribution stopped altogether. Unemployed workers could draw up to $10 per week from their former employer's account for up to 13 weeks. Commons had argued that a plan should do more than just provide for emergencies; it should also encourage employers to keep employment high.

Public hearings on the bill drew both advocates and opponents. Labor unions and farmers stood behind it. One farmer told the senate that he supported the bill because it meant that unemployed people would still be able to buy his milk and cheese. Manufacturers and other employers, however, were against the plan. They did not want to have to contribute their money to a state-run account. Instead, they promised that eventually they would set up their own unemployment compensation plans. Governor La Follette called the manufacturers' bluff when he promised that the program would not go into effect if at least 200,000 workers were covered under these voluntary plans within two years. Now manufacturers had to support the bill or appear to be schemers trying to avoid helping people in need!

Getting Started on Research

You can learn more about Wisconsin during the Great Depression in *The History of Wisconsin, Volume V: War, a New Era, and Depression, 1914–1940* by Paul W. Glad. Philip La Follette wrote about the unemployment compensation program in his memoir *Adventure in Politics*. Another good account of unemployment compensation is "The Origins of Unemployment Insurance in Wisconsin" by Daniel Nelson in the *Wisconsin Magazine of History* 51 (Winter 1967–68).

La Follette signed the unemployment compensation act on January 28, 1932, making Wisconsin the first state in the nation to establish such programs—another in a long line of innovations that made Wisconsin famous for its progressive legislation on behalf of its citizens. Three years later, the federal government followed Wisconsin's lead when President Franklin D. Roosevelt signed the Social Security Act, which provided benefits for the unemployed.

How did the Great Depression affect your community? What businesses in your community went bankrupt or laid off many workers? How did older adults in your community or their families make it through those tough years? Your public librarian can help you find newspapers from the 1930s that describe life at the time. What did local newspapers report about the unemployment compensation program? Which newspapers seemed to support Philip La Follette's program? Which ones opposed it? What reasons did both sides give?

Milwaukee Journal-Sentinel

Governor Philip La Follette signing the Unemployment Compensation Act, January 18, 1932.

Changing the Welfare State
Governor Tommy Thompson and the W-2 Program

One of the biggest state and national debates of the 1990s was the role of welfare. What obligation does society have to provide assistance to its poorest and most vulnerable citizens? Welfare is a product of the Great Depression. In 1935, the federal government created Aid to Families with Dependent Children (AFDC) to provide cash assistance for poor families. Qualifying families received $18 per month for one child and $12 for each additional child. By 1941, more than 360,000 families received assistance from AFDC, and the numbers increased steadily during the 1950s and 1960s. The "Great Society" programs enacted under President Lyndon Johnson in the 1960s added additional programs, including Medicaid, to aid the poor.

As more and more families depended on government assistance, some politicians and policymakers wondered whether federal and state welfare programs were truly effective in removing people from poverty. AFDC was meant to be temporary, but many AFDC critics asserted that the legislation allowed, even encouraged, individuals to remain on welfare rather than work. President Ronald Reagan made this charge a major issue when he talked about "welfare queens" who lived on food stamps and cash welfare payments. Those who agreed with this point of view resented tax funds being spent on welfare. Those who disagreed wanted to help people escape poverty and find jobs that would allow them to give up welfare payments.

Wisconsin Governor Tommy Thompson took the lead in reforming welfare. Beginning in 1987, Thompson sponsored changes to welfare programs in order to increase the welfare recipients' responsibilities. The state's Learnfare program required welfare recipients to send their children to school; the "Work Not Welfare" program of 1995 required welfare recipients to work, and it placed time limits on their benefits. In 1997, Wisconsin replaced AFDC with the Wisconsin Works program (W-2). Thompson characterized W-2 as an employment— rather than a welfare—program, because it

The Milwaukee Journal-Sentinel

Headline from the *Milwaukee Journal-Sentinel*, April 26, 1996

244

The Milwaukee Journal-Sentinel

A child is born in Milwaukee during the final days of the old welfare system. Her story gives us either reason to celebrate – or reason to dread – the long-promised...

END OF WELFARE AS WE KNOW IT

The *Milwaukee Journal-Sentinel*, August 31, 1997

was designed to encourage recipients to break their dependency on welfare, while providing them with opportunities to earn an education and find gainful work. W-2 provided money to families for education and childcare with the provision that recipients find work within five years. After that time, they would no longer be eligible for W-2 benefits.

The W-2 program succeeded in doing exactly what it was intended to do. It reduced the number of people on welfare. Between January 1987 and February 2000, Wisconsin reduced its welfare caseload by 93%, from 98,000 families to 6,700. But many critics of Thompson's initiative raised questions about unintended consequences of the W-2 program. Although people found jobs during the booming years of economic growth in the late 1990s, the critics countered that most of these jobs were minimum-wage, service-sector jobs that did not pay enough to support a family, especially when W-2 benefits ended.

So, the central questions of welfare remain. What responsibility does society have toward its most vulnerable citizens? Children do not choose to be poor, so how can society help parents provide for their children without promoting welfare dependency? Finally, in the wealthiest and most productive nation in the world, how

do we eliminate poverty and adequately equip people to help themselves? In 1937, President Franklin Roosevelt saw "one-third of a nation, ill-clad, ill-housed, ill-nourished" and called for a compassionate society. Today, the same problems plague our poorest people. How did people (social workers, politicians, vocational advisors, and school officials) in your community react to changes in state and federal government assistance? How do they feel it can better serve the poor?

Getting Started on Research

For secondary sources, consult Douglas J. Besharov's *Family and Child Well-Being after Welfare Reform* or Frances Fox Piven's *Work, Welfare, and Politics: Confronting Poverty in the Wake of Welfare Reform*. Tommy Thompson wrote his own account of welfare reform in his memoir *Power to the People*. Welfare reform was a big issue in 1996 under Governor Thompson's and President Bill Clinton's administrations. Ask your local public or school librarian to help you find state and national coverage of the issue. You can also consult the *Readers' Guide to Periodical Literature* (available at most libraries) for magazine articles on welfare in the 1990s. Read Tommy Thompson's papers in the Wisconsin Historical Society Archives.

Lee Sherman Dreyfus
Political Maverick in a Red Vest

Wisconsin voters encourage political mavericks. Early in the state's history, Bob La Follette and Walter Goodland were non-traditional politicians loved by state residents. In 1978, their love for mavericks expressed itself in the election of Lee Sherman Dreyfus as governor. He had never before held political office, but quickly gained a reputation as an informal but intelligent candidate who was in touch with the people.

Dreyfus never set out to be a politician. He was born in Milwaukee, and after serving in the Navy in World War II, he earned a bachelor's and a master's degree and. In 1952, he received a doctorate in communications from the University of Wisconsin. Ten years later, Dreyfus was teaching speech and radio/television courses at the university when he was appointed president of the Wisconsin State University–Stevens Point. In 1971, the state campuses merged into the University of Wisconsin system, and Dreyfus became the first chancellor of the University of Wisconsin–Stevens Point in 1972.

He and Governor Patrick Lucey were good friends, and he was well-liked by his students. Dreyfus made himself accessible to students during the tumultuous years of

Governor Lee Dreyfus

the Vietnam War. Dreyfus started wearing a red vest every day so that students and protestors alike would know who he was and would know exactly who to go to with questions, criticisms, or information.

Although a popular college chancellor, Dreyfus was an unlikely person to run for governor. He had identified with neither major party (sometimes referring to himself as a "republicrat") and was unknown to most state residents. Moreover, at that time, the leaders of both the Republican and Democratic parties essentially chose their candidates. The leading Democratic candidate was acting Governor Martin Schreiber, who had taken over the office when former Governor Patrick Lucey resigned in 1977 to become U.S. ambassador to Mexico. Schreiber had been planning to run for governor for years, and now he was the incumbent. Republican leaders had persuaded Congressman Robert Kasten to run for the Republican nomination. Kasten was a young and ambitious politician with a genius for organizing supporters and winning seemingly impossible races. Late in December 1977, Dreyfus formally joined the Republican Party, and a few weeks later, announced that he would seek the party's nomination for governor. The man in the red vest was off and running. Dreyfus toured the state in a bus with a group of supporters he called his "Rag Tag Band." He impressed people with his combination of folksiness and intellect. But more significantly, he struck a populist note on his campaign. Dreyfus not only understood the problems people faced, he easily persuaded them that he was sincere in his priorities and was not just trying to get elected for selfish gain.

The campaign took some interesting turns. First, Kasten refused to debate Dreyfus prior to the primary election. Then, Schreiber refused to debate his primary challenger David Carley, so Dreyfus and Carley debated each other! Dreyfus also aired 30-minute campaign programs to outline his platform. Kasten was the favorite going into the primary election in September and had been endorsed at the party convention. But Dreyfus won a major upset and went on to defeat Schreiber in the general election. The votes that November totaled 816,056 for Dreyfus to

Getting Started on Research

A general account of the 1978 campaign and election is *Let the People Decide* and was written by one of Dreyfus's advisors, William Kraus. You can find a wealth of material in the 1979–1980 *Wisconsin Blue Book* (available in most libraries) to see exactly how your town and county voted in both elections. The Wisconsin Historical Society archives contain the Lee Dreyfus papers, including video documents. Your public librarian can help you find newspaper coverage of the campaign, election, and administration of Lee Dreyfus. And don't forget to talk to people who remember the election and the Dreyfus administration!

Schreiber's 673,813. Once again, the people had entrusted the most important job in the state to a maverick.

How did your community vote in the primary and general elections of 1978? What were the major issues promoted by each candidate? What kind of coverage did your local newspaper give to the election? Did any of the candidates ever visit your town?

Inauguration of Lee Dreyfus in the Wisconsin State Capitol

The Battle for Fair Representation
Wisconsin's Redistricting Struggles

In a democracy, everyone is supposed to have an equal voice—"one person, one vote" goes the saying. But, ensuring equal representation is difficult when determining the number of seats in a legislature. The Wisconsin Constitution requires that after every U.S. Census Bureau tally (every 10 years), the legislature must apportion the seats "according to the number of its inhabitants," so that each assembly district seat and each senate district seat is equal, based upon population. If this formula sounds simple, carrying it out was anything but easy in the 1950s, 1960s, and 1970s in Wisconsin. In fact, redistricting became one of the most divisive political controversies of the last century.

By 1950, major differences existed among legislative districts. No reapportionment had been made since 1921, when Wisconsin was primarily rural. Nearly 30 years later, the population had become more urbanized. Rural areas were over-represented in the legislature, and urban areas under-represented. Bayfield County, for example, had a population of 13,715, while the assembly district that contained the city of Madison had a population of more than 95,000. Because each district had elected one representative, a voter in Bayfield County had seven times more say in the legislature than a voter in Madison!

Establishing districts according to the current population was the only way to put a stop to the disparity. But Democrats and Republicans could not agree on how to determine what constituted a just method of reapportionment. Democrats generally favored redrawing districts to give more representation to urban areas, because urban voters were more likely to vote for

Democrat candidates. Republicans saw this as a threat to the interests of rural voters. Rural voters tended to vote

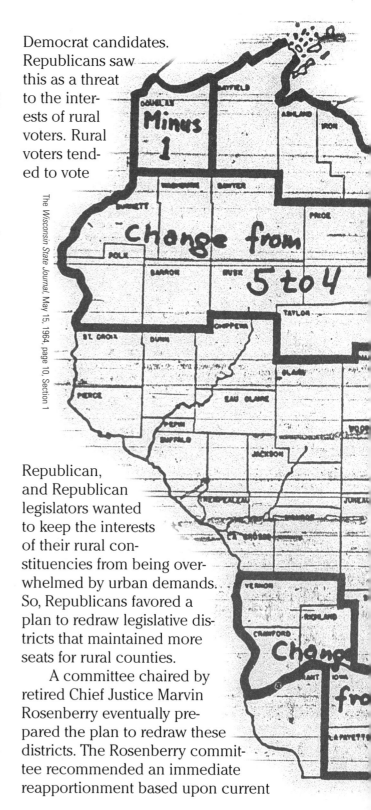

The *Wisconsin State Journal*, May 15, 1964, page 10, Section 1

Republican, and Republican legislators wanted to keep the interests of their rural constituencies from being overwhelmed by urban demands. So, Republicans favored a plan to redraw legislative districts that maintained more seats for rural counties.

A committee chaired by retired Chief Justice Marvin Rosenberry eventually prepared the plan to redraw these districts. The Rosenberry committee recommended an immediate reapportionment based upon current population. But, the committee also suggested that a constitutional amendment be established that would consider area in determining districts. Rosenberry believed that such an amendment would equalize representation for both rural and urban populations. For the rest of the 1950s, the legislature was apportioned based upon the 1950 U.S. Census Bureau's findings, and urban counties, including Milwaukee, gained more legislative seats.

After the 1960 census, however, the battle began again. This time, even more people had moved to cities, so Democrats insisted that population be used to determine seats. Milwaukee County, for example, contained 26.2% of the total population, so Democrats argued that it made sense to give it 26 out of 100 assembly seats. Not so, countered Republicans; giving Milwaukee County 26 seats would take away representation from northern, rural counties and leave them underrepresented. Because the legislature could not decide, the Wisconsin Supreme Court ordered the districts redrawn so as to provide the most equitable distribution

under the principle of "one person, one vote."

A similar situation occurred in 1971, and again the high court threatened to intervene if the legislature did not redistrict seats equitably. Because of this threat, Republicans and Democrats developed a plan that created remarkably equitable districts. Their new plan also changed the number of assembly representatives. Instead of 100 seats, there were now 99, and every senate district would contain three equal assembly districts. This is the situation today, but after every census, both parties renew the fight over the best way to ensure that each Wisconsin voter receives an equal voice in the way state government is run.

How did the 1950, 1960, and 1970 redistricting decision affect your community? Who were your legislators, and how many people did they represent? How has the population in your district changed over the past 50 years?

Getting Started on Research

An excellent overview of this complicated subject is "Equal Representation: A Study of Legislative and Congressional Apportionment in Wisconsin" by H. Rupert Theobald in the 1970 *Wisconsin Blue Book.* You can also learn more about these struggles in *The History of Wisconsin, Volume VI: Continuity and Change, 1940–1965* by William F. Thompson. Your public librarian can help you find local newspapers from the time that covered the reapportionment battles. These resources are great ways to find out about how the reapportionments directly affected your community. Other resources include *Working Files, 1970–1972* by the Wisconsin Governor's Commission on Reapportionment in State Government. These records include maps and 1970 census results.

Map depicting 1964's redrawn district boundaries.

From Milwaukee to the Promised Land

The Story of Golda Meir

How could a woman who grew up in Milwaukee become the Prime Minister of Israel? One of the most important world leaders of the twentieth century was a woman who did just that. Born Goldie Mabovitz on May 3, 1898, in Kiev, Russia (now Ukraine), Golda Meir grew up at a time when Jewish people in Russia endured violent anti-Semitism (hatred of Jews). Like millions of other Jews in Eastern Europe, the Mabovitz family longed for a better life, so they decided to move to the United States. They arrived in Milwaukee when Golda was eight, and she began a new life in Wisconsin.

Golda entered the Fourth Street Grade School and recalled that "Here I found freedom, kindness, and cleanliness." She was also pleased to find for the first time "a lack of prejudice," and she became a school leader. She also became an activist. At age 11, she organized a neighborhood meeting to raise money for books. Golda graduated as class valedictorian, and even as young woman, demonstrated her concern for the Jewish people. While she was studying at the Milwaukee Normal School (now UW–Milwaukee) to be a teacher, she taught at the Yiddish-speaking *Folks Schule*. While there, she became intrigued by the Zionist movement. Theodor Herzl first proposed Zionism, or Jewish Nationalism, in 1896, to encourage Jews to leave the anti-Semitism of Europe and return to Palestine, the home of their ancestors.

The Jewish people lived between the Mediterranean and the Jordan River from about 1200 BCE to 63 BCE. In some centuries, they were separated from one another mainly because of famine and military conquest. Their homeland has been called many names including Canaan, Israel, Judea, and Palestine. When the Romans destroyed the

The Golda Meir Collection, 1904–1987/University of Wisconsin–Milwaukee Manuscript Collection 21

Golda Meir, believed to be from her time as Israel's prime minister, 1969–1974

Getting Started on Research

Meir's 1975 autobiography *My Life* is a useful primary source. For secondary sources, read Louis Swichkow and Lloyd Gartner's *History of the Jews of Milwaukee*, Mitchell Bard's *The Founding of the State of Israel*, and Ahron Bregman's *A History of Israel*. The University of Wisconsin–Milwaukee's Manuscript Collection 21 contains press releases, oral interviews, photographs, and other primary materials. Check out their collection at http://www.uwm.edu/ Libraries/arch/findaids/uwmmss21.htm.

temple in the capital of Jerusalem in 70 CE, the Jewish people scattered even further. Those who remained in the area lived under the Romans, Muslims, the Christian Crusaders, and the Ottoman Empire, which lasted for 400 years. By then, Jews also lived in the Middle East and North Africa, and many more inhabited southern and eastern Europe and other continents. Throughout their diaspora, Jewish sacred texts continued to refer to their homeland as "Zion," or the promised land.

World War I destroyed the rule of the Ottoman Empire over "Zion," and the United Kingdom (Britain) ruled the area under the League of Nations. During World War I, the British government became increasingly committed to helping establish a Jewish home in Palestine. After discussions between British and Zionist leaders, the decision in favor of a homeland state was formulated in a letter written by Arthur James Lord Balfour. This famous document is known as the Balfour Declaration, and it represented the first significant political recognition of a Zionist state and its aims.

Soon after marrying, Meir and her husband moved to Palestine in 1921 to help build the vision of an independent nation for the Jewish people. Throughout the 1930s and 1940s, Meir served in various Zionist organizations, emerged as a forceful negotiator with British authorities during World War II, and eventually, she helped organize the new Israeli government. In November 1947, the United Nations partitioned Palestine into Jewish and Arab states, and Golda Meir was one of the Israelis who signed the independence proclamation on May 14, 1948. She held several jobs in the new government, and in 1969, she became the first woman ever elected prime minister of a nation. Golda Meir served until her resignation in 1974. The young girl who had longed for a new life had become one of the shapers of world history!

The Golda Meir Collection, 1904–1987. University of Wisconsin- Milwaukee Manuscript Collection 21

Golda Meir, believed to be from her time as Israel's prime minister, 1969–1974

The Right to Fish, Hunt, and Gather

Ojibwe Treaty Rights

Treaties are agreements between two or more sovereign nations. Between 1778 and 1871, Native people and the United States entered into more than 371 treaties. Most of these arrangements required Native people to give up (cede) land to the U.S. government in exchange for money, food, or goods.

Traditionally, the Ojibwe, like most Native inhabitants, cultivate a strong, respectful relationship with the natural world. Their existence has always depended upon seasonal activities such as hunting, fishing, harvesting (wild rice, for example), and making maple sugar. Ojibwe spiritual beliefs hold that natural resources should always be respected, the Ojibwe strongly feel that people should use resources, bearing in mind the needs of those seven generations in the future.

In the treaties of 1837 and 1842, the Ojibwe bands who signed the treaties forfeited their land titles, but retained the rights to hunt, fish, and gather on ceded territory. Because the Ojibwe possessed these rights before Europeans arrived (and they never relinquished them), the rights are "reserved rights," as opposed to special privileges. The Treaty of 1854 established reservations for the Ojibwe Nation, but did not cancel the rights guaranteed in earlier treaties. During the late nineteenth and early twentieth centuries, however, the state of Wisconsin denied the Ojibwe these lawfully protected "reserved rights."

In 1972, the Wisconsin Supreme Court ruled that the Bad River and Red Cliff Ojibwe Bands legally possessed the right to fish in Lake Superior without state regulation. In 1974, two brothers from the Lac Courte Oreilles (LCO) Band were arrested for off-reservation spearfishing. The LCO Band argued that the 1854 Treaty guaranteed them off-reservation hunting and fishing rights, but federal District Court Judge James Doyle ruled against the LCO Band in 1978, stating that the treaty's establishment of reservations canceled reserved treaty rights. The U.S. Court of Appeals for the Seventh Circuit overturned Doyle's deci-

Anti-treaty rights cartoon from the *Milwaukee Journal*, April 28, 1989

sion in 1983. This landmark decision is called the Voigt Decision or, more commonly, LCO I, and still stands today.

In the 1980s and 1990s, non-Indian anti-treaty protesters staged boat landing demonstrations, which sometimes resulted in violence. Some of the protestors argued that tribal sovereignty and treaty rights were outdated and no longer valid. Others believed rumors and propaganda claiming that the Ojibwe Band members would harvest all of the state's fish and game, thereby ruining the tourist industry. In response, groups sympathetic to the spearfishers began to act as "witnesses" at the boat landing protests. Their goal was to combat the rumors and educate the public about reserved rights guaranteed under treaty law.

Partially in response to the controversial nature of the issue, the Great Lakes Indian Fish and Wildlife Commission (GLIFWC) was formed in 1984. Its mission was to educate the public and assist its member bands in implementing and protecting off-reservation treaty rights. Strict rules govern off-reservation treaty harvests. Quotas, seasons, and permits regulate hunting and fishing. Nine of GLIFWC's 11 member bands maintain fish hatcheries from which they rear and stock fish. This often involves working in

WHS Museum 1991.161.2

People sympathetic to the Native American cause wore T-shirts such as this one.

WHS Museum 1988.203

Anti-treaty rights beer was sold in Wisconsin in the late 1980s.

lakes both on and off the reservations. GLIFWC and individual bands participate in annual resource assessment activities and share data with state and federal resource management organizations. Also, some bands help re-establish rice beds and assist with environmental monitoring activities.

To inform people and alleviate tensions about rights and other issues concerning the sovereign Indian nations of Wisconsin, the legislature passed Act 31 in 1989. This act requires Wisconsin Indian history, culture, and tribal sovereignty to be taught in public schools. The goal of these and other measures is to promote understanding among the people of the state of Wisconsin.

What disputes have arisen in your community over Native rights? How does the issue of treaty rights speak to larger issues about resource management, property rights, and the interaction between Native Americans and non-Natives in Wisconsin?

Getting Started on Research

Primary resources can be found on the opinion pages of most newspapers and in the WHS Archives, such as the papers of Jeff Peterson, a political activist from Luck, Wisconsin. Excellent secondary resources include Nancy Lurie's *Wisconsin Indians*, Ronald N. Satz' *Chippewa Treaty Rights: The Reserved Rights of Wisconsin's Chippewa Indians in Historical Perspective*, Rick Whaley and Walt Bresette's *Walleye Warriors: The Chippewa Treaty Rights Story*, and Larry Nesper's *The Walleye War: The Struggle for Ojibwe Spearfishing and Treaty Rights*.

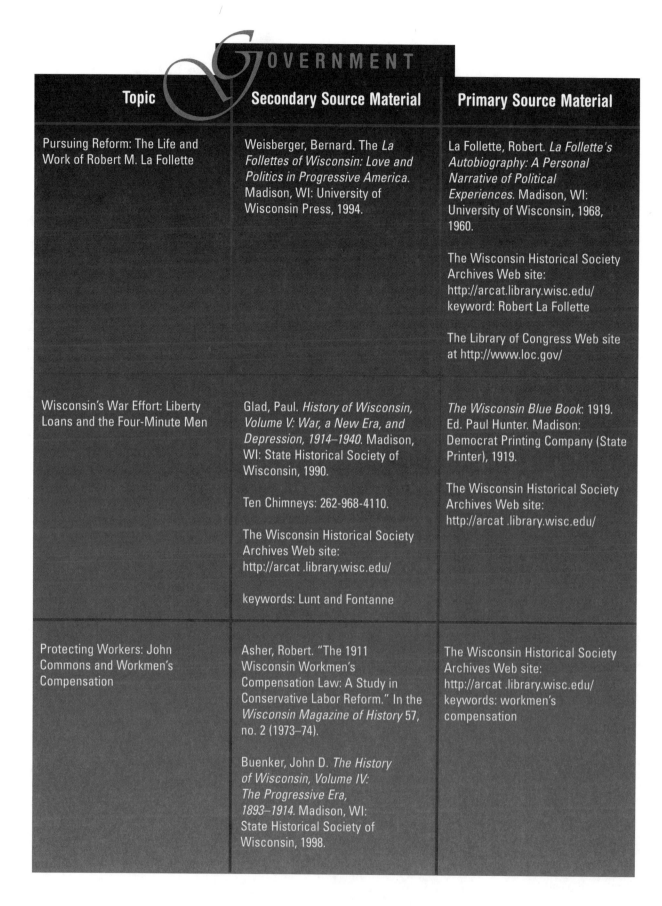

GOVERNMENT

Topic	Secondary Source Material	Primary Source Material
Pursuing Reform: The Life and Work of Robert M. La Follette	Weisberger, Bernard. The *La Follettes of Wisconsin: Love and Politics in Progressive America.* Madison, WI: University of Wisconsin Press, 1994.	La Follette, Robert. *La Follette's Autobiography: A Personal Narrative of Political Experiences.* Madison, WI: University of Wisconsin, 1968, 1960. The Wisconsin Historical Society Archives Web site: http://arcat.library.wisc.edu/ keyword: Robert La Follette The Library of Congress Web site at http://www.loc.gov/
Wisconsin's War Effort: Liberty Loans and the Four-Minute Men	Glad, Paul. *History of Wisconsin, Volume V: War, a New Era, and Depression, 1914–1940.* Madison, WI: State Historical Society of Wisconsin, 1990. Ten Chimneys: 262-968-4110. The Wisconsin Historical Society Archives Web site: http://arcat .library.wisc.edu/ keywords: Lunt and Fontanne	*The Wisconsin Blue Book*: 1919. Ed. Paul Hunter. Madison: Democrat Printing Company (State Printer), 1919. The Wisconsin Historical Society Archives Web site: http://arcat .library.wisc.edu/
Protecting Workers: John Commons and Workmen's Compensation	Asher, Robert. "The 1911 Wisconsin Workmen's Compensation Law: A Study in Conservative Labor Reform." In the *Wisconsin Magazine of History* 57, no. 2 (1973–74). Buenker, John D. *The History of Wisconsin, Volume IV: The Progressive Era, 1893–1914.* Madison, WI: State Historical Society of Wisconsin, 1998.	The Wisconsin Historical Society Archives Web site: http://arcat .library.wisc.edu/ keywords: workmen's compensation

Topic	Secondary Source Material	Primary Source Material
Edwin Witte and Social Security: A New Deal for American Workers	Glad, Paul. *History of Wisconsin, Volume V: War, a New Era, and Depression, 1914–1940*. Madison, WI: State Historical Society of Wisconsin, 1990.	Witte, Edwin. *The Development of the Social Security Act: A Memorandum on the History of the Committee on Economic Security and Drafting and Legislative History of the Social Security Act*. Madison, WI: University of Wisconsin Press, 1962. Altmeyer, Arthur. *The Formative Years of Social Security*. Madison, WI: University of Wisconsin Press, 1966. The Wisconsin Historical Society Archives Web site: http://arcat.library.wisc.edu/ keywords: Edwin Witte and Arthur Altmeyer
Mr. Berger Goes to Washington: Milwaukee Demands Representation	Miller, Sally M. *Victor Berger and the Promise of Constructive Socialism, 1910–1920*. Westport, CT: Greenwood Press, 1973.	Berger, Meta. *A Milwaukee Woman's Life on the Left: The Autobiography of Meta Berger*. Madison, WI: Wisconsin Historical Society Press, 2001.
Ending Vietnam: The Legacy of Melvin Laird, Secretary of Defense	Sheehan, Neil. *A Bright Shining Lie: John Paul Vann and America in Vietnam*. New York: Vintage Books, 1989, 1988.	A D.C. Everest HS interview with Laird can be found at http://www .dce.k12.wi.us/srhigh /socialstudies/histday/vietnam.htm The Wisconsin Historical Society Archives Web site: http://arcat .library.wisc.edu/ keywords: Melvin Laird
Help for the Unemployed: Wisconsin's Unemployment Compensation Law	Glad, Paul. *History of Wisconsin, Volume V: War, a New Era, and Depression, 1914–1940*. Madison, WI: State Historical Society of Wisconsin, 1990. Nelson, Daniel. "The Origins of Unemployment Insurance in Wisconsin." In the *Wisconsin Magazine of History* 51, no. 2 (1967–68).	La Follette, Philip. *Adventure in Politics: The Memoirs of Philip LaFollette*. New York, Holt, Rinehart, and Winston, 1970.

Topic	Secondary Source Material	Primary Source Material
Changing the Welfare State: Governor Tommy Thompson and the W-2 Program	"Family and Child Well-Being after Welfare Reform." Ed. Douglas J. Besharov. New Brunswick, N.J.: Transaction Publishers, 2003. Piven, Frances Fox. *Work, Welfare, and Politics: Confronting Poverty in the Wake of Welfare Reform.* Eugene, OR: University of Oregon Press, 2002.	Thompson, Tommy. *Power to the People: An American State at Work.* New York: HarperCollins Publishers, 1996.
Lee Sherman Dreyfus: Political Maverick in a Red Vest	Kraus, William. *Let the People Decide.* Aurora, IL: Caroline House Publishers, 1982.	1979–1980 *Wisconsin Blue Book* The Wisconsin Historical Society Archives Web site: http://arcat .library.wisc.edu/ keywords: Lee Dreyfus
The Battle for Fair Representation: Wisconsin's Redistricting Struggles	Theobald, H. Rupert. "Equal Representation: A Study of Legislative and Congressional Apportionment in Wisconsin." In the 1970 *Wisconsin Blue Book*. Compiled by the Wisconsin Legislative Reference Bureau, 1970. Thompson, William. *The History of Wisconsin, Volume VI: Continuity and Change, 1940–1965.* Madison, WI: State Historical Society of Wisconsin, 1988.	*Working Files, 1970–1972.* The Wisconsin Governor's Commission on Reapportionment. State Government records.

Topic	Secondary Source Material	Primary Source Material
From Milwaukee to the Promised Land: The Story of Golda Meir	Swichkow, Louis and Lloyd Gartner. *History of the Jews of Milwaukee*. Philadelphia, PA: Jewish Publication Society of America, 1963. *The Founding of the State of Israel.* Ed. Mitchell Bard. Farmington Hills, MI: Greenhaven Press, 2003. Bregman, Ahron. *A History of Israel.* New York: Palgrave Macmillan, 2003.	Meir, Golda. *My Life*. London: Weidenfeld and Nicolson, 1975. The University of Wisconsin-Milwaukee Manuscript Collection 21: http://www.uwm.edu/Libraries/ arch/findaids/uwmmss21.htm
The Right to Fish, Hunt, and Gather: Ojibwe Treaty Rights	Lurie, Nancy. *Wisconsin Indians.* Revised and expanded edition. Madison, WI: Wisconsin Historical Society Press, 2002. Satz, Ronald N. *Chippewa Treaty Rights: The Reserved Rights of Wisconsin's Chippewa Indians in Historical Perspective.* Madison, WI: Wisconsin Academy of Sciences, Arts and Letters, 1991. Whaley, Rick and Walt Bresette. *Walleye Warriors: The Chippewa Treaty Rights Story*. Philadelphia, PA: New Society Publishers, 1994. Nesper, Larry. *The Walleye War: The Struggle for Ojibwe Spearfishing and Treaty Rights.* Lincoln, NE: University of Nebraska Press, 2002.	

Linking Historic Research to the Wisconsin Model Academic Standards

The process of engendering independent student research projects forms an effective means of integrating a wide variety of standards in language arts and history. The following is a list of those that apply to many history-related projects.

ELA Standard A (Reading/Literature)

A.8.1 and A.12.1 Use effective reading strategies to achieve their purposes in reading.

A.8.3 and A.12.3 Read and discuss literary and nonliterary texts in order to understand human experience.

A.8.4, A.12.2, and A.12.4 Read to acquire information.

ELA Standard B (Writing)

B.8.1 and B.12.1 Create or produce writing to communicate with different audiences for a variety of purposes.

B.8.2 and B.12.2 Plan, revise, edit, and publish clear and effective writing.

ELA Standard C (Oral Language)

C.8.1 Orally communicate information, opinions, and ideas effectively to different audiences for a variety of purposes.

C.12.1 Prepare and deliver formal oral presentations appropriate to specific purposes and audiences.

ELA Standard C (Media and Technology)

E.8.1 and E.12.1 Use computers to acquire, organize, analyze, and communicate information.
E.8.2 and E.12.2 Make informed judgments about media and products.

E.8.3 and E.12.3 Create media products appropriate to audience and purpose.

E.8.5 and E.12.5 Analyze and edit media work as appropriate to audience and purpose.

ELA Standard F (Research/Inquiry)

F.8.1 and F.12.1 Conduct research and inquiry on self-selected or assigned topics, issues, or problems and use an appropriate form to communicate their findings.

Social Studies A (Geography)

A.8.3 Use an atlas to estimate distance, calculate scale, identify dominant patterns of climate and land use, and compute population density.

A.8.4 Conduct a historical study to analyze the use of the local environment in a Wisconsin community and to explain the effect of this use on the environment.

A.8.7 Describe the movement of people, ideas, diseases, and products throughout the world.

A.12.6 Collect and analyze geographic information to examine the effects that a geographic or environmental change in one part of the world, such as volcanic activity, river diversion, ozone depletion, air pollution, deforestation, or desertification, may have on other parts of the world.

A.12.9 Identify and analyze cultural factors, such as human needs, values, ideals, and public policies, that influence the design of places, such as an urban center, an industrial park, a public project, or a planned neighborhood.

Social Studies B (History: Time, Continuity, and Change)

B.8.1 Interpret the past using a variety of sources, such as biographies, diaries, journals, artifacts, eyewitness interviews, and other primary source materials, and evaluate the credibility of sources used.

B.8.2 Employ cause-and-effect arguments to demonstrate how significant events have influenced the past and the present in United States and world history.

B.8.3 Describe the relationships between and among significant events, such as the causes and consequences of wars in United States and world history.

B.8.4 Explain how and why events may be interpreted differently depending upon the perspectives of participants, witnesses, reporters, and historians.

B.8.5 Use historical evidence to determine and support a position
about important political values, such as freedom, democracy, equality, or justice, and express the position coherently.

B.8.6 Analyze important political values such as freedom, democracy, equality, and justice embodied in documents such as the Declaration of Independence, the United States Constitution, and the Bill of Rights.

B.8.7 Identify significant events and people in the major eras of United States and world history.

B.8.8 Identify major scientific discoveries and technological innovations and describe their social and economic effects on society.

B.8.10 Analyze examples of conflict, cooperation, and interdependence among groups, societies, or nations.

B.8.11 Summarize major issues associated with the history, culture, tribal sovereignty, and current status of the American Indian tribes and bands in Wisconsin.

B.12.1 Explain different points of view on the same historical event, using data gathered from various sources, such as letters, journals, diaries, newspapers, government documents, and speeches.

B.12.2 Analyze primary and secondary sources related to a historical question to evaluate their relevance, make comparisons, integrate new information with prior knowledge, and come to a reasoned conclusion.

B.12.3 Recall, select, and analyze significant historical periods and the relationships among them.

B.12.4 Assess the validity of different interpretations of significant historical events.

B.12.5 Gather various types of historical evidence, including visual and quantitative data, to analyze issues of freedom and equality, liberty and order, region and nation, individual and community, law and conscience, diversity and civic duty; form a reasoned conclusion in the light of other possible conclusions; and develop a coherent argument in the light of other possible arguments.

B.12.6 Select and analyze various documents that have influenced the legal, political, and constitutional heritage of the United States.

B.12.7 Identify major works of art and literature produced in the United States and elsewhere in the world and explain how they reflect the era in which they were created.

B.12.8 Recall, select, and explain the significance of important people, their work, and their ideas in the areas of political and intellectual leadership, inventions, discoveries, and the arts, within each major era of Wisconsin, United States, and world history.

B.12.9 Select significant changes caused by technology, industrialization, urbanization, and population growth, and analyze the effects of these changes in the United States and the world.

B.12.10 Select instances of scientific, intellectual, and religious change in various regions of the world at different times in history and discuss the impact those changes had on beliefs and values.

B.12.11 Compare examples and analyze why governments of various countries have sometimes sought peaceful resolution to conflicts and sometimes gone to war.

B.12.12 Analyze the history, culture, tribal sovereignty, and current status of the American Indian tribes and bands in Wisconsin.

B.12.13 Analyze examples of ongoing change within and across cultures, such as the development of ancient civilizations; the rise of nation-states; and social, economic, and political revolutions.

B.12.16 Describe the purpose and effects of treaties, alliances, and international organizations that characterize today's interconnected world.

B.12.18 Explain the history of slavery, racial and ethnic discrimination, and efforts to eliminate discrimination in the United States and elsewhere in the world.

Social Studies C (Political Science and Citizenship)

C.8.1 Identify and explain democracy's basic principles, including individual rights, responsibility for the common good, equal opportunity, equal protection of the laws, freedom of speech, justice, and majority rule with protection for minority rights.

C.8.3 Explain how laws are developed, how the purposes of government are established, and how the powers of government are acquired, maintained, justified, and sometimes abused.

C.8.7 Locate, organize, and use relevant information to understand an issue of public concern, take a position, and advocate the position in a debate.

C.12.1 Identify the sources, evaluate the justification, and analyze the implications of certain rights and responsibilities of citizens.

C.12.8 Locate, organize, analyze, and use information from various sources to understand an issue of public concern, take a position, and communicate the position.

C.12.10 Evaluate the ways in which public opinion can be used to influence and shape public policy.

C.12.15 Describe the evolution of movements to assert rights by people with disabilities, ethnic and racial groups, minorities, and women.

Where Highlights in

Wisconsin History

Happened

In this section we've listed all the stories in *Wisconsin History Highlights* by county. So you can find a story from your own county or one that's nearby that interests you!

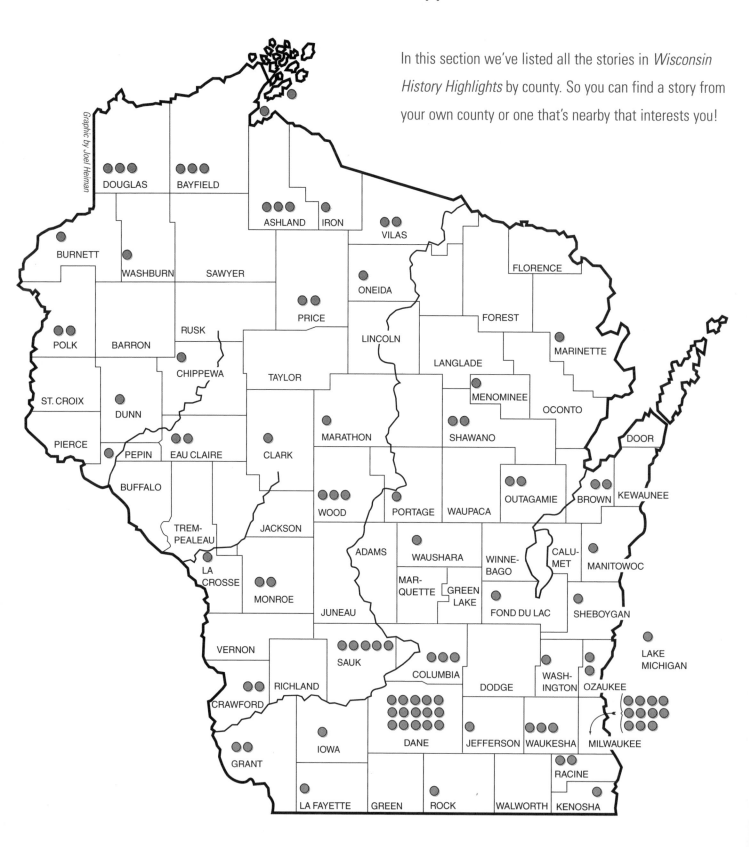

Graphic by Joel Heiman

FOREST

GRANT
Freedom Ride!: Grant County's African American Pioneers
The Ho-Chunk Bison Ranch: Restoration of Native Community

GREEN

GREEN LAKE

IOWA
In the English Language: The Bennett Law Controversy

IRON
Iron Mining and Italian Community Building in Hurley

JACKSON

JEFFERSON
Discovering Aztalan: Samuel Barrett and the Milwaukee Public Museum

JUNEAU

KENOSHA
Finding the Mammoth Hunters: Kenosha Public Museum

KEWAUNEE

LA CROSSE
Black Hawk's Return: "The Land Cannot Be Sold"

LAFAYETTE
From Lead to Zinc: The Mining Heyday in Southwest Wisconsin

LANGLADE

LINCOLN
Otter Spring: Protecting Wisconsin's Sacred Sites

MANITOWOC
Silent Service: Manitowoc's Submarine Industry in World War II

MARATHON
D.C. Everest: Building Wisconsin's Paper Industries

MARINETTE
The Great Peshtigo Fire: Logging Practices Create Deadly Firestorm

MARQUETTE

MENOMINEE
Menominee Tribal Enterprises and Sustained-Yield Forestry

MILWAUKEE
Increase Lapham: Wisconsin's First Scientist
Attracting Newcomers to a New State
Hogs on Wheels: The Evolution of the Harley-Davidson Motor Company
Allis-Chalmers: Manufacturing for Manufacturers
Soldiers without Guns: Milwaukee Women during World War II
Pursuing Freedom: Wisconsin Defies the Fugitive Slave Law
Breaking the Color Line: Milwaukee Housing Segregation
Lloyd Barbee: Fighting Segregation in Milwaukee Schools
School Vouchers: The Milwaukee Experiment
Mr. Berger Goes to Washington: Milwaukee Demands Representation
From Milwaukee to the Promised Land: The Story of Golda Meir

MONROE
Native Fruits: Wisconsin's Cranberry Industry
German POWs: Easing Wisconsin's Labor Shortages

OCONTO

ONEIDA
Dr. Kate Pelham Newcomb: Rural Healthcare on Snowshoes

OUTAGAMIE
Cleaning the Fox River: The Battle over PCB Removal
Senator Joseph McCarthy: The Rise and Fall of an Anti-Communist

OZAUKEE
German Music in a German State
We Won't Fight: German Immigrants Protest the Civil War Draft

PEPIN
Of Woods and Prairies: Children's Author Laura Ingalls Wilder

Index